SQL Statement Syntax

To help you find the syntax you need when you need it, this tear card list syntax for the most frequently used SQL operations. When reading statement syntax, remember the following:

- The ¦ symbol is used to indicate one of several options, so NULL¦NOT NULL means specify either NULL or NOT NULL.

- Keywords or clauses contained within square parentheses [like this] are optional.

- The syntax listed below will work with almost all DBMSs. You are advised to consult your own DBMS documentation for details of implementing specific syntactical changes.

ALTER TABLE

ALTER TABLE is used to update the schema of an existing table.

```
ALTER TABLE tablename
(
    ADD¦DROP    column    datatype    [NULL¦NOT NULL]    [CONSTRAINTS],
    ADD¦DROP    column    datatype    [NULL¦NOT NULL]    [CONSTRAINTS],
    ...
);
```

COMMIT

COMMIT is used to write a transaction to the database.

```
COMMIT [TRANSACTION];
```

CREATE INDEX

CREATE INDEX is used to create an index on one or more columns.

```
CREATE INDEX indexname
ON tablename (column, ...);
```

CREATE TABLE

CREATE TABLE is used to create new database tables.

```
CREATE TABLE tablename
(
    column    <datatype_definition>    [NULL¦NOT NULL]    [CONSTRAINTS],
    column    <datatype_definition>    [NULL¦NOT NULL]    [CONSTRAINTS],
    ...
);
```

CREATE VIEW

CREATE VIEW is used to create a new view of one or more tables.

```
CREATE VIEW viewname AS
SELECT columns, ...
FROM tables, ...
[WHERE ...]
[GROUP BY ...]
[HAVING ...];
```

DELETE

DELETE deletes one or more rows from a table.

```
DELETE FROM tablename
[WHERE ...];
```

CREATE DATABASE

CREATE DATABASE is used to create a database.

```
CREATE DATABASE <database_name>
    ON [PRIMARY]
    [ <filespec> [,...n] ]
    [, <filegroup> [,...n] ]
    [ LOG ON { <filespec> [,...n]} ]
    [ FOR LOAD ¦ FOR ATTACH ]
<filespec> ::=
    ( [ NAME = logical_file_name, ]
        FILENAME = 'os_file_name'
      [, SIZE = size]
      [, MAXSIZE = { max_size ¦ UNLIMITED } ]
      [, FILEGROWTH = growth_increment] ) [,...n]

<filegroup> ::=

    FILEGROUP filegroup_name <filespec> [,...n]
```

DROP

DROP permanently removes database objects (tables, views, indexes, and so forth).

```
DROP INDEX¦TABLE¦VIEW indexname¦tablename¦viewname;
```

INSERT

INSERT adds a single row to a table.

```
INSERT INTO tablename [(columns, ...)]
VALUES(values, ...);
```

INSERT SELECT

INSERT SELECT inserts the results of a SELECT into a table.

```
INSERT INTO tablename [(columns, ...)]
SELECT columns, ... FROM tablename, ...
[WHERE ...];
```

ROLLBACK

ROLLBACK is used to undo a transaction block.

```
ROLLBACK [ TO savepointname];    Or    ROLLBACK TRANSACTION;
```

SELECT

SELECT is used to retrieve data from one or more tables (or views).

```
SELECT columnname, ...
FROM tablename, ...
[WHERE ...]
[GROUP BY ...]
[HAVING ...]
[ORDER BY ...];
```

UPDATE

UPDATE updates one or more rows in a table. S

```
UPDATE tablename
SET columnname = value, ...
[WHERE ...];
```

Matthew Shepker

SAMS
Teach Yourself

SQL Server® 7

in **24** Hours

SAMS

A Division of Macmillan USA
201 West 103rd Street, Indianapolis, Indiana, 46290 USA

Sams Teach Yourself SQL Server 7 in 24 Hours

Copyright © 2000 by Sams Publishing

International Standard Book Number: 0-672-31715-X

Library of Congress Catalog Card Number: 99-63166

Printed in the United States of America

First Printing: October 1999

01 00 99   4   3   2   1

Trademarks

Warning and Disclaimer

ASSOCIATE PUBLISHER
Bradley L. Jones

ACQUISITIONS EDITOR
Sharon Cox

DEVELOPMENT EDITOR
Matt Purcell

MANAGING EDITOR
Lisa Wilson

PROJECT EDITOR
Dawn Pearson

COPY EDITOR
Rhonda Tinch-Mize

INDEXER
Eric Schroeder

PROOFREADER
Megan Wade

TECHNICAL EDITOR
Sundar Rajan

TEAM COORDINATOR
Meggo Barthlow

SOFTWARE DEVELOPMENT SPECIALIST
John Warriner

INTERIOR DESIGN
Gary Adair

COVER DESIGN
Aren Howell

COPY WRITER
Eric Borgert

PRODUCTION
Cyndi Davis-Hubler
Dan Harris
Heather Moseman

Overview

Contents

About the Author

Matthew Shepker is the director of Technology and Development for Diversified Consulting Resources, Inc., in Overland Park, Kansas. He is a Microsoft Certified Systems Engineer and a Microsoft Certified Trainer holding 11 certifications. Matthew is currently working on completing the Microsoft Certified Database Administrator and Microsoft Certified Solutions Developer certifications. Matthew has been working with SQL Server for more than four years in a variety of business applications including online transaction processing, decision support systems, and other custom software.

Matthew has authored one other book, New Riders's *MCSE Core NT Exams*, and has co-authored five other books, including Sams's *Microsoft SQL Server 7.0 Programming Unleashed* and Que's *Using SQL Server 7.0*.

Matthew lives with his wife, Misty. Other living things in the house include one permanent dog, Sam, and an occasional rotating foster dog. Matthew can be reached at shepker@planetkc.com.

Dedication

To my dearest wife, Misty. I know you want to know, you'll just have to wait. I love you.

Acknowledgments

It is a difficult thing to imagine how many people you want to thank when you write a book, and almost all of them are behind the scenes.

First of all, I need to thank all the people who worked to help me get this book from the initial good idea phase into the book that you now hold in your hand. Thanks to Sharon Cox, who signed me up to write the book. Matt Purcell is the person who is responsible for ensuring that I got all the important little things included. Also, thanks to all the technical and copy editors who ensured that I was telling the truth and that everything is readable. I could have never made it this far without all of your help.

For all my writing and publishing skills, I have three teachers that I must thank. The first was one of my high school English teachers, Pat Fellers. Mrs. Fellers made it very clear that if you were going to succeed both in life and in her class, you had to be able to write well. The person who picked up where Mrs. Fellers left off was a college composition instructor I had named Sharon Wilson. Mrs. Wilson probably killed a few red pens on my papers alone. Last, I have to thank Lynn Ann Huntington for all the journalism experience I have.

On the work front, I have to thank Michael Walsh for taking a chance on me. Chris Herbig gets a nod for being the best HR manager that I have ever worked with. And to Mark, Doug, Chris, Mark, Joel, and Blake—you have to admit that it has been an interesting ride.

Finally, I have to thank all the people who have helped me in general, both past and present. To my parents, without you, I wouldn't be. You have supported me through all my choices in life and you have to be commended for that. To my grandfather, Ehrhard Weinman, you helped spark my creativity. How many other men would have let me loose in a basement with power tools? Not many. Believe me. It would take guts... even today. I have to thank Becky and Norby for providing the occasional weekend distractions that Misty and I needed during this process. All work and no play makes Matt a dull boy... Last, to my wonderful wife Misty. It always seems that you get left holding the short straw whenever I write, and you do so without complaint. Well, not much, at least. Thank you for putting up with all the time that I spend glued to a computer screen.

Thank you all...

Tell Us What You Think!

As the reader of this book, *you* are our most important critic and commentator. We value your opinion and want to know what we're doing right, what we could do better, what areas you'd like to see us publish in, and any other words of wisdom you're willing to pass our way.

As an Associate Publisher for Sams Publishing, I welcome your comments. You can fax, email, or write me directly to let me know what you did or didn't like about this book— as well as what we can do to make our books stronger.

Please note that I cannot help you with technical problems related to the topic of this book, and that due to the high volume of mail I receive, I might not be able to reply to every message.

When you write, please be sure to include this book's title and author as well as your name and phone or fax number. I will carefully review your comments and share them with the author and editors who worked on the book.

Fax: 317.581.4770
E-mail: adv_prop@mcp.com
Mail: Bradley L. Jones
          Associate Publisher
          Sams Publishing
          201 West 103rd Street
          Indianapolis, IN 46290 USA

Introduction

I realize that you are probably very excited to tear into SQL Server 7.0. You are about to embark on an exciting journey through just about all the basics you will need to know to be a SQL Server database administrator. Before you get into it, you should take a few minutes to acquaint yourself with some of the design of this book.

Who Should Read This Book?

This book is intended for anyone who does not have a great deal of knowledge about SQL Server and wants to learn about SQL Server 7.0 in a short amount of time. SQL Server 7.0 is a very powerful server application that can be used to create business tools that can be implemented in almost any business. For anyone who has been a DBA in any other database management system, there will be parts of this book that you will find old hat, but most of it will be new to you.

In this book, you will learn SQL Server at several different levels. First, you will learn how to manage SQL Server from a purely database management standpoint. This means you will learn how to set up, back up, and manage SQL Server. Next, we will look at SQL Server from a more development standpoint. You will learn how to query and modify data that is stored in the database as well as create tables, indexes, and stored procedures.

When you become familiar with how SQL Server works and the majority of the functionality that you have with it, you will be able to hone your skills. You should be able to effectively manage a SQL Server and the databases that are contained on that server.

This 24-hour book concentrates on SQL Server 7.0, which is the latest version of Microsoft's database server product. This product will run on Windows NT as well as Windows 95/98.

What You Will Learn

In this book, you will learn how to work with SQL Server. We will go over a large number of advanced concepts, but we will not go over these in too much depth. The reason we do this is that you will really want to get up to speed with SQL Server 7.0 as quickly as possible. You will learn some of the theory and history behind SQL Server and how you can make all of this work for you.

Can I Really Learn SQL Server in 24 Hours?

You will be able to learn what you need to get up and running with SQL Server, but you will not learn anything else. I have been working with SQL Server for six years, and I am still learning things. You should be able to cover each chapter, called either lessons or hours, in about an hour. For the most part, the longer chapters contain tutorial type lessons for you to cover, and the shorter chapters contain background and theoretical information.

What Do I Need?

For starters, you will need a copy of SQL Server 7.0. This can be the full version or the evaluation edition of SQL Server 7.0 that can be downloaded from Microsoft's Web site. The exact location of this download changes quite frequently, but you should be able to get to it from http://www.microsoft.com/sql. You will be able to perform most of the exercises in this book if you install the software on a Windows 95/98 computer; but some of them, such as the replication section, will require a Windows NT Server computer to perform the exercises.

Conventions Used in this Book

Each lesson in this book covers new terms and contains a question-and-answer section at the end of each lesson to help you answer questions that you might have. Also, there is a quiz section and exercise at the end of the section to help reinforce what has been covered.

Several conventions are used in this book that you will run into. Here is a summary of the typographical conventions:

- Any commands and output from the computer will appear in a monospaced font.
- Any words that you type will appear in monospace.
- When dealing with syntax, monospaced words are keywords that must match exactly.
- When dealing with syntax, *italicized monospaced* words indicate placeholders that must be replaced with your own values.
- When dealing with syntax, [bracketed monospaced] words indicate terms or commands that are optional.

HOUR 1

Introducing SQL Server

You are about to enter the wide world of Microsoft SQL Server 7.0. SQL Server is one of the most powerful database engines on the market today. From the outside, learning SQL Server can be a very daunting task. As you will find over the next 24 hours, there is a large quantity of information to learn, but it is not that difficult to master. Although this book will not make you an SQL Server expert, when you have completed all 24 hours, you should have a solid understanding of how it works and the major capabilities of the software.

The highlights of this hour include

- Introduction to SQL Server
- The history of SQL Server
- Major features of SQL Server 7.0
- SQL Server and the Client/Server Model
- Introduction to the DBA Role

An Introduction to SQL Server

Before you get too far into how SQL Server works, it is important to understand what it is. First and foremost, SQL Server is not a database. SQL Server is a Relational Database Management System, or RDBMS. Although this might sound confusing, it really isn't. SQL Server, or any other RDBMS, is an engine that you build databases on top of. I will cover more on RDBMSs in a minute. It is something like Microsoft Word. Word is not a document. It is a tool for creating and managing documents.

NEW TERM A *database* is a collection of data stored in one location.

NEW TERM A *Relational Database Management System*, or *RDBMS*, is an engine that is used to store and manage databases.

SQL Server is a Windows application that runs as a service. This means that it runs in the background and requires very little user interaction after it has been set up. SQL Server provides all of the functionality for managing user connections, providing data security, and servicing query requests. All you have to do is create the database and the application that interacts with it, and you don't have to worry about any of the background processes.

The History of SQL Server

SQL Server has been around for quite some time, in one form or another. SQL Server was originally introduced in 1988. This first version was a joint venture between Sybase and Microsoft and ran only on OS/2, and was a complete flop in the marketplace. In 1993, SQL Server 4.2 for Windows NT Advanced Server 3.1 was released. This version made some small advances in the marketplace, but still did not have what it needed to make it an enterprise class RDBMS. Microsoft and Sybase went separate ways in 1994. Shortly after, in 1995, Microsoft released SQL Server 6.0. In 1996, SQL Server 6.5 was released. SQL Server 6.5 had the speed, power, ease-of-use, and low cost that the marketplace was looking for.

In addition to the features that administrators were looking for, part of SQL Server's success had to do with the direction that the marketplace took around the same time that it was released. For the most part, the market was moving toward faster and cheaper Intel-based servers running Windows NT Server. This meant that, upon abandoning other network operating systems, when there was a need for an RDBMS, SQL Server became the natural selection.

NEW TERM A *Network Operating System* is a special type of operating system that is specifically designed to provide network services such as file and print servers.

1

SQL Server 7.0, which was released in early 1999, thrusts SQL Server into the enterprise database arena. Although previous versions of SQL Server contained large amounts of the original Sybase code, SQL Server 7.0 is said to be 100 percent Microsoft code. It is even said that Microsoft developers threw a party when the final lines of original code were removed. This means that SQL Server 7.0 is, if not a complete rewrite, pretty close.

Relational Database Management Systems

Before I jump into the main features of SQL Server 7.0, you should be familiar with important features of all RDBMSs. These features are the basics of what make up any RDBMSs. These include

- As the name implies, RDBMSs manage relational databases. A relational database is a grouping of tables. The tables are broken down into rows, also known as records, and these are broken down into columns, also known as fields. Without these, you would have nothing to manage.

NEW TERM A *table* is a grouping of records that is all related. For example, you might have a table that contains information about every employee who works at your company.

NEW TERM A *record*, or row, is a grouping of data that is related. For example, a single record might contain data about an employee of a company including name, address, hire data, and pay rate.

NEW TERM A *field*, or column, is a single piece of data that is contained in a record. For example, this might be the name or address of a certain employee.

- All RDBMSs use SQL, or a variation of it, to manipulate the data that is contained in any of the databases. SQL, which is pronounced S-Q-L, was developed at IBM in the late 1970s.

- RDBMSs must maintain data integrity. In other words, any relational databases need to ensure that if data in multiple tables is updated, all of the updates take place. For example, imagine a banking system that contains two tables, one for your savings account and one for your checking account. You call your bank and ask them to transfer $100 from savings into checking. This process involves subtracting $100 from savings and adding $100 to checking. If after the $100 is deleted from the table, the bank loses power, what happens? If data integrity didn't exist, you would have just lost $100. With data integrity, when the server is powered back on, the server will realize that the subtract was completed—but the addition was not—and it would cancel the whole thing. I will cover more about data integrity in Hour 4, "Database Architecture Fundamentals."

- Most RDBMSs strive to maintain separation between the actual data and the business logic, which ensures that the data in the database is maintained in a constant state. In most cases, you only want to store data in the database.

- Many RDBMSs store data in such a way that redundant data is eliminated through some type of compression. This does not mean that data is lost; rather, it means that less storage space is needed.

- Every RDBMS provides some sort of security for the databases that it manages. This is usually through the use of some sort of login process.

Major Features of SQL Server 7.0

Now that you have an idea of the major features of almost all RDBMSs, you are probably wondering what makes SQL Server so special. If all these features are available in any RDBMS, why should you consider SQL Server? A host of features are available in SQL Server that makes it stand out from all its competitors.

Graphically Based Management Tools

As a newcomer to SQL Server, the graphical management tools make it extremely easy to manage the server. The major graphical user interface, or GUI, tool that you will use is the SQL Enterprise Manager. This tool takes advantage of the Microsoft Management Console, or MMC. MMC is a tool Microsoft released that allows you to manage all the services on a Windows NT Server from one place. This tool allows you to manage Windows NT, Internet Information Server, SQL Server, and many other products from a single application.

 A *GUI*, or Graphical User Interface, is a graphical way of interacting with an application. Windows is an example of a GUI. To contrast this, any DOS application does not have a GUI. These types of applications are commonly known as text based or command-line applications.

 Microsoft Management Console, or MMC, is a tool that can be used to manage all server services running on a Windows NT computer. This application provides a single point of administration for all services.

Centralized Management

No matter how far apart your SQL Servers are, using SQL Enterprise Manager, you can manage all your servers from one central location. For example, you might have ten different SQL Servers, each separated by hundreds of miles, but you can still manage these servers from one computer. This helps lower the cost of maintaining multiple servers—you only need one administrator for all those servers.

Supports Multiple Client Applications

SQL Server 7.0 supports almost any type of client application. SQL Server ships with a standard suite of applications that you can use to manage the server and modify your data. I will cover these applications in Hour 5, "Using the Tools and Utilities." SQL Server also supports a standard known as Open Database Connectivity, or ODBC. Using this, you can create custom applications that can connect to SQL Server and any other type of RDBMS for which a driver is available.

NEW TERM *Open Database Connectivity*, or *ODBC*, is a set of drivers designed to make development for different database platforms faster and easier.

Supports Many Different Development Platforms

When creating new applications to access SQL Server, you can use almost any development platform that is currently available. This means that no matter what programming language you know, you can write applications tailored to SQL Server. The best suite of development applications available for SQL Server is a Microsoft Product known as Visual Studio. This suite contains several tools that allow you to quickly and easily create new SQL Server applications. Through the use of ODBC, several third-party programming suites can be used to create applications that run on SQL Server.

Can Support Enterprise Class Applications

In the world of databases, SQL Server is sometimes looked at as the stepchild of enterprise class database servers. With the release of SQL Server 7.0, SQL Server has truly stepped into the world of enterprise class database servers. SQL Server 7.0 Enterprise Edition can support databases larger than several terabytes with more than 32 processors.

Runs on Windows NT and Windows 95/98

For large-scale production purposes, SQL Server 7.0 usually runs on Windows NT. Unlike previous versions of SQL Server, version 7.0 will also run on a computer that is running Windows 95/98. Although this might not sound like it is a big improvement, for developers, this is one of the largest timesavers you can imagine. This means that a developer can create an application which communicates with a single database type. An example of this need would be an application that supports mobile users. These users might need to view and modify data when they are offline, or not connected to the network. Later, when they are plugged into the network, the changes they made are synchronized with the main data source. With previous versions of SQL Server, the developer would use SQL Server for the main data source and then rely on a smaller and less robust database type, such as Access, for the offline data source. SQL Server 7.0 makes this much easier.

Supports Data Replication

As with previous versions of SQL Server, version 7.0 supports data replication. Replication is a process which ensures that data your users need is where they need it when they need it. SQL Server 7.0 has added a great deal of functionality into the newest version. This version allows for a new type of replication known as merge replication. For your Microsoft Access users, merge replication is nothing new. Merge replication allows users at any site to make changes to the data. The changes that the users make are sent to the master copy and then replicated out to any other subscribers. Although this might not seem like a big deal, having multiple up-to-date copies of your data can be a very useful thing. Not only can replication reduce the amount of network bandwidth it takes to return data to your users, but it can also lower the overall frustration level of your users by lowering the amount of time it takes to get the data they need.

> **NEW TERM** *Replication* is the process of making copies of data contained in a master database and moving it out to other subscriber servers.

Supports Distributed Transactions

SQL Server 7.0 supports distributed transactions. A distributed transaction is a transaction that occurs on several servers at the same time. If any of the servers that are involved in a distributed transaction cannot make the requested changes, the changes are not made on any of the servers. Going back to the bank example from earlier this hour, your bank has merged several times over the past couple of months, and instead of the thousands of customers it used to have, they now number in the millions. The bank has placed all the customers' savings accounts on one server and all their checking accounts on another. A distributed transaction would need to be involved to ensure that both servers get updated, and no data is lost.

> **NEW TERM** A *distributed transaction* is a transaction that occurs on several different servers at the same time. In order for a distributed transaction to take place, all computers must be able to make the requested changes. Otherwise, all requested changes are cancelled.

Can Support Data Warehouses

SQL Server 7.0 has made many advances in the way it handles large quantities of data. This makes SQL Server 7.0 perfect for managing large data warehouses. Data warehouses are usually extremely large databases that contain data from transactional oriented databases. These huge databases are used to search for trends that are not apparent from a cursory examination. SQL Server 7.0 has built in several online analytical processing tools (OLAP) known as the Microsoft Decision Support Services.

Online Analytical Processing Is Built-in

One of the largest advantages to SQL Server 7.0 is that OLAP services are built into the server. These services are known as Microsoft Decision Support Services. Unlike other servers on the market, you do not have to purchase other third-party, and frequently very expensive, applications. This lowers the overall cost of SQL Server and raises the bar for other database platforms.

Total Cost of Ownership Is Less than Its Competitors

Last but not least, when you compare all the features of SQL Server with its competitors, you get more bang for your buck from SQL Server. Hardware, software, and client licenses; ongoing management costs; and development costs are all less expensive than any other RDBMS on the market right now. With the amount of money that can be in-vested into RDBMSs, sometimes numbering in the millions of dollars, it is a good idea to get the best RDBMS that money can buy with the least amount of money.

SQL Server and the Client/Server Model

Although the client/server model is not extremely new to the technology world, it is still considered to be the new kid on the block. The roots of the client/server model extend back into the mainframe world. With a mainframe, all the processing and data resided on one large, and usually very expensive, mainframe. When interacting with a mainframe, you can have clients that have absolutely no processing power. All processing is done on the mainframe, and only the results are sent back to the clients. When the prices of computers began to drop, it didn't take people very long to realize that they could save a lot of money if they could figure out a way to take some of the processing off of the main computer and put it on the client computer. In this way, they could spend less money on the central computer. This was the first evolution of the client/server model.

When you think of the client/server model, traditionally you think of two sides—the client and the server. The client machines usually display the data, perform some data validation, and handle any error messages that are sent back from the RDBMS. The server computer stores the data, responds to user requests, and maintains the data in a logical state. The main problem with this type of model is that the business logic and rules reside on either the client or the server. An example of a business rule might be the format in which your business requires a customer's phone number to be entered. A fact of life in business is that the rules change. In this type of situation, you would either have to make changes to all the client computers, which is an administrative nightmare, or you would have to maintain all your business rules on the server, which can be an extreme resource drain.

NEW TERM   *Business rules* are definitions for the way that your business creates, manages, and stores data.

The next evolution of the client/server model is what is known as the N-Tier model. This model relies on several different computers performing different functions. The RDBMS resides in what is known as the data layer. This computer only stores data and responds to requests for data. The client computer resides in a layer known as the presentation layer. The client computer only displays the data. The big difference comes in the middle layer. The middle layer is known as the data services layer. The data services layer contains all the business logic and rules. When the rules change, you modify the middle layer and never have to touch the data layer or the presentation layer. This layer can be written in any programming language, such as Visual Basic or Visual C++. The problem with the N-Tier architecture is the cost. To create a successful N-Tier solution, it is going to cost more than a simple two-tier client server architecture. The payoff, though, is in ongoing maintenance costs. Changes that, in two-tier architectures, would have required you to rebuild and redistribute the client application, which could take days or months, can now be made in minutes.

NEW TERM   *N-Tier architecture* is the process of dividing the processing that your computers must do into separate layers that each perform specific functions.

Introduction to the DBA Role

You have probably heard the term DBA thrown around quite a bit with little regard to what it is and why it is there. The simplest definition of a DBA, or Database Administrator, is a person who manages a database or a database server. As you can probably imagine, there is a lot more to a DBA than it sounds. In order to be a good SQL Server DBA, there are quite a few things you need to know. This knowledge is not just about SQL Server either. With the way that SQL Server is tied into Windows NT, it is a really good idea for you to have at least a cursory understanding of Windows NT.

NEW TERM   A *DBA*, or *Database Administrator*, is a person who manages a database or a database server.

So what skill are important for a SQL Server DBA? There are quite a few. Some are more important than others, and many of them you will pick up the more you use the product. The following are some of the skills that you should have in order to be the consummate SQL Server DBA:

- SQL Server—In order to be a good SQL Server DBA, you must live and breath SQL Server. A SQL Server DBA will need to know how to install, configure, maintain, and troubleshoot SQL Server. Now that might not seem like a lot, but you must understand that SQL Server is a huge product. The good part about this is that Microsoft has added a great deal of functionality which will help you perform all of these tasks.

- Windows NT—As mentioned before, a SQL Server DBA should have, at a minimum, a cursory understanding of the way Windows NT works. SQL Server 7.0 is tied into Windows NT more than any previous release. Some of the basic skills a SQL Server DBA should be familiar with is managing users and groups; creating, modifying, and managing shares; modifying and managing permissions; starting and stopping Windows NT Services; and using the Event Viewer.

- Relational Databases—Because the main function of SQL Server is to manage relational databases, it is extremely important for a SQL Server DBA to understand how relational databases work and their basic structure.

- SQL—Every DBA needs to have a basic understanding of the SQL language. This does not mean that you have to be a programmer, but it does mean that you need to know how to piece together an occasional SELECT statement. The good part about this is that the more you use the SQL language, the better off you will be.

- Backup and Restore Processes—As you will find with more experience in databases, the question you should have is not whether a database or server will crash, but when. When a database crashes, usually your best option for recovery is to restore the database from the most recent backup. If a database crashes and you haven't been making frequent backups, usually the two most important skills you can have are resume writing and job hunting.

- Business Processes—Every DBA, no matter which RDBMS is being used, needs to have a good understanding of the underlying business processes. It is a good bet that, whatever the business you are in, your database will mimic the processes of your business. For example, a business that sells products over the Internet would have a database that tracks products, customer accounts, and billing information.

Now that you have an idea of what an SQL Server DBA must know, you are probably wondering what an SQL Server DBA is going to do. As an SQL Server DBA, you are going to have a great deal of responsibilities and, potentially, a great deal of stress. Some of the basic responsibilities of a DBA are as follows:

- Install SQL Server—This is probably going to be one of the first jobs you perform as an SQL Server DBA. Installing an SQL Server is relatively simple, but if you do not properly plan, it will make life very difficult further down the road. It is not uncommon that you install an SQL Server and have it up and running for a while, only to find out that the server on which you installed the software is not powerful enough to handle the load you place on it. At this point, you have to look at upgrading the hardware or replacing the server.

- Create and Maintain Databases—Creating new databases on your SQL Server is another rather routine task you will have to perform because you do not want your everyday person performing this task. Maintaining current databases is one of the most important tasks that you will have. If your databases are not properly maintained, they will start to fail, which will mean more work for you anyway.

- Perform Database Maintenance—This task falls under maintaining databases. It involves things such as running utilities against the database to ensure that everything is created and allocated correctly. The whole point behind this is to find and fix errors in your databases before they become problems for you and your users.

- Manage Users—Whenever a new person joins or leaves your company, it is the database administrator's job to add or remove the user login ID. This is extremely important, especially when you consider what some people could potentially do to your database when they leave your company.

- Manage Permissions—Another important security issue that you will have to handle as an SQL Server DBA is managing permissions. This is important because frequently data is stored in databases you do not want made available to the general population of your company. A good example of this is salary information. An SQL Server DBA will assign permissions on tables that contain this type of data, so it is only available to people who need to access it.

- Backup and Restore Databases—This is quite possibly one of the most important tasks you will perform as a DBA. At some point, any one of the databases that you have will crash. There is no way around that, except to make frequent backups of your databases. When databases crash, usually the fastest way to get your users back up and running is to restore from a backup.

- Schedule Tasks—One of the most useful features of SQL Server is the capability to schedule tasks. This makes it possible to automate tasks to occur at off-hours of the day when your users are not running. This is especially useful for running backups, maintenance tasks, and batch processes. These types of processes usually take a large amount of server overhead, and can severely impact your users if they are run while users are active in the database.

- Import and Export Data—Frequently, SQL Server has to interoperate with other database management systems on platforms anywhere from mainframes, to UNIX servers, to PC databases. In order to get this interoperation working, you will need to move data between systems. This data transfer can be a one-time-only process, or it can be a daily process.

- Manage SQL Server Replication—SQL Server Replication is a tool that you can use to make several copies of your data and move it out to different locations. As DBA, you will probably be the person who sets up and monitors replication.

- Monitor and Tune the Server—SQL Server 7.0 has made many advances in server tuning. In fact, SQL Server 7.0 will autotune most options for you. Nevertheless, there are still times that you will want to make your own decisions about how SQL Server will use its resources. This can be one of the most difficult tasks to pick up because there are so many options you can configure. After you get a good feel for what can be configured, you can try different settings and see how they affect the performance of the server.

- Troubleshoot SQL Server—When you encounter a problem with your SQL Server, the first thing you will probably do is panic. As you become more experienced, you will begin to recognize how to deal with problems. One thing you will notice is that as soon as you solve one problem, you will eventually come up with a new problem to solve.

Summary

In this hour, I have covered the overall features of SQL Server and what it takes to be an SQL Server DBA. A large number of associated technologies are used in SQL Server, and it might seem difficult to get through them all. In the following hours, you will look at all the technologies that I have discussed and how to implement them.

Q&A

Q Is SQL Server difficult to master?

A It can be. This should not discourage you from learning as much as you can and actually moving towards mastering this product. The main reason that SQL Server is difficult to master is that it crosses so many different disciplines. In order to completely master all of SQL Server, you must know about development, networking, infrastructure, and business.

Q After I am done with this book, what should I do?

A The best thing that you can do is to practice. If you have a development server, do everything you can to that server to master all the concepts I talk about. If you do not have a development server, I would not recommend messing with any productional server that you may have, set up a development server instead.

Workshop

The quiz and the exercise are provided for your further understanding. The answers can be found in Appendix A, "Answers."

Quiz

1. What is an RDBMS?
2. What platforms does SQL Server 7.0 run on?
3. What is a DBA?
4. What management tool is used to manage SQL Server?
5. How did SQL Server get started?
6. What does it mean to have an N-Tier application?

Exercises

Look around your business for a computer that can be used throughout the rest of this book. You will need to have Windows NT or Windows 95/98 installed on it.

HOUR 2

Installing SQL Server

SQL Server 7.0 is a relatively simple product to install. Nevertheless, you should be familiar with all the options that are available to you during the installation process. In this hour, I will go over the different hardware and software requirements for installing SQL Server, and then walk through the actual installation process.

The highlights of this hour include

- The Steps to Installing SQL Server
- SQL Server Versions
- Verifying SQL Server Installation
- Troubleshooting Installation
- Uninstalling SQL Server

The Steps to Installing SQL Server

Three basic portions to the SQL Server installation process exist. The first step is a preinstallation checklist in which you ensure that the hardware and software installed on your machine meets the minimum requirements and then create the requisite user accounts. The second step is the actual installation process. During this process, the server software itself is installed, and the default databases are created. The last step is to review all the installed options and ensure that everything works correctly.

Preinstallation

The preinstallation process is probably the most important portion of the SQL Server installation process. If this process is not properly completed, your installation might fail, or you might have problems with performance. Before you install, you must check the hardware and software to ensure that it meets the minimum requirements and then create the user account that SQL Server will use when it is running.

Hardware Requirements

SQL Server 7.0 requires a relatively powerful machine in order to work properly. As with all server products, the more users you are going to support and the faster performance you require, the bigger, better, and, of course, more expensive machine is needed. The minimum requirements are outlined in Table 2.1.

TABLE 2.1   Hardware Requirements

Category	Minimum Requirement
Processor	SQL Server 7.0 requires an Alpha-based processor or an Intel Pentium-based (Pentium, Pentium Pro, Pentium II, or Pentium III) or other compatible running at 166 MHz or faster. SQL Server 7.0 does not support the MIPS or PowerPC platforms. As of Windows NT Service Pack 3, Microsoft is phasing out all support for these processor platforms.
Memory	SQL Server 7.0 has two different memory requirements depending on which version you are installing. SQL Server Enterprise Edition requires a minimum of 64MB. All other versions require a minimum of 32MB.
Hard Disk Space	Several different requirements are available depending on which installation type you choose: Full—180MB Typical—170MB Minimum—65MB Management Tools Only—90MB OLAP Services—50MB English Query—12MB

Category	Minimum Requirement
CD-ROM	A CD-ROM is required to install SQL Server 7.0.
Network	A network infrastructure of some type is required for interaction with clients. SQL Server 7.0 supports Named Pipes, TCP/IP, Multiprotocol (which supports Named Pipes, TCP/IP, and Novell IPX/SPX), Novell IPX/SPX, AppleTalk, and Banyan VINES.

Software Requirements

Like all software products, there are several requirements for which versions of operating system software and other required pieces must be installed before installing SQL Server 7.0. These software requirements are outlined in Table 2.2.

TABLE 2.2   Software Requirements

Category	Minimum Requirement
Operating System	Depending on which version of SQL Server 7.0 you plan to install, there are different requirements for the base operating system that must be installed:
	Enterprise Edition—This version requires a minimum of Windows NT Server 4.0 Enterprise Edition with Service Pack 4 or higher.
	Standard/Small Business Server Edition—These versions require a minimum of Windows NT Server 4.0 with Service Pack 4 or higher, or Microsoft Small Business Server.
	Desktop Version—This version requires Windows NT Workstation 4.0 with Service Pack 4 or higher, Windows 95/98, or any other operating system listed previously.
	Management Tools—The management tools require Windows NT Workstation 4.0 with Service Pack 4 or higher, Windows 95/98, or any other operating system listed previously.
Internet Browser	SQL Server 7.0 requires a minimum version of Microsoft Internet Explorer 4.01 with Service Pack 1. This is required for Microsoft Management Console (MMC) and HTML Help to work. You can install a minimum version of Internet Explorer (IE) 4.01, and it does not have to be your default browser.
Network Software	Depending on the network support that you require, you must ensure that the correct network drivers are loaded. Additional network support will not be needed unless you are using Banyan VINES or AppleTalk. Novell IPX/SPX support is provided by NWLink IPX/SPX.

continues

TABLE 2.2 continued

Category	Minimum Requirement
Client Software	SQL Server 7.0 can support Windows 95/98, Windows NT Workstation, Windows NT Server, UNIX, Apple Macintosh, and OS/2 clients. UNIX, Macintosh, and OS/2 client support is provided through the use of third-party ODBC drivers.

Creating Windows NT User Accounts

When running SQL Server on a Windows NT computer, SQL Server and the SQL Server agent run as services. This means that they run in the background with very little user interaction. In order for these services to run, they must be assigned to a Windows NT user account. This is for security purposes. When SQL Server is running on a Windows 95/98 machine, SQL Server simulates Windows NT services. You do not have to create Windows NT user accounts for these accounts.

SQL Server can run under the following types of user accounts:

- Local System—The local system account is a built-in account that can be used primarily for services. This account does not have access to network resources.
- Local User—A local user account is one that is set up by the administrator of the local computer. This account is available only on the local computer and has no access to network resources.
- Domain User—A domain user account is one that is set up by the domain administrator in the domain that the SQL Server resides in. A domain account is usually the best type of account to use with SQL Server.

Several problems with using the local system and local user accounts exist. The primary problem is that these accounts have no network access privileges, which means that servers set up to use these cannot interact with other SQL Servers. This means you cannot perform certain server to server activities, such as:

- Replication
- Remote procedure calls
- Distributed transactions
- Backing up to network drives
- Heterogeneous joins
- SQL Server mail features and SQL Mail

If you are planning on using any of the preceding features, you must set up SQL Server to use a domain account. Several things must be done in order for a domain account to work, but all of these are taken care of if you create the SQL Server account as an administrator. The following tutorial will walk you through creating a Windows NT user account for use with SQL Server. This will only work on Windows NT Servers and Workstations that are in a domain. You must be logged in as an administrator for this to work. If you cannot log in as an administrator, have your network administrator perform these steps for you.

2

1. Click the Start menu, go to Programs, Administrative Tools, and then click User Manager for Domains. This opens up the User Managers, as seen in Figure 2.1.

FIGURE 2.1

The User Manager for Domains screen.

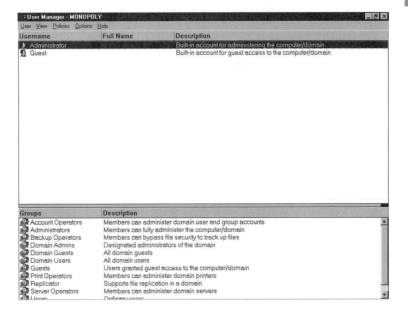

2. Click on the User Menu and choose New User. This opens the New User dialog, as seen in Figure 2.2.

3. In the Username box, you can type any valid Windows NT user account. It is best to type a name in there that you will recognize. For these purposes, type MSSQLServerService in this box.

4. The Full Name and Description boxes are both optional, but it is best to document this information as much as possible. For these purposes, put SQL Server Service Account.

FIGURE 2.2

The New User dialog.

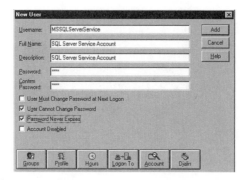

5. In the password boxes, choose a password that will be very difficult to guess and enter it in both boxes.

6. By default, the User Must Change Password At Next Login box is checked. You must uncheck this box, or SQL Server will fail on startup.

7. The next two boxes, User Cannot Change Password and Account Never Expires, should be checked. The User Cannot Change Password is not that big of a deal because SQL Server will never try to change its password. But if there is a security breach, someone changing this password can be rather difficult to troubleshoot. The Account Never Expires option is a big deal though because many organizations set up policies that make user accounts expire frequently to ensure that users change their passwords.

8. Ensure that the Account Disabled box is not checked.

9. Click the Groups button, add the Domain Admins group, as shown in Figure 2.3, and then click the OK button.

FIGURE 2.3

The Group Memberships dialog.

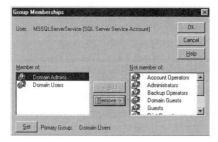

10. Click the OK button to add the user and then close the User Manager for Domains.

You can repeat the preceding steps to make a second account for the SQL Server Agent, although this is not necessary. If you do not create a second account, you can assign both services the same account.

Now that you have ensured that your hardware and software are up to snuff and have created the Windows NT User account that you are going to use, it is time to perform some final steps and then install SQL Server. The following steps are the last few things you have to do before you install SQL Server:

- Shut down all services that are dependent upon SQL Server. These services include Internet Information Server (IIS), Microsoft Transaction Server, and any services that use ODBC connections.
- Shut down Windows NT Event Viewer and regedt32.exe, if they are running.
- Log into the computer on which you are going to install SQL Server as an account that has administrative privileges.

SQL Server Versions

Now that you know how to prepare the server on which you will install SQL Server, you should consider which version of SQL Server you will install. Four different versions of SQL Server exist that you can install, depending on what your business needs are. These versions and the differences between them are outlined as follows:

- Standard Edition—The standard edition of SQL Server 7.0 is what you will normally install. This version supports four processors and unlimited database size. This version will only run on Windows NT Server machines.

- Enterprise Edition—The enterprise edition of SQL Server is a special version that you would install in situations where you need your servers to be highly available. This means that the server is up and running under almost any circumstances. Although this sounds simple, it is not. When set up correctly, SQL Server Enterprise Edition supports cluster failover. This means that in the event of a hardware failure on one server, SQL Server will start up on another computer and continue to service clients with little down time. SQL Server Enterprise Edition also supports extended memory (greater than 2GB) and up to 32 processors. This version will run only on Windows NT Server Enterprise Edition.

- Small Business Server Edition—The Small Business Server edition of SQL Server 7.0 is the version that is shipped with Small Business Server. This version supports four processors and a maximum database size of 10GB. Because this version runs only on Small Business Server, it is optimized for 50 or fewer concurrent connections.

- Desktop Edition—The desktop edition of SQL Server is what you get when you install SQL Server on a Windows NT Workstation or Windows 95/98 computer. This version supports two processors and a maximum database size of 4GB.

Installing SQL Server

You have made it this far, and now it is time to actually install SQL Server on the computer. At this point, you must have the server that you are installing on prepared as I discussed earlier. Three different options, like all Microsoft products, exist for installing SQL Server. These are Typical, Minimum, and Custom. You must choose which type of installation you are going to perform during Setup Wizard. They are described in the following:

- Typical—The typical installation installs SQL server and the client utilities using the default options. If you choose this method, you will have to make very few decisions during the installation process. This option automatically installs the SQL Server Engine and Management Tools, Books Online, the Quick Tour, and What's New. It does not install the Full Text Search, the development tools, or the sample files. This option will take about 165MB of disk space, not including your user databases.

- Minimum—Like the typical installation, the minimum installation installs SQL Server using the default options. The difference is that this option installs SQL Server with the fewest possible files, thus taking up a lot less disk space—about 74MB. The minimum installation does not install the Management Tools, Books Online, the Quick Tour, or What's New.

- Custom—This option allows you to choose which SQL Server options are installed as well as exactly how they are installed. In order for this option to work, you must know exactly how you want SQL Server to work. During this option, you will have to choose which network protocols to use, the characterset, the default sort order, which utilities to install, where to place all the files, which documentation to install, which accounts SQL Server will run under, and how SQL Server will start.

SQL Server Install Process

During this section, I will discuss the installation of SQL Server Standard Edition on a Windows NT Server version 4.0 from a local CD-ROM. Because of the number of options that are available, I will cover the custom setup. The overall directions, though, will be similar to installing any of the other versions. For more information on installing and configuring failover support for SQL Server Enterprise Edition, you can search in Books Online. Implement the following steps:

1. Log into the server on which you will be installing SQL Server using an account that has administrative privileges.

2. Insert the SQL Server CD-ROM. If autorun is enabled on the server, the screen shown in Figure 2.4 is displayed. If the screen is not displayed, open Windows NT Explorer and run start.bat off the root of the CD-ROM.

FIGURE 2.4

The initial SQL Server Setup screen.

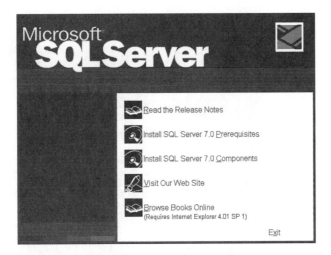

3. From this screen, select the Install SQL Server Components option. This opens the Install SQL Server 7.0 Components screen, as seen in Figure 2.5.

FIGURE 2.5

The Install SQL Server 7.0 Components screen.

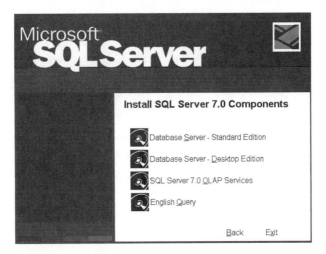

4. From the Install SQL Server 7.0 Components screen, select the Database Server—Full Product. This opens the Install Method dialog, as seen in Figure 2.6. At this screen, you will normally choose that you want to install SQL Server on the local machine.

FIGURE 2.6

*The Select Install
Method dialog.*

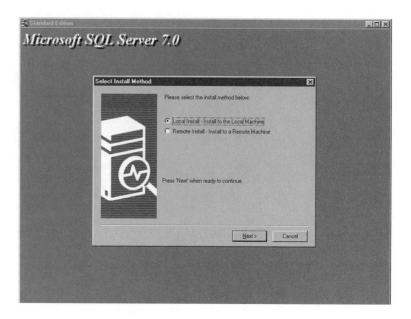

5. The next screen is the Welcome screen. This is the start of the SQL Server Setup Wizard. This wizard gathers information about you, your computer, and the options you want to install, and then actually installs the software.

6. The next screen is the Software License Agreement. If you agree with the license, select Yes. Otherwise, select No. If you select No, the SQL Server installation process halts.

7. The next screen is the User Information Screen. In this dialog, you must enter your name and your company's name. Select Next to continue.

8. The next screen is labeled the SQL Server Setup Dialog. In this screen, you have to type in your CD Key. This is the 10-digit number that is on the yellow or orange sticker on the back of your SQL Server CD-ROM case.

9. The following screen is the Select Type screen, as seen in Figure 2.7. From this screen, you must select the installation type, as I discussed earlier. For the purposes of this tutorial, I will choose the Custom installation option. You can also use the two browse buttons to choose the locations that you are going to install both the Program Files and the Data Files.

FIGURE 2.7

The Select Type dialog.

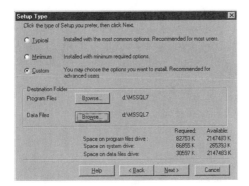

10. From the next screen, the Select Components Screen, as seen in Figure 2.8, you can select the components you are going to install. By default, the same options that are installed with the Typical installation option are already selected.

FIGURE 2.8

The Select Components screen.

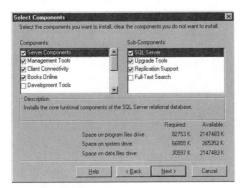

11. After selecting the Next button, the Character Set/Sort Order/Unicode Collation Screen appears, as seen in Figure 2.9. For the purposes of this installation, you should select the default options. For more information on the other options, you should refer to Books Online.

FIGURE 2.9

The Character Set/Sort Order/Unicode Collation screen.

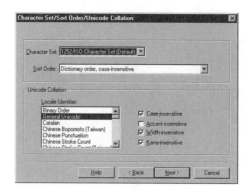

12. The next screen is the Network Libraries screen, as seen in Figure 2.10. From this screen, you can select any of the available network protocols. As you can see, the default protocols are Named Pipes and TCP/IP. For the purposes of this installation, you should select the default options. For more information on the other options, you should refer to Books Online.

FIGURE 2.10

The Network Libraries screen.

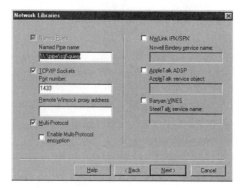

13. After selecting the Next button, the Services Account screen, as seen in Figure 2.11, is displayed. In this screen you can select to use the same service account for all SQL Server services, or you can specify different accounts for each service. You can also select whether SQL Server will start when the server is started. For the purposes of this installation, select the Use the Same Account for each service, Auto start SQL Server Service option, and enter the username and password for the account that you created earlier.

FIGURE 2.11

The Services Account screen.

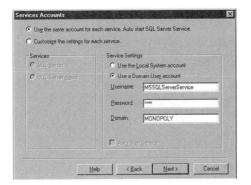

14. The next screen is the Choose Licensing Mode screen, as seen in Figure 2.12. From this screen, you can choose Per Seat or Per Server licensing. In a Per Seat licensing scheme, the client licenses are assigned to the individual clients, and the administrator must track license usage. When using Per Server, all client licenses are assigned to an individual server, and when additional servers are brought in, you must buy more licenses for each server.

FIGURE 2.12

The Choose Licensing Mode screen.

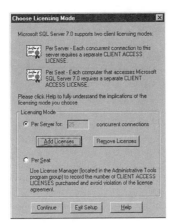

15. The next screen that you get is the Start Copying files screen. When you click the Next button, the SQL Server Installation Wizard begins copying files. This process can take up to 20 minutes. When this process is complete, the installation is complete.

16. The last screen you get is the confirmation that SQL Server has been installed and an option to reboot the server now or later. After you have rebooted the server, the SQL Server installation process will be complete.

Verifying SQL Server Installation

Now that you have completed the SQL Server installation process, it is time to verify that SQL Server was installed properly. Several different things need to be checked. You should check each of the following to ensure that SQL Server is installed properly:

- Were the correct directories created?
- Were all the appropriate Management Tools loaded?
- Did the SQL Server services get installed?
- Were there any errors in installation or was your installation verification correct?

Program and Data Directories

One of the first steps in verifying that SQL Server was installed correctly is to check and ensure that all the correct directories were created. Open Windows NT Explorer and browse out to the location on the hard drive where SQL Server was installed. The directory structure should look like those shown in Figure 2.13. If you installed the data directory in a different location than the default, you should also check to ensure that it also exists.

FIGURE 2.13

You can use Windows NT Explorer to check the SQL Server directory structure.

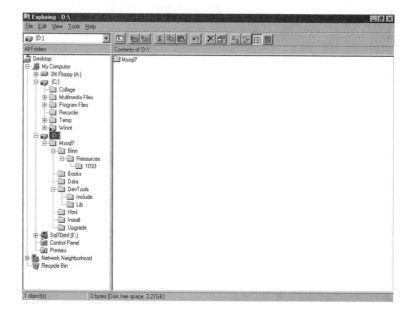

All Management Tools Loaded

Another important step is to ensure that all appropriate Management Tools were loaded during the installation process. The best way to do this is to click the Start Button, go to Programs, and choose the Microsoft SQL Server 7.0 program group. Look and ensure that all the tools that you selected are contained in this group.

SQL Server Services Loaded

The last step is to make sure that the SQL Server services were installed. When SQL Server is installed, two new services are installed—SQLServerAgent and MSSQLServer. You can check these services by performing the following:

1. Click the Start Menu, choose Setting, and then click on the Control Panel. Double-click on the Services icon. This opens the Services Control Panel, as shown in Figure 2.14.

FIGURE 2.14

The Services Control Panel.

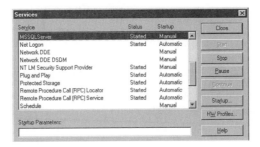

2. Look in the list of services, for both the MSSQLServer services and the SQLServerAgent service. If these are not in the list, you will have to reinstall SQL Server. If you have not yet rebooted the server, these two services will have no status.

3. After you have verified that the services are in the list, click the Close button.

Troubleshooting Installation

If, for some reason, SQL Server did not properly install, there are several things for you to check. If you receive any errors during the installation process, you should copy down any errors and text associated with those errors. You should also be sure to verify the installation as outlined in the previous section.

Error Messages

Whenever you get an error message, you should copy down the exact text of the message and any numbers that are associated with the errors. As with all error messages, the text of the error is often quite cryptic and difficult to understand. After you have copied down the error, you can go to three different places to get information about the error and how to fix it. The first place to look would be *SQL Server Books Online*. If you cannot find anything helpful there, the next place to look is *Microsoft TechNet* or *Microsoft Support Online*. *TechNet* is a subscription service that sends out CD-ROMs that contain all public Knowledge Base Articles. *Microsoft Support Online*, which used to be known as the *Knowledge Base*, also contains a great deal of information. You can find Microsoft Support Online at http://www.microsoft.com/support.

Installation Verification

If any of your verification steps do not work, you should also begin to investigate your installation. You should look at all the steps you performed and make sure that everything was done correctly. If you are not sure, you have two options to try. You can reinstall SQL Server over your current installation, or you can uninstall and then reinstall SQL Server. If you cannot find any information on any of these resources and still can't get SQL Server to install, the next best thing is to call Microsoft. The Microsoft technical support people have access to information that has not been made public yet, as well as one of the greatest resources—access to the developers.

Uninstalling SQL Server

Uninstalling SQL Server is a very simple process. Before you perform the uninstall, you should back up all your databases, user and system, in the event that you have to rebuild the server. After you have completed this, perform the following steps to remove SQL Server:

1. Insert the SQL Server 7.0 CD-ROM and run the SQL Server 7.0 installation program. This program will look at the computer, detect the installation of SQL Server, and give you the option to uninstall SQL Server.

2. At the Welcome screen, click the Next button.

3. The next screen gives you the option to choose the computer from which you are going to remove SQL Server. The local computer is highlighted by default. Click the Next button to continue.

4. The next screen gives you several options. Select the Work with Existing SQL Server option and then click the Next button.

5. From the next screen, click the Remove SQL Server option and then click the Next button.

6. The last screen gives you a confirmation screen. Click the Yes button, and SQL Server will be removed from your computer.

Summary

In this section, you have gone over the installation requirements, installation options, and the actual installation of SQL Server. You have also gone over the post installation issues that can arise with SQL Server. Finally, you looked over troubleshooting and uninstalling SQL Server.

Q&A

Q I have an old 486 server that is running an older version of SQL Server. Is it possible for me to upgrade this computer to SQL Server 7.0?

A No. The minimum processor requirement for SQL Server 7.0 is a Pentium 166 or faster. If you have an older computer, you will have to upgrade to a faster computer before installing SQL Server 7.0.

Q When I first installed SQL Server 7.0, I used the local system account. I now need to set up this server to participate in replication. How can I change from using the local system account to a domain account?

A In the Services Control panel, click the Startup button and enter the Domain Username and Password in the Log On As section.

Workshop

The quiz and the exercises are provided for your further understanding. The answers can be found in Appendix A, "Answers."

Quiz

1. What are the minimum processor requirements for SQL Server 7.0?

2. How much disk space does a typical installation of SQL Server 7.0 take?

3. What operating system does SQL Server 7.0 Enterprise Edition run on?

4. What is the major limitation that you must take into account when you are using SQL Server 7.0 Desktop Edition?

5. When installing SQL Server, you get an error message; what should you do?

6. What is the biggest limitation that you have when you install SQL Server using the local system account?

7. What type of privileges must you be logged in with in order to install SQL Server 7.0?

Exercises

1. Prepare a Windows NT Server for the installation of SQL Server 7.0. Check to make sure that the computer has a fast enough processor, enough memory, and hard drive space. You should also create a domain user account called MSSQLServerService.

2. Install SQL Server 7.0 on the computer that you prepared in exercise 1. Perform a Custom installation using the default Character Set and Sort Order. When the installation process has completed, verify the installation as outlined earlier in the chapter.

Hour **3**

Introducing Relational Databases

Before we jump into everything you need to know about SQL Server, you will first need to understand relational databases and how they work. There is a lot to relational databases. Aside from the logical and physical portions of the database, many objects can be contained in the database. These objects can be anything from tables to stored procedures. In this hour, you will be introduced to a lot of these, and then in future hours, you will learn how they work and how to create them.

The highlights of this hour include

- All About Relational Databases
- Database Architecture
- Database Objects

All About Relational Databases

A huge amount of theory exists out there about databases and the objects that can be contained in them. Two levels are going to be covered in this section. The first is the actual database itself. Then, we will look at the objects in the database and what they are used for.

Database Architecture

Databases are where everything in your SQL Server is stored. These databases are actually composed of both physical and logical components. The logical components are what the users who interact with the database actually see. The physical components of the database are not directly seen by the user; instead, these components are what SQL Server interacts with to form the logical components.

Physical Database Components

Every database on an SQL Server will contain at least two physical components. These components are files on the hard drive of the server. These two files contain all the information that your users enter into the server as well as a great deal of information that SQL Server needs to keep itself running. Your users will rarely, if ever, interact with the files. Rather, the database administrator will be the person who works with them. Two different types of files exist: data files and log files.

Data files are what SQL Server uses to store all the information that your users enter into the database as well as all the objects created in the database. You will learn more about objects here in a few minutes. These files will grow and shrink, if they are configured to do so, as needed.

The log files in a database is where SQL Server stored the transaction log of a database. The transaction log is what SQL Server uses to maintain the consistency of the database by ensuring that all modifications to the database are either completely made or cancelled. In the event that the server crashes, SQL Server will examine the transaction logs to make sure that all data modifications are complete. You will learn a great deal about transaction logging in Hour 4, "Database Architecture Fundamentals."

Logical Database Components

Databases are similar to data files in that they are places to store data. Users can enter data into databases and then retrieve data from the databases. Also similar to data files, users rarely access the data that is stored in the database directly. Rather, they will run an application that retrieves data from the database, or data files, and presents it to the users in a readable and understandable format.

The major differences between databases and data files is that the data in a database is highly organized, making retrieval much easier. In correctly designed databases, little or no redundant data is stored. This make life extremely easy on database developers because if they need to update one piece of data, like an address, they only have to go to one place to update it. This brings us to relational databases.

Relational databases are one of the most effective ways to organize data. Relational database management systems are applications of mathematical theories that solve how data can be effectively stored. In all relational database systems, all the data that is stored in the database is grouped into tables. A table, also known as a relation in database theory, is a representation of some amount of data that is important to the organization collecting the data. For example, many companies will track employee information in a database. Each table in the database will contain information that is important to tracking information about the employees. These tables will contain columns, also called attributes, and rows, also called tuples or records. Back to the employee tracking database, you might have one table that tracks basic information about the employee, such as employee number, name, address, phone number and department. Another table in the database might contain information about current assignments that the employee has. Employees can have more than one assignment at a time. One of the most important parts of relational database design is to have very little repeating data in the tables. For example, it is bad database design to have more than one column containing a phone number at which your employee might be reached. Because each employee can be assigned to multiple projects, you will need to relate the employee to the project through a unique ID, such as the employee number. Figure 3.1 outlines some of this for you.

FIGURE 3.1

An example of a relational database.

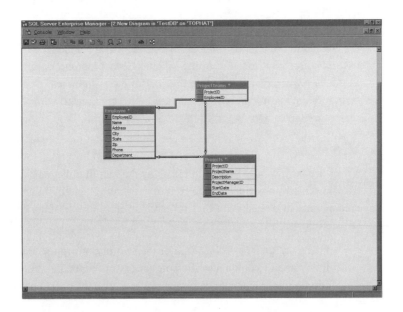

Database Objects

Now that you have somewhat of an idea about exactly what a relational database is, we need to go over the things that can be in the database. These different things, called objects, can be anything from tables to small pieces of code that can be used to perform application functions in the database. In this section, we will look at and define what these different database objects are, and in later hours, we will look at creating most of these objects.

Tables

A table is simply a database object made up of columns and rows that can be used to store data. As many as two billion tables can be in a database with as many as 1,024 columns per table. The only limiting factor to the number of rows in the database is the amount of disk space that you have to allocate to that database. The maximum row length in an SQL Server table is 8,060 bytes long. Each column in the table will contain data only of a specific datatype. SQL Server supports two different types of tables—permanent and temporary.

Permanent tables are created in the database and remain there until they are dropped. Normally, these tables are used to store permanent data, such as anything that is created by your users. These tables are created in the database that you specify.

The other type of table is temporary tables. These tables are usually created by the user application for temporary storage space. Two types of temporary table exist. The first is local temporary tables. These tables are created by one user and accessible only by that user. The other type of temporary table is a global temporary table. These types of tables are create by one user and then accessible by any user who is on the system. These tables are created in the tempdb database. Local temporary tables are dropped as soon as the user who created it logs out of the system. Global temporary tables are dropped as soon as the user who created the table logs out of the system, and any other users who had been referencing it logs out. Temporary tables are created with a prefix of # for local temporary tables and ## for global temporary tables.

Views

Views are intrinsically related to tables by the fact that they are essentially virtual tables. Views are used to represent data from one or more table in an alternative way. Views are created only in the database that you are currently using. Many reasons for using views are as follows:

- Focus on Specific Data—One of the best reasons to use a view is to focus the user's attention on a specific amount of data in the database that he needs to perform his job. This can be extremely useful as the users can only get to the data that they need and no other data in the database. For example, you might create a view based on your employees' name and phone numbers to create a phone list.

- Query Simplification—Views are created and based on queries that can often be quite complex. These queries can span multiple tables, create aggregates of several columns, and perform subqueries. The view simplifies this because instead of submitting the complex query, the user only has to query the view. An example of this would be to create a view that retrieves data out of several tables that tells management which employees are working on which projects under which project managers.

- Data Customization—Views allow users with different skill sets and job functions to view the same data in different ways based on their needs. An example of this would be to create a view that retrieves only the data about employees who a manager handles.

- Security—Views are useful when you are dealing with highly sensitive data. It is possible to create a view that allows users to look at specific portions of the data in a table and to not allow them to look at the table itself. In other words, your users will be able to access the data through the view, but if they would try to access the data in the table itself, it would fail. An example of this would be payroll information. You could create a view that allows people to view basic information such as name and department while blocking those users from seeing the amount of money that those people make.

- Exporting Data—It is possible to create a view that is based on several tables and then use the SQL Server Bulk Copy Program, or BCP, to copy the rows that are referenced by the view out to a flat file. This file can then be loaded into Excel or any other similar program for analysis.

- Simplify Access to Partitioned Data—Many times with very active databases, you will partition large tables into smaller tables based on criteria such as a date. This makes queries somewhat difficult. To simplify this, you can create a view and simply query the view.

It is important for you to realize that there is no data at all stored in the view itself. The view is only a simpler way to access the data that is contained in other tables in the database.

Indexes

An index is a special type of database object that is associated with a table directly. An index is used to speed up access to the data in that table and can enforce some data integrity issues, such as uniqueness of rows in that table. Indexes contain keys that are made up of at least one column in the table. The keys allow SQL Server to pinpoint rows in the table quickly without needing to scan the entire table for the requested rows. If you create a table that contains no indexes on it, SQL Server will store the data in that table in no particular order.

Two types of indexes that can be created on tables in SQL Server are as follows:

- Clustered—A clustered index is one in which SQL Server stored the data in the same order that it is indexed. For example, on a table that contains last names, if the index is on the last name, SQL Server will store the names in alphabetical order. If the key is built based on a numeric column, SQL Server will store the data in numeric order. These type of indexes are very useful for finding specific rows as well as ranges of rows. The only time that the data in the table is sorted in any type of order is when there is a clustered index on the table. You can only place one clustered index on each table because the data cannot be sorted in different ways.

- Nonclustered—A nonclustered index provides a completely different structure for sorting data than a clustered index. Nonclustered indexes have an index key that is associated with the value in the row and then a pointer to where that row actually resides in the database. The data in the table is not stored in the order that the non-clustered index dictates. You will commonly see this type of index used on tables that have a clustered index on one set of columns, but the table is also frequently searched on another set, so it becomes important to have an index on those values as well.

When working with indexes, it is important to remember that the columns which are frequently searched on, such as an employee's ID number or last name, should be indexed. This will speed the process of getting at the data.

Datatypes

A datatype is a definition for the type of data that you are going to be placing in a table or variable. These are used for several purposes. First, they tell SQL Server what type of data to expect, thereby allowing space allocation to be optimized for that specific datatype. Secondly, it allows the developer to determine what type of data needs to be collected—for example, numeric data or character data—and forces the user to input that type of data. Any attempt to input data not of that type results in an error. Lastly, datatypes ensure consistency across all the rows in the table.

Many different datatypes are available in SQL Server. If these datatypes are not enough for you, though, you can also create your own based off the original ones provided to you by SQL Server. We are not going to go into the different datatypes in this hour, but we will go into them in depth in Hour 7, "Working with Tables."

Constraints

Constraints are a way to ensure that data in your databases is in the form that you expect it to be. Constraints can be used to define rules on the format of data, ensure uniqueness in a table, ensure that data is actually entered into a column, and ensure that columns maintain integrity between tables. Five types of constraints that can be used in SQL Server are as follows:

- NOT NULL—This type of constraint is used to force the user adding data to a table to enter a value into a specific column. You can have more than one NOT NULL constraint per table. For example, in an electronic phone book application, you would want to ensure that any new name added to the phone book had a name and a phone number. To do this, you would mark the columns containing that data as NOT NULL and, if the user tries to enter a row into the table that contains a NULL value for either of these columns, the entry will fail.

- CHECK—A CHECK constraint is used to specify a Boolean operator that tells SQL Server to limit the number of values that can be entered into the table. If the Boolean expression evaluates to False, the row is rejected and an error is produced. An example of a CHECK constraint would be to tell SQL Server that the bonus column must contain a numeric value between 2 and 15 percent. This way, anytime a value is entered into this column, it is checked against this constraint to ensure that it is valid. You can create multiple check constraints per table and per column.

- UNIQUE—The UNIQUE constraint is used to force the users of the application to always enter unique values into a column. If the user attempts to enter a value into the column that is already contained in the column, the row is rejected and an error is produced. UNIQUE constraints allow NULL values if the columns contained in the constraint allow NULL values.

- PRIMARY KEY—A PRIMARY KEY constraint is used to create a column or combination of columns that can be used by SQL Server to identify the rows in that table. The PRIMARY KEY is used to enforce what is known as entity integrity, which means that the columns in a PRIMARY KEY must be unique. You can only have one PRIMARY KEY per table and all the columns in the PRIMARY KEY cannot accept NULL values. If a PRIMARY KEY is defined on several columns, it is important to note that the combination of the columns must be unique.

- FOREIGN KEY—A FOREIGN KEY constraint is used to establish a link between two tables. This link is created when the column that is the PRIMARY KEY in one table is added to the second table. The primary function of a FOREIGN KEY constraint is to keep users from entering data into one table without having a relating row in another. For example, in an order processing environment, you could have two tables called Customers and Orders. The Orders table would have a FOREIGN KEY

3

constraint put on it referencing the Customers table. The reason behind this is that you would always want any record in the Orders table to have a corresponding row in the Customers table. Otherwise, your shipping department will have product to ship, but no where to ship it to.

Constraints are very powerful tools if you use them correctly.

Stored Procedures

Stored procedures are groupings of SQL statements that have been compiled together into a single execution plan. These can be used to return data to the user and to achieve a consistent implementation of logic across applications. A great deal of advantages to using stored procedures are as follows:

- SQL statements and logic that is used to perform similar tasks can be designed, coded, and tested at one place. Then, when applications need that functionality, all they have to do is execute the stored procedure.

- Stored procedures can increase performance on the server by eliminating large amounts of network traffic required to execute large SQL scripts. Instead, all the client needs to do is to execute the single stored procedure.

- Stored procedures can keep your users from having to know everything about the underlying table structure. All they need to know is that they have to execute a particular stored procedure to attain a specific result.

You can do a great deal of things with stored procedures. You will learn how to work with stored procedures in Hour 21, "Programming SQL Server."

Triggers

Last but not least, you need to learn about triggers. Triggers are similar to stored procedures by the fact that they are a grouping of SQL statements. The major difference is how triggers are executed. Triggers are executed when a row is inserted, updated, or deleted from a table, depending on how the trigger was created. Triggers are a powerful way to enforce business rules when data is modified. A single table can have up to three different triggers on it. You can have a trigger that fires when an UPDATE occurs, one that fires when an INSERT occurs, and one that fires when a DELETE occurs. Triggers can be a way that the SQL Server automates business processes. For example, when an author has sold enough books to cover the advance that the publishing company paid, a trigger could be used to automatically begin calculating the royalty payments. Triggers fire after the record has been successfully modified in the table. If the modification fails because of a syntax error or constraint violation, the trigger is not fired.

You need to be aware of one point of caution when dealing with triggers. Although triggers can be very powerful, they can also be very damaging to the performance of your server. Be very careful that you do not try to put too much functionality into your triggers because it will slow down response and can really frustrate your users.

Summary

In this hour, we have covered a lot of the little details about databases that you need to be aware of before you get too far into dealing with databases. First, we covered databases in general. Then we covered all the objects that can be placed into a database and what they can do.

Q&A

Q **What circumstances should I not consider a view that spans several tables?**

A One of the major issues that you have in dealing with views is when you are performing INSERTs, UPDATEs, and DELETEs. You cannot perform any of these data modifications into a view that spans several tables.

Q **What types of performance problems could I expect if I create a trigger that contains too much functionality?**

A The biggest problem with triggers is the amount of time that they can take to run. If there is too much functionality in the trigger, it will cause other users to wait. When a user performs any sort of data modification that causes a trigger to fire, the rows effected by the trigger are held until the trigger has completed running. For example, if the trigger takes 10 seconds to run, it will be 10 seconds until any other user can access the rows the original user was running.

Workshop

The quiz and the exercise are provided for your further understanding. The answers can be found in Appendix A, "Answers."

Quiz

1. Physically, how is a database implemented?

2. What is a table?

3. What can a view do for you?

4. What type of constraint could you use to make sure that all the rows in the table are different from each other?

5. What type of constraint could you use to ensure that all the rows in one table have a matching row in another table?

6. What is a stored procedure?

7. What functionality does a trigger perform for you?

Exercise

Look through the databases on the server that you have registered and look to see what objects are contained in the database.

HOUR 4

Database Architecture Fundamentals

When dealing with SQL Server, it is very important to not only know how things work, but also why they work. Although this might seem odd, you must understand several things about SQL Server databases in order to properly work with them. In this section, I will cover some of the different aspects of how SQL Server databases work.

The highlights of this hour include

- Database 101
- Physical Space Allocation
- System Databases
- User Databases
- The System Catalog
- The Transaction Log

Database 101

As I mentioned before, it is important for you to understand the basic architecture of SQL Server databases. It should come as no surprise to you that all data in SQL Server is stored in databases. On a physical level, these databases are implemented as at least two files on the server's hard disk drives. On a logical level, you and your users work with tables, stored procedures, views, and other objects. From your user's standpoint, the physical implementation should be pretty much invisible.

When you first install SQL Server, several databases are automatically installed. Four of these databases are known as system databases. System databases contain information that is vital to making SQL Server work. These databases contain configuration information, maintenance history, temporary space for data sorting, and a basic structure for creating all user databases. Two user databases are also installed during the initial setup. These two databases are used for testing and user training.

Unlike other RDBMSs, you do not have to run multiple instances of SQL Server to allow users to access different databases on the same server. SQL Server is very good at managing server resources, allowing multiple users the ability to access multiple databases. Each user connection is associated with a single database, but each user can open up several different connections to different databases.

Physical Space Allocation

When I talk about how SQL Server uses space, you are going to hear quite a bit about two terms. Before I get into any of the logical implementations of databases, you must understand what these two terms are and how they interact with each other. They are page and extent.

Page

A *page* is the smallest unit of space allocation in SQL Server. A single page is 8KB in length and is where the actual data in the database is written. Each page can contain at least one row, and a row cannot extend past the length of a single page. A page can only contain data from a single table because the page itself is owned by a specific table. To keep SQL Server from having to allocate individual pages when space is needed, which would cause a great deal of system overhead, space is allocated in units called extents.

Extent

An *extent* is the smallest unit of space that SQL Server can allocate at one shot. An extent is eight contiguous pages, or 64KB of space. To save space in the database, each object in the database is not allocated an entire extent. If this were the case, very small objects that contain little data would take up a minimum of 64KB of space. To solve this, SQL Server uses two different types of extents:

- Mixed—A mixed extent is a 64KB allocation that can contain pages from up to eight different objects.
- Uniform—A uniform extent is a 64KB allocation in which all pages contained in it are owned by the same object.

When you first create an object, SQL Server assigns that object space from a mixed extent. If the object grows to the point that it contains eight or more pages, SQL Server will then move the existing data into a uniform extent.

Files and Filegroups

When you create a SQL Server database, the actual storage for the database is mapped across several operating system files. Unlike previous versions of SQL Server, transaction log and database information are never stored on the same file, and more than one database is never stored on the same file. Also, unlike previous versions of SQL Server, database files will automatically grow when they become full, until they reach a specified size that you define. The three types of SQL Server database files are as follows:

- Primary Database Files—Primary database files are the starting point for all databases. These files not only contain the information that is gathered by the database users, but they also contain information about all the other files that are contained in the database. Every database will have a primary database file. The default, and recommended, extension for primary database files is .mdf.
- Secondary Database Files—Secondary database files are any other database files that you add to a database. These can be added to give the database the capability to grow on multiple drives on your server. Not all databases will have secondary database files, but they are required if you want your database to extend across several physical hard drives. The default, and recommended, extension for secondary database files is .ndf.
- Log Files—Log files are used to hold the transaction log of the database. Every database will have at least one log file, but you can have multiple log files in a database. The default, and recommended, extension for log files is .ldf.

An advanced feature of database files is the capability to assign files to filegroups for allocation and administrative purposes. Filegroups can be used to allocate tables, indexes, and other data to specific locations on the server. This can allow large or infrequently accessed data to be moved off of the main filegroup, which will speed up access for the other data. I will go over creating files and filegroups in Hour 6, "Creating Databases, Files, and Filegroups."

System Databases

Four system databases are installed with SQL Server. These system databases are called master, model, tempdb, and msdb. These databases are the heart and soul of SQL Server and, without them, SQL Server would not work. Each one of these databases performs a specific function within the servers.

Master

The master database controls all aspects of SQL Server. This database contains all the configuration information, user login information, and information about current processes that are going on in the server. The first thing that SQL Server does when it starts up is to find the master database and open it up. Because the master database contains all the information about the existence of all other databases, it is really the most important database on the whole system. If you lose the master database, it is very difficult to recover all of your user databases. Therefore, it is very important that you keep recent backups of the master database in case something does happen.

Model

The model database, as the name implies, is the model from which all user databases are created. When you create a new database, SQL Server makes copies of all the objects that are contained in the model database and moves them into the new database. Any extra space that is contained in the new user database after the model objects are copied is filled with empty pages.

tempdb

tempdb is a very special database that is used by all users who are accessing your SQL Server. This database is used to hold all temporary tables, stored procedures, and any other temporary worktables that are created by SQL Server. One example of when tempdb is used is when you sort data. This data is selected into a temporary worktable in tempdb, sorted, and then the results are returned to the user. Every time SQL Server is restarted, it clears any data that is in tempdb and rebuilds it. You should never create any tables in tempdb that are going to be needed permanently.

msdb

The msdb database is a special case in SQL Server. If you look at the actual definition of this database, it is really a user database. The difference comes in with what SQL Server does with this database. Any scheduled task, alert, and operator is stored in the msdb database. Another function with this database is that it stores all backup history. The process that uses this database is the SQL Server Agent.

User Databases

Along with any user databases that you create, SQL Server will always create two user databases during the initial installation process. These databases do not affect the performance and operation of the server, but they do make good places to learn and experiment with new concepts without having to worry about changing productional data. These two databases are called pubs and Northwind.

pubs

Anyone who is familiar with previous versions of SQL Server should have an idea about, or at least have seen, the pubs database. This database contains information about a publishing company and is used to demonstrate many of the key features and concepts of SQL Server. You can make any changes you want to this database, and it will not affect the way that your SQL Server runs. If you have made changes and you want to restore the database to its original state, Microsoft has provided the installation script for the database. This script, called instpubs.sql, is stored in the \MSSQL7\Install directory. To reinstall the pubs database, perform the following steps. Do not worry, at this point, about understanding the syntax of this command. I will go over it in Hour 5, "Using the Tools and Utilities."

1. Click the Start Button, go to Programs, and select the Command Prompt.

2. At the command prompt, change directories to the \MSSQL7\Install directory using the following command:

   ```
   cd \MSSQL7\Install
   ```

3. Using the OSQL utility, run the instpubs.sql script using the following command:

   ```
   osql /Usa /Psapassword /Sservername /iinstpubs.sql /oinstpubs.rpt
   ```

4. When this command has completed running, exit the command prompt and use Notepad to view the contents of the instpubs.rpt file. If there were any errors during the execution of this script, they will be contained in this file.

4

Northwind

Like the pubs database, the Northwind database is a preinstalled user database that
you can use to learn the concepts of SQL Server. Like the Microsoft Access database
of the same name, this database contains information about a trading company called
Northwind Traders. This fictitious company imports and exports specialty foods from
across the world. You can make any changes to this database without having to worry
about impacting your productional systems. If you do make any changes to this database,
you can restore it to its original condition by running the script called instnwnd.sql using
the following steps. Like the pubs example, do not worry about understanding this yet, I
will go over the syntax later. I will refer back to this reinstallation process several times
over the course of this book, after I have made changes to these databases.

1. Click the Start Button, go to Programs, and select the Command Prompt.

2. At the command prompt, change directories to the \MSSQL7\Install directory
   using the following command:

   ```
   cd \MSSQL7\Install
   ```

3. Using the OSQL utility, run the instpubs.sql script using the following command:

   ```
   osql /Usa /Psapassword /Sservername /iinstnwnd.sql /oinstnwnd.rpt
   ```

4. When this command has completed running, exit the command prompt and use
   Notepad to view the contents of the instnwnd.rpt file. If there were any errors
   during the execution of this script, they will be contained in this file.

The System Catalog

Contained in all user and system databases are a set of special tables, known as the system
catalog. These tables contain all the information SQL Server uses to find out information
about the objects that are contained within each database. When querying data from the
system catalog, Microsoft wants you to avoid accessing the tables directly. SQL Server
has provided a way for you to view the information from these tables using Information
Schema Views. Information Schema Views do two major things for you. First of all, they
shield any applications from any changes that are made in the system catalog. Frequently,
when Microsoft adds new functionality into SQL Server, they have to make changes to
the layout of the system catalog. If an application is hard coded to look at certain tables,
the application will fail because they are not prepared to handle those changes. If the
application points at the Informational Schema Views, they will continue to work. The
second thing that these views do for you is make SQL Server compliant with the SQL-92
standard. The SQL-92 standard defines how a SQL database server should look. This
ensures that SQL Server applications will be compatible with other applications on other

database management platforms. If your applications are coded to work with these views, the applications will be able to be ported between different systems.

The Transaction Log

In SQL Server, the transaction log is what is responsible for maintaining your database in a consistent state. What this means is it makes sure that data modifications are either completely made or they are cancelled. All of these data modifications are based on transactions. A transaction is a logical unit of work within SQL Server. Within a transaction, you want either everything or nothing to work. If only part of a transaction works, you leave the database in an inconsistent state.

An example that might make more sense would be a banking example. Imagine that your bank maintains all of its accounts on an SQL Server. You balance your checkbook one day and realize that your balance is getting a little bit low. Your response is to call your bank and ask them to transfer $1,000 from your savings account into your checking account. You would want this entire process to be a single transaction. If your bank's computer were to fail for some reason between the time that it removes the $1,000 from your savings account and before it adds it to your checking account, you would be out $1,000.

When a transaction begins, and before any actual data is modified, a row is written to the transaction log, showing the beginning of the transaction. All changes made are then logged to the transaction log. SQL Server then finds the data, either in memory or on disk. If the data is on disk, it is loaded into memory. The data modifications are actually made in memory and then written to disk at a later point when SQL Server is not as busy. When the transaction has completed, an end transaction row is written to the log. The begin and end records are how SQL Server delimitates the beginning and end of a transaction.

A transaction can fail for any reason. It can fail if one of the tables that it is trying to write to cannot be written to. It can fail because of hardware failure. Or, it could fail because someone accidentally kicks the power cord out of the wall.

If this is the case, when SQL Server is restarted, the automatic recovery process goes through the transaction logs of each database and searches for the begin and end records of transactions and compares that to the data in the database. Transactions that have not been committed at the time of the system crash are cancelled, or rolled back. When both begin and end transaction records are found in the transaction log, the transactions are re-executed, or rolled forward.

The automatic recovery process begins with the master database, and then moves on to the model database. After the model database has been recovered, the automatic recovery process clears tempdb of all objects in it. Next, msdb is recovered; then pubs is recovered. If the server is set up as a distribution server, the distribution database is recovered next. After all the system databases have been recovered, the user databases are recovered. Users can log into the server after the system databases have been recovered, but they cannot use any user database until it has completed recovering.

The automatic recovery process cannot be turned off, but two configuration options affect automatic recovery. During the automatic recovery process, the databases that are being recovered are grayed out in SQL Enterprise Manager with the word Recovering next to them. The recovery flags option determines what information SQL Server displays during the recovery process. The recovery interval option controls the maximum amount of time that SQL Server should take to recover the database. The value that you set here is used by SQL Server to determine the frequency of the checkpoint process. These options can be set using SQL Enterprise Manager or the sp_configure stored procedure.

To speed the automatic recovery process, SQL Server performs a process called the checkpoint. This is where SQL Server writes all pages that have been changed to disk. After this has completed, it writes a record to the transaction log. This is the identifying point, which tells SQL Server that all completed transactions were guaranteed to have been written to the disk.

Two types of checkpoints exist: user initiated and automatic checkpoint. A user-initiated checkpoint is issued by the database owner. The automatic checkpoint is issued by SQL Server and based on the amount of system activity and the recovery interval value that you configured. The recovery interval determines the amount of time that it should take the server to recover after a failure.

At two other times, the databases are checkpointed. When you use the sp_dboption stored procedure to change a database, it will automatically be checkpointed. Also, when you issue the shutdown command, SQL Server will automatically checkpoint all databases on the server.

Summary

In this hour, I have covered how SQL Server allocates space and maintains information about itself. I have also covered information about how SQL Server maintains consistency in the database using the transaction log. This information will help you out later on when you are looking at transactions.

Q&A

Q **I have created a database in which no data will ever be modified; it will only be queried. Because no data will ever be modified and I do not want to manage the overhead of transaction logging, is it possible to turn this off?**

A It is not possible to turn off transaction logging. This part of SQL Server is vitally important to the way it works, so Microsoft doesn't allow it. What is more, on a read-only database, SQL Server will not be incurring any overhead of transaction logging anyway because you will not be modifying data.

Q **I have just installed SQL Server 7.0 and have discovered that there are already six databases installed on the server. They are taking up space and I want to delete them. Is that okay?**

A No. It is not OK to delete these databases, or at least all of them. Only two databases can be deleted, and these are the pubs and Northwind databases. All the other databases on the system are vital to the operation of the server.

Workshop

The quiz and the exercise are provided for your further understanding. The answers can be found in Appendix A, "Answers."

Quiz

1. What is the smallest amount that SQL Server allocates space to the database in, and how large is it?
2. When SQL Server first allocates space to a new database object, how does it do it?
3. What is an extent, and how large is it?
4. What is the purpose of the master database?
5. What is the purpose of the msdb database?
6. What is tempdb used for?
7. What are primary database files used for?
8. How many primary database files can you add to a database?
9. What is the transaction log used for?
10. What is a transaction?

Exercise

Explore your installation of SQL Server. Find the master, msdb, and model databases on your system. Investigate the size of their data and log segments.

HOUR 5

Using the Tools and Utilities

Now that you have installed SQL Server on your computer and you know a little more about SQL Server and relational databases, you need to learn all the tools that are available to you and how to use them. Most of these tools are used for specific purposes, such as importing and exporting data or monitoring the server. Other tools, such as SQL Enterprise Manager, are multipurpose tools that you can use to perform a large number of functions.

The highlights of this hour include

- All These Tools
- The SQL Server 7.0 Program Group
- Microsoft SQL Server—Switch Group
- Other Tools

All These Tools

When you install SQL Server 7.0, it installs a host of tools and utilities that perform many different functions. Like most other products, some of the functionality of these products crosses functionality boundaries. Also, like most other products, of all the products that are installed with SQL Server 7.0, you will use only a few on a daily basis. The rest of these tools are used in special circumstances. Depending on the platform you have installed SQL Server on and whether you have had a previous version of SQL Server installed on your machine, you might not have all the tools that we are going to cover here. If all the right circumstances have been met, you will have SQL Server installed with two program groups. These are the Microsoft SQL Server 7.0 group and the Microsoft SQL Server 7.0—Switch group.

The SQL Server 7.0 Program Group

Within this folder, shortcuts to most of the tools that you will commonly use exist. Out of this, you will use probably only two tools on a daily basis—only one if you do not want to mess with writing SQL Scripts. We will go over each of the utilities in the order that they are listed in the group.

Books Online

The SQL Server Books Online are probably your biggest ally when you are trying to research a problem or determine the correct course of action when given a specific problem. Microsoft has taken what would have been the printed documents that could have shipped with the product and placed them all on the hard drive of your computer. This document is a special type of HTML code called compiled HTML. The reason that Microsoft has done this is threefold. First, to actually produce these books in hard copy would be extremely expensive. If you have worked with any previous versions of SQL Server and you ordered the documentation kit, you know that it was expensive and comprised of around 10 books. Secondly, it was difficult to have this number of books because it is difficult to keep track of them all. Lastly, it is so much easier to be able to search the Books Online to find the topic that you are looking for.

In the older, hard copy versions of the books, you actually had a separate book comprised of the index that told you which book you needed to look at. The problem with this was that book indexers are human beings and do not always pick up all the keywords in a section. When you search Books Online, you actually search every word on every page unless you specify otherwise. This can be a double-edged sword for you though. It you do not narrow your search sufficiently, Books Online will return hundreds of responses for you to look through to find the topic that you were actually looking for. For example, if you want to find information on the snapshot replication with immediate updating subscribers, you need to make sure to specify that as your search phrase. If you make your search phrase too generic, you will get too many hits to sort through. Take a look at Table 5.1 to see how your search phrase can make all the difference.

TABLE 5.1 Narrowing Your Search

Phrase Searched	Hits
replication	500
snapshot replication	210
snapshot replication updating subscribers	54
snapshot replication immediate updating subscribers	33
snapshot replication immediate updating subscribers	10

As you can see, the more specific you can make your search phrase, the better off you are going to be.

Client Network Utility

The Client Network Utility is used to manage what network protocols the client computers are going to use to connect to the SQL Server. This is also used to control which protocols the SQL Server will use to connect to other SQL Servers.

There are three tabs to the Client Network Utility. The first tab, as seen in Figure 5.1, is the General Tab. On this tab, you can choose the default network library for the client. The default network library is used to connect to any server when you do not specify a different library to use when connecting. The default for this setting is Named Pipes. If the server that you are connecting to is on a Windows 95/98 computer, you should change this value to something else because Windows 95/98 cannot create Named Pipes.

The other section in this tab is the Server Alias Configurations area. With this, you can actually do some really useful things. First of all, it allows you to specify the location of a server on the network for your users. This is useful when your users are having a difficult time connecting to a server. Another useful function in this is that you can set up multiple connections to the same server under different names. This might not seem to be such a big deal, but there are two scenarios in which this can be extremely useful.

5

FIGURE 5.1

*The General Tab of the
Client Network Utility.*

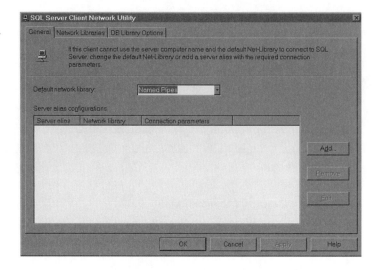

The first is when you are developing an application and want to certify that it will work under all network protocols. It is not totally unheard of to find an application that works perfectly under some network protocols but not as well under others. As a developer, all I have to do is create different server aliases and connect to the server using those different protocols.

The second scenario in which this is useful is when you need to connect to the same server within SQL Enterprise Manager using different login credentials. When you register a server in SQL Enterprise Manager, a user name and password are usually associated with that, and to change it is not always easy. All that needs to be done is to create a new server alias for each login with which you are going to connect to the server.

The other two tabs in the Client Network utility are useful during those few times that you will need the functionality they provide, but for the most part will sit untouched by you. The first tab is the Network Libraries tab. From this tab, you can view the version information and build date of each network library that is installed on the machine. The last tab, the DB Library Options tab, allows you to view version information and build date of the DB-Library. The DB-Library is the library that SQL Server clients actually use to communicate with the server. The other options that are available on this page deal with international charactersets and options. These settings are rarely changed.

SQL Enterprise Manager

SQL Enterprise Manager will become your close companion when you are working with SQL Server. SQL Enterprise Manager is a graphical way to manage all the SQL Servers that you have access to from one central point. SQL Enterprise Manager is actually an extension of the Microsoft Management Console, or MMC. MMC is one of the newest tools in Microsoft's arsenal to make administration easier. Basically, MMC is a framework that can be used for managing almost all BackOffice applications.

When you start SQL Enterprise Manager for the first time, you will notice that the SQL Server you installed has already been detected and registered. The process of registration is a fairly common one of which you need to be aware. Registration is simply the process of telling SQL Server that there is an SQL Server running on a specific machine and telling it what username and password to use when connecting to that server. All of this is performed through the Registered SQL Server Properties dialog, as seen in Figure 5.2.

FIGURE 5.2

The Registered SQL Server Properties dialog.

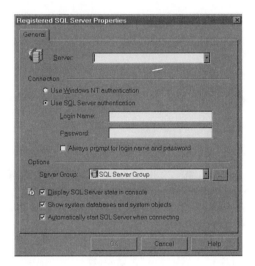

You can do a lot with SQL Enterprise Manager. We will get into most of the functionality in the different sections throughout the book, but there are a couple of things that you should keep in mind when using SQL Enterprise Manager. First of all, try to right-click on everything. This is because you will be able to perform most actions dealing with specific objects by right-clicking on them. The other thing you need to remember is that there are two sets of menus, as you can see in Figure 5.3. The top set of menus, which includes the Console, Window, and Help items, will be almost useless to you when you are managing SQL Servers. The lower set of menus is the ones you will use when you manage your servers.

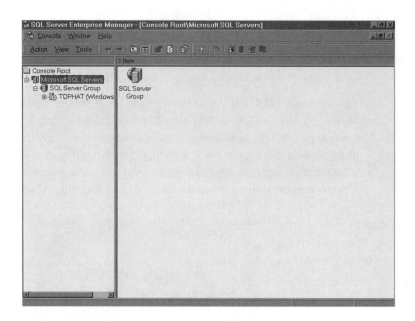

FIGURE 5.3

Multiple menus are available in SQL Enterprise Manager.

Import and Export Data

The Import and Export Data shortcut actually opens the Data Transformation Services Wizard. This tool is used to import, export, and transform data from one data source to another. For example, it is possible to migrate data into an SQL Server from an Oracle database, an Excel spreadsheet, or a text file. This is a very powerful tool that we will go over in more detail in Hour 12, "Importing and Exporting Data."

MSDTC Administrative Console

The MSDTC Administrative Console is used to manage the Microsoft Distributed Transaction Coordinator. This service is installed with SQL Server, but is really an entirely separate animal. This product can be used to create distributed transactions, which are transactions that are spread across different servers. If, for some reason, the transaction cannot be committed on one server, it will not be committed on any server. This ensures that the data on all servers remains consistent. In this book, you will not learn a great deal about the Distributed Transaction Coordinator. It is a very powerful tool, and its usage could easily fill a book this size. We will, however, go over distributed transactions in more detail in the sections on replication. One book you can check out that contains more information about the Distributed Transaction Coordinator is *MTS Programming with Visual Basic* by Sams Publishing (0-672-31425-8).

Profiler

SQL Server Profiler is one of the most powerful tools available to you in monitoring users and optimizing your server. The types of events that SQL Server Profiler can track are login attempts, connects and disconnects, SQL INSERTs, UPDATEs and DELETEs, and Remote Procedure Call batch status. After collecting information in the form of traces, you can then use the traces to analyze and fix server resource issues, monitor login attempts and correct locking and blocking issues. A trace is a file in which you capture server activity and events for later use. We will look at using the SQL Server Profiler in Hour 23, "Optimization and Tuning."

Query Analyzer

The SQL Server Query Analyzer is the other tool you will rely on to help you administer your server. Unlike SQL Enterprise Manager, this tool is not a graphical one, per se, although it does have one very useful graphical component. Although this tool does have a graphical interface, you must type in SQL command and scripts directly in order to use this tool. The one very useful graphical part of this tool is the ability to view statement execution plans. When SQL Server runs any SQL Server commands, it generates a plan that it will use to access all the tables referenced in the command. This is useful to allow you to determine how indexes are used. Depending on what your comfort level is and how much SQL you want to learn, this can actually be a more powerful tool than SQL Enterprise Manager. This is because SQL Enterprise Manager provides you a smaller, more frequently used, set of functionality, whereas if you know the right commands, Query Analyzer allows you to have more control than you have with SQL Enterprise Manager. Like SQL Enterprise Manager, we will cover a great deal of information on the SQL Server Query Analyzer throughout the rest of the book.

5

readme.txt

This shortcut is not exactly an actual application that can be used to run SQL Server. Rather, this is a text file that contains vital information that did not make it into SQL Server Books Online when it was created. It also contains corrections to data that changed after Books Online were finished. If this is your first time working with SQL Server 7.0, you should open this file up and skim through it. Even if you do not know understand all the information presented to you, it is important that you at least know what is in there, so when you do run across something that is incorrect in Books Online, it might spark your memory.

Server Network Utility

The Server Network Utility is used to control what network protocols that the SQL Server itself will communicate on. This is an important utility because, of course, if SQL Server is not listening on the protocol that your clients are expecting, they will not be able to communicate with the server.

The Server Network Utility is comprised of two tabs. The first tab is the General tab, as seen in Figure 5.4. This tab shows you which network libraries are already set up on the server. If you have the Shared Memory library on the computer, this library allows for client/server connections on the same computer on Windows 95/98. To add other network libraries, click on the Add button and choose the network library you want to add. Most of these libraries require that you supply some configuration options. The best thing you can do is get with your network administrator to help you fill out these options.

FIGURE 5.4

The Server Network Utility.

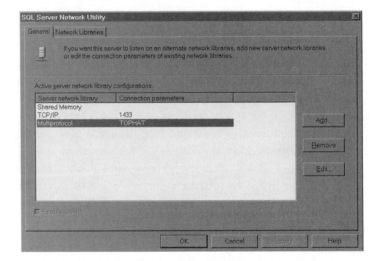

Service Manager

The SQL Server Service Manager, as seen in Figure 5.5, is used to start, pause and stop the MSSQLServer service, the SQLServerAgent service, and the MSDTC service. These are all integral portions to SQL Server. On Windows NT computers, all of these run as services, and on Windows 95/98, they run as applications in the background.

FIGURE 5.5

The SQL Server Service Manager.

The following is the functionality provided by each service:

- MSSQLServer—This service is the actual database server that provides access to the databases.
- SQLServerAgent—This service is responsible for running all scheduled tasks on the server, sending alerts, and managing operators.
- MSDTC—This is the Distributed Transaction Coordinator as we discussed earlier.

As mentioned earlier, you can use the SQL Server Service Manager to stop and start the services. The MSSQLServer services can also be paused. The following outlines the different states:

- Stopped—When the service is in this state, it is not running at all. In the case of the MSSQLServer service, any client who is connected to the server when it is shut down will be disconnected and all their processes will be killed. In the case of all other services, processing simply halts.
- Started—This service state indicates that the service is running and processing normally. In the case of the MSSQLServer service, this indicates that the server is accepting user connections and processing data. In the case of all other services, it means that they are alive and running.
- Paused—This service state is only available to the MSSQLServer service. When the MSSQLServer service is paused, any client who has been connected to the server before it was paused will be allowed to remain connected to the server as if nothing changed. The major difference is that new clients connections are refused until the service has been started. This option is useful when you are running processes in which you do not want your users to be connected to the server, such as batch processing and troubleshooting.

After you have installed SQL Server on a computer, the SQL Server Service Manager will be available to you in the SysTray of the computer on which it is installed. Aside from accessing this application through the SQL Server 7.0 group, you can also access the application by double-clicking on the icon.

5

Uninstall SQL Server 7.0

This option in the SQL Server 7.0 program group does exactly what it says. It allows you to remove the installation of SQL Server 7.0 from your computer. Note that when SQL Server 7.0 is uninstalled, pretty much everything is deleted, so you really need to make sure that you want to actually uninstall before you click on this option.

Microsoft SQL Server—Switch Group

The Microsoft SQL Server—Switch group is only available to you if you have installed SQL Server 7.0 on a machine that had SQL Server 6.5 on it. The reason that this is available is that SQL Server 7.0 and SQL Server 6.5 cannot run on the same machine simultaneously. If you have upgraded the server and left the original DAT files from the SQL Server 6.5 installation on the server, you can use the Microsoft SQL Server—Switch application to switch back to the previous version of SQL Server. This allows you to troubleshoot issues with the upgrade as well as allowing the ability to back off the upgrade if it produces an unexpected result from your user applications.

Other Tools

Microsoft has provided a number of other tools that you can use to manage and work with your servers. These tools, although extremely powerful, are not listed in the previous sections because, for the most part, they are command-line applications. In other words, you will have to break out your DOS hat in order to run these. Because there are a very large number of these applications available, we are only going to cover those that are frequently used.

BCP

The BCP application is an extremely useful utility that is used to move data in and out of SQL Server. BCP will write data out of an SQL Server table or view and into a flat file on the hard drive of the computer where it is being executed. BCP can also be used to write data back into an SQL Server table. We will go over the BCP utility in Hour 12.

isql

The isql application is one that you can use to execute SQL scripts and stored procedures. Primarily, this stored procedure remains in this version of SQL Server for backwards compatibility. This utility connects to SQL Server using DB-Library. SQL Server 7.0 includes a new version of this tool, called osql, which we will go over in a few minutes. Because this version remains for backward compatibility reasons, there are several functions that you cannot perform. For example, you cannot work with any of the Unicode datatypes. The syntax of the isql command is as follows:

```
isql -U login_id [-e] [-E] [-p] [-n] [-d db_name]
[-Q "query"] [-q "query"]
[-c cmd_end] [-h headers] [-w column_width] [-s col_separator]
[-t time_out] [-m error_level] [-L] [-?] [-r {0 ¦ 1}]
[-H wksta_name] [-P password]
[-S server_name] [-i input_file] [-o output_file] [-a packet_size]
[-b] [-O] [-l time_out] [-x max_text_size]
```

Where the options are:

Option	Description
-U login_id	This it the login ID you will use to access the server.
-e	This specifies that all input into the server will be echoed back to the screen.
-E	This option specifies that you want to connect to the server using a trusted connection.
-p	The option tells SQL Server to return any query statistics it generates from the running of the query.
-n	This is used to specify that the numbers associated with each line of returned information are to be stripped off.
-d db_name	This option is used to specify an initial database that SQL Server should use.
-Q "query"	This specifies that the "query" text is to be executed by isql as soon as it connects to the database and it is to disconnect as soon as it has completed running the query.
-q "query"	This specifies that the "query" text is to be executed as soon as isql connects to the server.
-c cmd_end	This is used to specify a new command terminator. By default, SQL Server uses the GO keyword to indicate this.
-h headers	This option is used to specify the number of rows that are to be returned to the user before the column headers are displayed. The default is to display the headers as soon as the query is executed.

5

continues

Option	Description
-v *column_width*	This option is used to specify the number of characters to be displayed on a single line.
-s *col_separator*	This is used to specify a character for SQL Server to place between each column.
-t *time_out*	This option specifies the amount of time SQL Server will wait during the execution of a command before it times it out.
-m *error_level*	This option is used to determine whether error messages are shown.
-L	This option will list all SQL Servers that are currently broadcasting on the network.
-?	This option will return a list of all the switches that can be used in conjunction with isql.
-r	Specifies that error messages are to be redirected to the screen.
-H *wksta_name*	This option is used to specify the name of the local work-station.
-P *password*	This specifies the password associated with the login that we are passing in.
-S *server_name*	This option specifies the name of the server that we are going to connect to.
-i *input_file*	This specifies a file that contains commands that isql will execute against the database.
-o *output_file*	This specifies a file that isql will write any results that are returned to.
-a *packet_size*	This option specifies the size of the packet to be sent on the network.
-b	This option specifies that isql should exit with a DOS error code when it has completed processing.
-0	This option is used to force isql into a compatibility mode that works with SQL Server 6.0.

Option	Description
-l *time_out*	This option specifies the number of seconds that isql will wait before a login attempt times out.
-x *max_text_size*	This is the maximum number of bytes that SQL Server will return from text fields.

osql

The osql utility is the preferred method of accessing SQL Server through a command prompt. This contains much of the same functionality that the isql application does, except that it allows you to work with Unicode data. This application uses ODBC to connect to the server. The syntax of this command is as follows:

```
osql -U login_id [-e] [-E] [-p] [-n] [-d db_name]
[-Q "query"] [-q "query"]
[-c cmd_end] [-h headers] [-w column_width] [-s col_separator]
[-t time_out] [-m error_level] [-L] [-?] [-r {0 ¦ 1}]
[-H wksta_name] [-P password]
[-S server_name] [-i input_file] [-o output_file] [-a packet_size]
[-b] [-O] [-l time_out] [-x max_text_size]
```

Where the options are

Option	Description
-U *login_id*	This is the login ID you will use to access the server.
-e	This specifies that all input into the server will be echoed back to the screen.
-E	This option specifies that you want to connect to the server using a trusted connection.
-p	The option tells SQL Server to return any query statistics it generates from the running of the query.
-n	This is used to specify that the numbers associated with each line of returned information are to be stripped off.
-d *db_name*	This option is used to specify an initial database that SQL Server should use.

continues

5

Option	Description
-Q "query"	This specifies that the "query" text is to be executed by isql as soon as it connects to the database, and it is to disconnect as soon as it has completed running the query.
-q "query"	This specifies that the "query" text is to be executed as soon as isql connects to the server.
-c cmd_end	This is used to specify a new command terminator. By default, SQL Server uses the GO keyword to indicate this.
-h headers	This option is used to specify the number of rows that are to be returned to the user before the column headers are displayed. The default is to display the headers as soon as the query is executed.
-v column_width	This option is used to specify the number of characters to be displayed on a single line.
-s col_separator	This is used to specify a character for SQL Server to place between each column.
-t time_out	This option specifies the amount of time SQL Server will wait during the execution of a command before it times it out.
-m error_level	This option is used to determine whether error messages are shown.
-L	This option will list all SQL Servers that are currently broadcasting on the network.
-?	This option will return a list of all the switches that can be used in conjunction with isql.
-r	Specifies that error messages are to be redirected to the screen.
-H wksta_name	This option is used to specify the name of the local workstation.
-P password	This specifies the password associated with the login that we are passing in.

Option	Description
-S *server_name*	This option specifies the name of the server to which we are going to connect.
-i *input_file*	This specifies a file containing commands that isql will execute against the database.
-o *output_file*	This specifies a file to which isql will write any results that are returned.
-a *packet_size*	This option specifies the size of the packet to be sent on the network.
-b	This option specifies that isql should exit with a DOS error code when it has completed processing.
-0	This option is used to force isql into a compatibility mode that works with SQL Server 6.0.
-l *time_out*	This option specifies the number of seconds that isql will wait before a login attempt times out.
-x *max_text_size*	This is the maximum number of bytes that SQL Server will return from text fields.

makepipe and readpipe

These utilities are used for troubleshooting Named Pipes. They must be used together to test the desired functionality. Because you are only able to create a Named Pipe on a Windows NT computer, you can only run the makepipe utility on that platform. When a client is not connecting to the SQL Server and you suspect that the problem lies in the Named Pipe connections, you can use this tool to determine that. On the Windows NT computer, you would run the makepipe utility. What this does is open a Named Pipe on the server on which it was run. From the client computer, you would run the readpipe utility, telling it which Named Pipe to connect to.

5

Summary

In this hour, we have gone over most of the utilities that are installed when you set up SQL Server 7.0. The two tools that you will probably use more than any others are SQL Enterprise Manager and SQL Query Analyzer. All the rest of the tools are great to have when you need them, but for the most part, you will rarely use them.

Q&A

Q **I have just started SQL Enterprise Manager, and it looks like the server is not running. Where can I check that?**

A The first place to check would be the SQL Server Service Manager and see what is going on there.

Q **I have heard people say that the BCP utility is a dead piece of technology. What is that and is it true?**

A People have been calling for the death of BCP for quite some time. The problem with that is that too many people rely on this technology for it to die. Plus, it is a really useful tool and, if Microsoft is thinking about getting rid of it, they should rethink that stance.

Workshop

The quiz and the exercise are provided for your further understanding. The answers can be found in Appendix A, "Answers."

Quiz

1. What is the Client Configuration Utility used for?

2. What is SQL Enterprise Manager?

3. What is MMC?

4. What can you do with the SQL Server Profiler?

5. What functionality is provided to you through SQL Query Analyzer?

6. Is it possible to run SQL Server 6.5 and SQL Server 7.0 on the same machine at the same time?

7. What tools to you have to troubleshoot Named Pipe issues?

Exercise

Explore the SQL Enterprise Manager, remembering to right-click on the objects that it contains to see what options you have. If you have access to any other SQL Servers, register them.

Hour 6

Creating Databases, Files, and Filegroups

In Hour 4, "Database Architecture Fundamentals," we covered much of what a database is and how it works. This is very important knowledge to take forward with you into this hour. When you are setting up most user applications that run on SQL Server, you will have to create the database and then the installation process that came with the application will create all the associated tables and other objects. When you first create a database, it is basically an empty shell that is ready for you to create tables in. A couple of preexisting tables, the system tables, are already in the database, but for the most part, there is nothing that you or your users will interact with directly.

The highlights of this hour include

- What Are Files and Filegroups?
- Creating Databases
- Database Options
- Resizing Databases
- Dropping Databases

What Are Files and Filegroups?

Before we get too far into creating and managing databases, you need to be familiar with the concept of files and filegroups. Basically, files are the physical implementation of the database and filegroups are groupings of associated files.

Database Files

In SQL Server, all databases will be mapped directly to files that are on the hard drive of the computer. These files will contain either data from the database or information out of the transaction log. Unlike previous versions of SQL Server, data and log information cannot be stored in the same file, and data from more than one database cannot be stored in the same file. One of the best advances in SQL Server 7.0 is that the database files will automatically grow as they get full. You are probably thinking, "So what?" but in previous versions of SQL Server, you would define a database file and give it a size, and SQL Server would allocate that whole file. This is pretty inefficient. SQL Server 7.0 will always make sure that enough space is in the file for what is happening in the database, but will not grab all the space to start with. This feature is known as autogrow.

Three types of database files in SQL Server are as follows:

- Primary Database Files—Primary database files are the starting point for all databases. These files not only contain the information that is gathered by the database users, they also contain information about all the other files contained in the database. Every database will have a primary database file. The default, and recommended, extension for primary database files is .mdf.

- Secondary Database Files—Secondary database files are any other database files that you add to a database. These can be added to give the database the capability to grow on multiple drives on your server. Not all databases will have secondary database files, but they are required if you want your database to extend across several physical hard drives. The default, and recommended, extension for secondary database files is .ndf.

- Log Files—Log files are used to hold the transaction log of the database. Every database will have at least one log file, but you can have multiple log files in a database. The default, and recommended, extension for log files is .ldf.

Each file will actually have two names associated with it. This first will be the logical name that you assign it. For example, the pubs database that we have discussed has a primary database file simply called pubs. The transaction log device for the pubs database is called pubs_log. The second part of the name is the physical name of the database file. This is the name of the file that is on the hard drive of the computer, including the path

to the file. For the pubs database, on this computer, the files are called
C:\MSSQL7\DATA\pubs.mdf and C:\MSSQL7\DATA\pubs_log.ldf. These could change
on your computer depending on which drive you installed SQL Server on and what path
you chose for your installation.

Any type of database file can be assigned to a filegroup for administrative ease.

Filegroups

The main purpose of filegroups is to ease administration. The other purpose for creating
a filegroup would be for space allocation purposes. After you have created file groups,
you can assign tables, indexes, or text or image data to those filegroups. This will allow
you to control which data resides on which drives. This might seem odd, but some systems can benefit from moving highly accessed data onto its own drive. SQL Server 7.0
will still work even if you do not create your own filegroups. If you choose not to create
your own filegroups, SQL Server will create a single primary filegroup and use that to
allocate data in the database.

Three rules that you must be familiar with when creating filegroups are as follows:

- No database file can be associated with more than one filegroup. When you assign
  a table or index to a filegroup, all pages that are associated with that table or index
  are then associated with that filegroup.

- Log files cannot be added to a filegroup. Transaction log data is managed differently from database data.

- No file in a filegroup will autogrow unless there is no space in any of the files in
  the filegroup.

As with files, three different types of filegroups that you can create exist, and are as
follows:

- Primary—The primary filegroup contains the primary file and any other database
  files that you do not assign to any other filegroup. When you create a database
  without defining a filegroup, SQL Server will create this filegroup. All information
  in the system tables is stored in this filegroup.

- User-defined—A user-defined filegroup is one that is created by the database
  administrator. After you have created a user-defined filegroup, you can assign database files to it as you wish.

- Default—The default filegroup is really not a type of filegroup in and of itself.
  Instead, it is either a user-defined filegroup or the primary filegroup. The default
  filegroup will contain all tables and indexes that are created without being assigned

6

to a different filegroup. Only one default filegroup can be in a database at a time. If you do not explicitly specify a default filegroup, SQL Server will use the primary filegroup as the default filegroup for this purpose.

Now that you have an idea of what files and filegroups are and understand how they work, it is time to look at creating databases. You will not create files by themselves; instead, they are created when you create a database.

Creating Databases

Creating databases, like almost every other object in a database, can be accomplished in one of two ways. The first way that you can create a database is through SQL Server Enterprise Manager. This is really the easiest way to create databases, but it does have one major drawback: it is difficult to reproduce on a large scale. In other words, if you create a database that is going to be redistributed around the world, it is not that easy to get inexperienced users to walk through Enterprise Manager and build the database. The second way to create the database would be to use SQL statements and execute them in SQL Server Query Analyzer. This approach allows the database to be reproduced easily, but the statements are somewhat difficult to master. We will cover each of these methods in this hour.

Creating a Database Using SQL Enterprise Manager

As we discussed earlier, creating a database from within SQL Enterprise Manager is the easiest way to go about it. When creating a database with the default options, all you have to do is provide the name of the database. In the next section, we will create a database called OrderCenter. It is important that you create this database because we will be using it throughout the rest of the book for our examples. The following will walk you through creating a database using SQL Enterprise Manager:

1. Click the Start button, choose Programs, Microsoft SQL Server 7.0, and then click SQL Server Enterprise Manager. From the list of servers, double-click the name of the server on which you will be creating the database. This connects you to the server.

2. Click the plus sign next to the server name. This opens up a list of folders you can use to access different objects on the SQL Server.

3. Click the plus sign next to the Databases folder. This opens up a list of all the databases on the computer that you are connected to, as seen in Figure 6.1. A few extra databases are listed in the figure, but yours will look similar.

FIGURE **6.1**

The Databases folder in SQL Enterprise Manager.

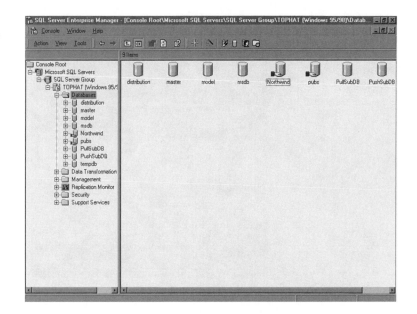

4. Right-click in the right pane of SQL Enterprise Manager. This opens a menu, as seen in Figure 6.2, from which you can choose the New Database option.

FIGURE **6.2**

The New Database option.

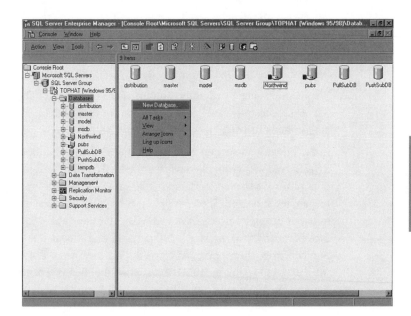

6

5. After you have selected the New Database option, the Database Properties screen opens up, as seen in Figure 6.3.

FIGURE 6.3

The Database Properties screen.

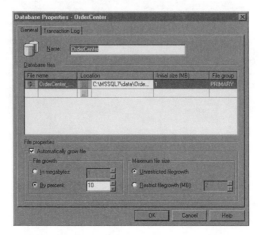

6. In the Name box, you can type the name of the database that you are creating. For these purposes, type in the name OrderCenter. As you start typing, you will notice that SQL Server begins to fill out the name of the database: SQL Server will start to create the name of the primary database file. By default, it is the name of the database with _data attached to the end of it.

7. If you want to create multiple files, all you have to do is type in the name of the file. If you want to create a filegroup, all you need to do is type the name of the filegroup after the database file.

8. Some options are listed at the bottom of the dialog box. These involve how SQL Server handles physical space allocation for the database. Neither of these options are available to you unless you select the Automatically Grow File checkbox.

9. In the Filegrowth section, you are presented with the option of what increments SQL Server will grow the database file in. The first option that you have, and the option that is selected by default, is to grow the database by a certain number of megabytes at a time. The next option is to grow the database at a certain percentage rate. For example, if you have a 10MB database and it gets full, you can have SQL Server expand the database by 10 percent, or 1 megabyte. On small, rapidly growing databases, this option can cause a lot of overhead. For example, you might have the database expand by 10MB every time it gets full. For these purposes, leave these options alone.

10. The second section is the Maximum File Size section. If SQL Server is automatically growing the file, these options allow you to specify a size in which SQL Server will stop growing the file. You have two options if you should choose to do this. The first option, Unrestricted Filegrowth, tells SQL Server to continue to grow the file forever. The only restriction to the size that this will have is the size of the hard disk drives. The next option, Restrict Filegrowth is where you specify the maximum size. For these purposes, leave these options alone as well.

11. The next tab in the dialog, as shown in Figure 6.4, is the Transaction Log tag. This tab gives you the same options that the Database tab did and should be treated the same.

FIGURE 6.4

The Transaction Log tab of the Database Properties screen.

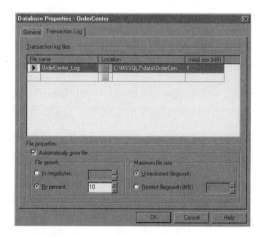

12. After you have filled in the options as previously listed, click the OK button and SQL Server will create the database for you.

As you can see, creating databases in SQL Enterprise Manager is extremely easy. Next we will cover how to create databases using SQL statements.

Creating a Database Using SQL Statements

The other option in creating databases is to create them through SQL statements and then execute them using SQL Query Analyzer. A large number of options must be used when creating a database using the CREATE DATABASE statement. The syntax of the CREATE DATABASE statement is as follows:

```
CREATE DATABASE <database_name>
    ON [PRIMARY]
    [ <filespec> [,...n] ]
    [, <filegroup> [,...n] ]
```

```
[ LOG ON { <filespec> [,...n]} ]
[ FOR LOAD ¦ FOR ATTACH ]

<filespec> ::=
    ( [ NAME = logical_file_name, ]
        FILENAME = 'os_file_name'
      [, SIZE = size][sr]
      [, MAXSIZE = { max_size ¦ UNLIMITED } ]
      [, FILEGROWTH = growth_increment] ) [,...n]

<filegroup> ::=
    FILEGROUP filegroup_name <filespec> [,...n]
```

Where the following are the options:

Option	Description
<database_name>	This is the name of the database that you want to create. The database name can be up to 128 characters long, unless you do not specify a logical name for the log. If you do not specify a logical name for the log, the name of the database is limited to 123 characters.
[PRIMARY]	This optional keyword is used to specify that the database file you are creating is the primary file. Only one primary file can exist in each database.
<filespec>	This is a placeholder for all the information required to create a file. The information required for the filespec is listed below the CREATE DATABASE statement.
<filegroup>	This is a placeholder for the information required to create a filegroup. The information required to create a filegroup is listed below the filespec information.
LOG ON	This optional keyword is used to specify the disk files to store the log files. The keyword is followed by a list of filespec information.
FOR LOAD	The FOR LOAD option is included for backwards compatibility. This option has become outdated because an SQL Server 7.0 restore will recreate a database.
FOR ATTACH	The FOR ATTACH option is used to create a database from an existing set of operating system files. You should use the sp_attach_db stored procedure to create this type of database except when you have more than 16 files to attach.

Option	Description
NAME	The NAME option is used as a part of the filespec. This is the logical name of the file, as we discussed in the section on database files.
FILENAME	The FILENAME option is used as a part of the filespec. This is the name of the physical file on the hard disk drive, as we discussed in the section on database files.
SIZE	The SIZE option is used as a part of the filespec. This is the initial size of the database file on the hard disk drive.
MAXSIZE	The MAXSIZE option is used as a part of the filespec. This is the maximum size that the file can grow to be on the hard disk drive. You can either specify an actual size or use the UNLIMITED keyword to specify that it can grow forever.
FILEGROWTH	The FILEGROWTH option is used as a part of the filespec. This is the factor either in megabytes or percentage that the file will grow to be.
FILEGROUP	The FILEGROUP option is used to create a filegroup. You will give it a name and then a list of filespecs.
[...]	This is used to indicate that you can add multiple files or filegroups to a database.

Admittedly, this looks really complicated, and with all the options available to you, it can be. For the most part, when you are creating a database, you will use very few options. In the following example, you will create a database called Test on a database file called Test_Data and a log file called Test_Log:

```
CREATE DATABASE Test
ON PRIMARY
(       NAME = 'Test_Data',
        FILENAME = 'c:\mssql7\data\Test_Data.mdf',
        SIZE = 10MB,
        MAXSIZE = 50MB,
        FILEGROWTH = 5MB )
LOG ON
(       NAME = 'Test_Log',
        FILENAME = 'c:\mssql7\data\Test_Log.ldf',
        SIZE = 5MB,
        MAXSIZE = 25MB,
        FILEGROWTH = 5MB )
GO
```

6

If you would execute this script, the results would look like the following:

```
The CREATE DATABASE process is allocating 10 MB on disk 'Test_Data'.
The CREATE DATABASE process is allocating 5 MB on disk 'Test_Log'.
```

The following steps will walk you through creating a database called Script_Test on a 5MB primary database file called Script_Data with a maximum size of 25MB and a file growth of 5MB. The log file will be a 2MB file called Script_Log with a maximum size of 12MB and a file growth of 20 percent.

1. Click the Start button, go to Programs, to Microsoft SQL Server 7.0, and then click SQL Server Query Analyzer. This opens the SQL Server Query Analyzer at the Connect to SQL Server dialog.

2. Log into SQL Server and type in the script required to create the Products table. The script is as follows:

```
CREATE DATABASE ScriptTest
ON
(       NAME = 'ScriptTest_Data',
        FILENAME = 'c:\mssql7\data\ScriptTest_Data.mdf',
        SIZE = 5MB,
        MAXSIZE = 25MB,
        FILEGROWTH = 5MB )
LOG ON
(       NAME = 'ScriptTest_Log',
        FILENAME = 'c:\mssql7\data\ScriptTest_Log.ldf',
        SIZE = 2MB,
        MAXSIZE = 12MB,
        FILEGROWTH = 20% )
GO
```

3. After you have typed in the script, click the green play button, and, if you have typed in everything correctly, you should receive the following message:

```
The CREATE DATABASE process is allocating 5 MB on disk 'ScriptTest_Data'.
The CREATE DATABASE process is allocating 2 MB on disk 'ScriptTest_Log'.
```

4. When you have completed this, you can exit SQL Query Analyzer.

Now that you have created a few databases, we should look at database options.

Database Options

Several database options can be set to control such things as how the database is accessed and how the database manages itself. Table 6.1 outlines the different database options.

TABLE 6.1   Database Options

Option	Description
DBO Use Only	A database option that you can set that only allows the DBO, or Database Owner, to access the database. This can be a very useful option when you are troubleshooting a database.
Single User	A database option that forces SQL Server to only allow one user into the database at a time. This sounds like a great option for troubleshooting and batch processing, but if any users are in the database when this option is set, the set will fail. Also, if you are setting this option to allow only yourself the ability to access the database, any user who accesses the database before you do will lock you out.
Read Only	The option allows you to mark the database as only being able to be read. No data modification can occur while this option is set.
ANSI NULL Default	This option is used to specify the default column nullability behavior when creating a table. When this option is set, SQL Server will create columns as NULL by default.
Recursive Triggers	This option allows you to specify whether triggers on tables in the database will be fired recursively. In other words, if a trigger is fired on a table that inserts into a table that has an insert trigger defined on it, this option will allow or disallow that trigger's firing.
Select Into/Bulk Copy	This option allows you to turn on and off the ability to perform non-logged operations against the database. A non-logged operation is one in which the actual inserts into the tables are not logged, making them nonrecoverable.
Truncate Log on Checkpoint	This option specifies that the transaction log of the database will be truncated every time the server performs a checkpoint. This option is very useful when you are working on development servers or on databases in which the data is not very important. You should never turn this option on in a productional environment.
Torn Page Detection	This optionallows SQL Server to detect pages that were not correctly written to the hard disk drive because of power failures or other problems. This option causes SQL Server to perform extra reads and writes to the hard drive, thus causing a little extra overhead on the server. You should probably enable this option on your databases if the server is in an unstable environment.

continues

6

TABLE 6.1 continued

Option	Description
Auto Close	This option forces SQL Server to gracefully shut down the database after all users have exited the database and all processes in that database have shut down. This allows SQL Server to free up any resources that are being utilized in the database for use by other processes.
Auto Shrink	When the Auto Shrink option is turned on in a database, the files of the database will be examined and any free space in those files will be reclaimed. This is especially useful when you are working with databases in which large amounts of data are deleted.
Auto Create Statistics	This option forces SQL Server to automatically create statistics on the tables that are contained in the database. These statistics are used by SQL Server to speed up data access and modification processes. If the statistics are not used for a period of time, SQL Server will delete them.
Auto Update Statistics	This option forces SQL Server to automatically maintain the table statistics when they become out-of-date because the data in the table has changed.
Use Quoted Identifiers	The Use Quoted Identifiers option is used to force the users to delimit object identifiers with single quotation marks. All strings that are referenced in the database then must be enclosed in double quotation marks. This option must be turned on when tables or other objects in the database have been created, using characters that SQL Server considers to be invalid.

Just like creating the tables, there are two ways to modify the options in any database. One is through the use of SQL Enterprise Manager. To access this, connect to the SQL Server and open the Databases folder on that server. Double-click the name of the database on which you want to change the options. This will open the database properties box. Click the Options tab, as seen in Figure 6.5. From here, you can access all the options that are previously outlined.

The other option that you have is to use the sp_dboption system stored procedure in SQL Query Analyzer. This will allow you to access all the options that we previously outlined, along with some other more advanced options. You can get more information on the other options by searching for "Setting Database Options" in SQL Server Books Online. The syntax of the sp_dboption stored procedure is as follows:

```
sp_dboption <database_name>, <option_name>, <value>
```

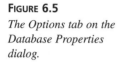

Figure 6.5

The Options tab on the Database Properties dialog.

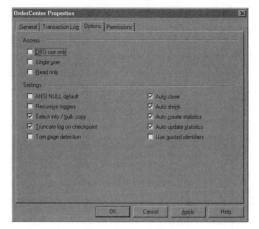

Where the options are

Option	Description
<database_name>	This is the name of the database in which you want to change the options. This will be an existing database on the server.
<option_name>	This is the name of the database option that you want to change. You do not have to type the full option name because SQL Server will recognize any portion of the name that is unique.
<value>	This is the value to which you want to set the option. You will either use True or False here.

To get a complete list of options, you can simply type the name of the stored procedure into the SQL Query Analyzer window and execute it. This will bring back the names of all supported options.

Resizing Databases

As we have mentioned over the past few sections, SQL Server will automatically grow and shrink your databases for you, if they need to and if you have configured them to do so. Sometimes, though, you will have to take on this task manually.

6

Shrinking a Database

You can manually shrink a database to free up pages that have been allocated which are no longer in use. This will shrink the files on the disk and free up space to the operating system. You would want to shrink the database manually only if you have configured the database not to shrink automatically. The biggest restriction to this is that you cannot shrink a database to a size smaller than it was originally created. If you created a database that was originally 50MB and it has grown to be 500MB, you cannot shrink it to less than 50MB, even if all the data in the database has been deleted. You can either use SQL Server Enterprise Manager or SQL Query Analyzer to shrink a database. To shrink a database using SQL Server Enterprise Manager, perform the following steps:

1. Connect to the server in SQL Enterprise Manager. Click the plus sign next to the name of the server that contains the database and then click the database's folder under that server.

2. Right-click the name of the database that you want to shrink, choose All Tasks, and then choose Shrink Database. This opens the Shrink Database dialog, as seen in Figure 6.6.

FIGURE 6.6

The Shrink Database dialog.

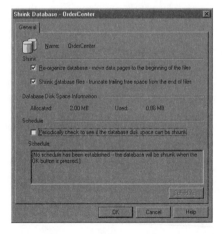

3. Two main options are available to you from this screen. The Re-organize Database option tells SQL Server to consolidate partially filled pages together at the beginning of the database. The Shrink Database Files option tells SQL Server to truncate the empty space at the end of the database files.

4. Under the schedule option, you can schedule the shrinkage process to occur at specific times. If you have selected this option, the schedule button becomes available for you to select.

5. When you press the OK button, SQL Server begins to shrink the database files, and a dialog box will pop up telling you the current size of the database.

The other option in shrinking the database is to use the DBCC SHRINKDATABSE command in the SQL Query Analyzer. The following is the syntax of the command:

```
DBCC SHRINKDATABASE (<database_name> [, <target_percent>]
[ic:ccc] [, NOTRUNCATE¦TRUNCATEONLY}])
```

Where the options are

Option	Description
<database_name>	This is the name of the database that you want to shrink. This will be an existing database on the server.
<target_percent>	This option is used to specify the percentage of free space currently in the database that is to be left in it after you have shrunk it.
NOTRUNCATE	This option specifies that all free space in the database is to remain allocated.
TRUNCATEONLY	This option specifies that all unused space in the database is released to the operating system.

Expanding a Database

If you have set up the database to not automatically grow, you will have to perform this function for yourself. You can expand both the database or the log. You can do this through SQL Server Enterprise Manager or SQL Query Analyzer. To expand the database, you will add extra database files to the database.

The easiest way to expand the database is to use SQL Server Enterprise Manager. To do this, perform the following steps:

1. Connect to the server in SQL Enterprise Manager. Click the plus sign next to the name of the server that contains the database and then click the databases folder under that server.

2. Double-click the name of the database that you want to expand. This opens the Database Options dialog.

3. Under the list of files, click the empty slot and type in the name of the new file and the size that you want to expand the database by. This can be another partition or disk drive on the server.

6

4. After you have added this, click the OK button, and SQL Server expands the database.

The other option you have is to use the ALTER DATABASE command from SQL Query Analyzer. The syntax of the command is as follows:

```
ALTER DATABASE <database_name>
{ ADD FILE <filespec> [,...n] [TO FILEGROUP filegroup_name]
¦ ADD LOG FILE <filespec> [,...n]
}
<filespec> ::=
(NAME = logical_file_name
[, FILENAME = 'os_file_name' ]
[, SIZE = size]
[, MAXSIZE = { max_size ¦ UNLIMITED } ]
[, FILEGROWTH = growth_increment] )
```

Where the following are the options:

Option	Description
<database_name>	This is the name of the database to which you want to add the file.
ADD FILE	This option tells SQL Server to add a database file to the database.
TO FILEGROUP	You can use this keyword to specify that the database file you are adding is to be added to a specific filegroup.
ADD LOG FILE	This option is used to tell SQL Server to add a log file to the database.
<filespec>	This is a placeholder for all the information required to create a file. The information required for the filespec is listed below the ALTER DATABASE statement.
NAME	The NAME option is used as a part of the filespec. This is the logical name of the file, as we discussed in the section on database files.
FILENAME	The FILE name option is used as a part of the filespec. This is the name of the physical file on the hard disk drive, as we discussed in the section on database files.
SIZE	The SIZE option is used as a part of the filespec. This is the initial size of the database file on the hard disk drive.

MAXSIZE	The MAXSIZE option is used as a part of the filespec. This is the maximum size that the file can grow to be on the hard disk drive. You can either specify an actual size or use UNLIMITED keyword to specify that it can grow forever.
FILEGROWTH	The FILEGROWTH option is used as a part of the filespec. This is the factor either in megabytes or percentage that the file will grow to be.
[...]	This is used to indicate that you can add multiple files or filegroups to a database.

For example, let's expand the theoretical database that we created earlier called Test. We need to add a file to the database called Test_Expand with a size of 10MB and a max size of 20MB. The following will do this for you:

```
ALTER DATABASE Test
ADD FILE
(
    NAME = Test_Expand,
    FILENAME = 'c:\mssql7\data\Test_Expand.ndf',
    SIZE = 10MB,
    MAXSIZE = 20MB,
    FILEGROWTH = 5MB
)
```

Dropping Databases

Finally, the last thing that you need to be familiar with is how to get rid of any databases that you do not need anymore. You must be very careful about performing this process, called dropping the database, because if the database is still being used for anything, it will no longer be accessible. Like the rest of these processes, there are two ways to perform this process: SQL Enterprise Manager and SQL Query Analyzer.

To drop a database in SQL Enterprise Manager, connect to the server that contains the database you want to drop. Expand the databases folder by clicking the plus sign, and then click the database you want to drop. When the database is selected, right-click and choose the Delete option. SQL Server pops up a box asking if you really want to do this. If you do, click the Yes button, and the database is deleted from the system.

6

To drop a database using SQL statements from within SQL Query Analyzer, use the DROP DATABASE command. The syntax of the command is

```
DROP DATABASE <database_name>
```

Where <database_name> is the name of the database you want to drop.

Summary

In this hour, we have gone over all the information that you need to manage databases in SQL Server. First we went over how to create the database, how to expand them manually, and how to drop them. Finally, you created a database that you will use in many of the following hours.

Q&A

Q I would like to use filegroups for the management of my transaction log files. How can I do this?

A You cannot add transaction log files to filegroups. The data in transaction log files is managed differently than that in database files.

Q I have a database that is created on a single hard disk drive that is 3GB. I want to expand the database another 3GB. How can I do this?

A This is one of those situations in which you have to manually expand the database. You would follow the steps that we previously outlined for manually expanding the database and simply specify a new hard drive to hold the data.

Workshop

The quiz and the exercises are provided for your further understanding. The answers can be found in Appendix A, "Answers."

Quiz

1. What is a database file?
2. What is the difference between a database file and a log file?
3. What is a filegroup?
4. If you do not specify the logical name for the log file when creating a database using the CREATE DATABASE statement, what is the maximum length of the name of the database?
5. What is the Auto Create Statistics database option used for?
6. What database option would you use if the database you are working on is a non-productional development database?
7. When shrinking a database, how would you tell SQL Server to leave 50 percent of the existing free space in the database available.

Exercises

Create a 10MB database with a 2MB transaction log called Exercise using SQL Enterprise Manager. After you have completed this, use SQL Enterprise Manager to expand the database by 5MB by adding a file. After you have performed that step, use the DROP DATABASE in SQL Query Analyzer to drop the database.

6

Hour 7

Creating Tables

All data storage in an SQL Server database revolves around tables. Data is not stored in any other location in the database. You can access data through a variety of methods, but it all comes from the tables. Most premade database applications you install will not require much knowledge of how SQL Server tables work. If you ever create a custom SQL Server solution, though, intimate knowledge of SQL Server tables is very important.

The highlights of this hour include

- What Is a Table?
- Database Table Fundamentals
- Designing Tables
- Creating Tables
- Altering Tables
- Dropping Tables

What Is a Table?

By now, you have probably heard the term table thrown around quite a bit, and you probably have a good idea about what it means. To put it simply, a table is a collection of similar data, called columns. Tables are organized in rows and columns. The rows in a table, sometimes called a record, represent a collection of data about a single entity. For example, in a table that contains information about employees, a row would contain all relevant information about an employee. Each row in the table can be broken down in columns. Columns represent a single piece of information in that record. For example, in your employee tracking database, you might have columns that contain name, address, phone number, and salary.

SQL Server can contain up to 2 billion tables per database with up to 1,024 columns per table. The number of rows and size of the tables is only limited by the amount of storage space available on the servers.

Database Table Fundamentals

As I have mentioned before, all data storage in SQL Server is based around the table. Good tables contain only a certain well-defined amount of corresponding data with little or no repeating data. This sounds complicated, but it really is not.

One way to think of this is to imagine a set of filing cabinets at a school. In this school, of course, we have teachers, students, and classes that are taught. If we go by the preceding rules, we would have different filing cabinets to track the students, teachers, and classes. We would not want to look through all the student names to find the folder that pertains to a specific class. This would be extremely inefficient. To fulfill the second part of this rule, you would want to limit the amount of repeating data. An example of this would be not to record all information about a class that a student is taking into his folder. Instead, you might record the class name and number, and if the person wants to find a class description and associated fees, she can look up the class in the class's filing cabinet.

Entire full semester classes can be taken at the collegiate level on good database design, and I have just scratched the surface here. In the next few sections, I will cover creating and modifying tables.

Designing Tables

When you have decided what data you are going to store in your database and have divided it up into the logical components that you are going to store as tables, you need to begin designing the tables themselves. Several things need to be taken into consideration when you are designing tables:

- How the tables and columns are going to be named.

- What types of data are going to be stored in each column.

- Whether columns will accept NULL values.

Identifiers

Every object in SQL Server has a name, called an identifier. SQL Server has a well-defined set of rules for how object identifiers are created and what they look like. Most of the time, when you create an object, you are required to give the object a name. Some variations to this rule exist. For example, when you create a constraint, SQL Server does not require that you give it a name. Nevertheless, when SQL Server creates the constraint, it gives it a name for you. The rules for creating identifiers are as follows:

- The length of the identifier must be 128 characters or fewer. This gives you a great deal of space to name your objects in a way that allows you to remember what they are. This can be a double-edged sword, though. Keep your object names descriptive enough for you to know what they are and short enough so you do not have to type in extremely long names every time you need to access the object.

- The first character of the identifier must be a letter (the letters A–Z, a–z, and any letter characters from other languages), the _ (underscore), the @ (at sign), or # (number sign). There are certain restrictions to this, though. When an object starts with an @ sign, it means that it is a local variable. Objects that start with a # sign are denoted as being local temporary tables or stored procedures. Objects that start with ## are global temporary objects. Finally, SQL Server has many functions that begin with @@. It is recommended that you not begin any object names with @@ to avoid confusion with these functions.

- Any following characters can be a letter (the letters A–Z, a–z, and any letter characters from other languages), a number (0–9 and any other number characters from other languages) , the @ (at sign), the $ (dollar sign), the # (number sign), or the _ (underscore).

- SQL Server reserved words, such as the word order, are not allowed.

- Imbedded spaces or any special characters are not allowed in identifiers.

7

The preceding rules are prettysimple and allow you a great deal of latitude when creating identifiers. But, like all rules, ways to break some of them exist. Any of these rules, except the length restriction, can be broken if you use delimited identifiers. A delimited identifier means that whenever you refer to that identifier, either directly in SQL Server or through an application, you must enclose the identifier in either double quotes (" ") or square brackets([ ]). The best thing that you can do, though, is to follow the naming convention I have previously outlined. This will save you, other database administrators, and developers who will hit the database a lot of headaches.

Datatypes

One of the biggest decisions you will make regarding your tables is what type of data you are going to want to store in each column of the table. For example, in a table that is tracking orders, you would not want to store the word Yes in the order quantity column. This could throw off any calculations you are making as well as make life difficult for your shipping center when they are trying to determine what to ship. You make this distinction by telling SQL Server what datatype to store in a column. Every column must have a declared datatype. Table 7.1 outlines the different SQL Server standard datatypes.

TABLE 7.1 SQL Server Standard Datatypes

Datatype	Type	Description
bit	Integer	The bit datatype is an integer that can only store a 0, 1, or NULL value. This datatype is useful when you are storing data that can only have two answers such as Yes and No, True and False, or On and Off.
int	Integer	The int datatype can store whole number values from -2[af]31 (-2,147,483,648) to 2[af]31 (2,147,483,647). This datatype is the one you will use for almost all numeric data that you store in your database. This datatype takes up 4 bytes of space within your database.
smallint	Integer	The smallint datatype can store whole number values from -2[af]15 (-32,768) to 2[af]15 (32,767). This datatype is useful when you are storing numeric data that you know will always be within the specified range. This datatype takes up 2 bytes of space in your database.
tinyint	Integer	The tinyint datatype can store whole number values from 0 to 255. This is useful when you only have a limited number of values that you are going to store. This datatype takes up 1 byte in your database.

Datatype	Type	Description
decimal	Decimal	The decimal datatype can be used to store fixed precision and scale numeric data from `-10[af]38-1` to `10[af]38-1`. When using the decimal datatype, you must specify a scale and precision. The scale is the total number of decimal digits that can be stored to the left and right of the decimal point. The precision is the number of digits that can be stored to the right of the decimal point.
numeric	Decimal	Numeric is a synonym for the decimal datatype.
money	Monetary	The money datatype is used to represent money and currency values. This datatype can store data from `-922` billion to `922` billion with an accuracy to a ten-thousandth of a unit.
smallmoney	Monetary	The smallmoney datatype is used to represent money and currency values. This datatype can store data from `-214,748.3648` to `214,748.3647` with an accuracy to ten-thousandth of a unit.
float	Approximate Numeric	The float datatype is an approximate numeric datatype for use with floating point numeric data. Floating point data is approximate because not all values in the range can be precisely represented. Float data can be any numeric data from `-1.79E+308` through `1.79E+308`.
real	Approximate Numeric	The real datatype is, like the float datatype, an approximate numeric datatype. A real is a floating point number from `-3.40E+38` through `3.40E+38`.
datetime	Date	The datetime datatype is used for representing dates and times. This datatype stores date and time data from January 1, 1753 through December 31, 9999 with an accuracy to one three hundredths of a second, or 3.33 milliseconds.
smalldatetime	Date	The smalldatetime datatype is used for representing dates and times from January 1, 1900 through June 6, 2079 with an accuracy to a minute.
cursor	Numeric	The cursor datatype is a special datatype that contains a reference to a cursor. This datatype is used in stored procedures and cannot be used when creating tables.
timestamp	Numeric	The timestamp datatype is a special datatype that is used to create a database-wide unique number. A table can have only one timestamp column in it. Every time a row is inserted or updated, the value in the timestamp column is updated. Despite the name, the timestamp column is not a human readable date. A timestamp value is unique within a database.

7

continues

TABLE 7.1 continued

Datatype	Type	Description
uniqueidentifier	Numeric	The uniqueidentifier datatype is used to store a globally unique identifier, or GUID. A GUID is a truly globally unique id. Almost no chance exists for this number to be recreated on another system. A column with the uniqueidentifier can be initialized by using the NEWID function or by converting a string into a uniqueidentifier.
char	Character	The char datatype is used to store fixed length non-Unicode data of a specified length. When defining a column of char type, you must specify the length of the column. The char datatype is useful when you always know the length of the data that is going to be stored. For example, when you are storing zip codes in a zip plus four format, you know that you will always be using 10 characters. A char column can be up to 8,000 characters in length.
varchar	Character	The varchar datatype, like the char datatype, is used to stored non-Unicode character data. Unlike the char datatype, the varchar datatype is of variable length. When you define a varchar column, you specify a maximum length for that column. The biggest difference with this datatype over the char datatype is that the stored length is the length of the data, not the length of the column.
text	Character	The text datatype is used for storing large amounts of non-Unicode character data. This datatype has a maximum length of $2^{31} - 1$ or 2 billion characters.
nchar	Unicode Character	The nchar datatype is used to store fixed length Unicode character data. Unicode is the process of storing each character in a two byte structure instead of a single byte, like in normal text. This allows for a larger number of represented characters. This datatype can store up to 4,000 characters using two times the number of characters of storage space in bytes.
nvarchar	Unicode Character	The nvarchar datatype is used to variable length Unicode character data. This datatype can store up to 4,000 characters using two times the number of characters of storage space in bytes.
ntext	Unicode Character	The ntext datatype is used to store large amounts of Unicode character data. This data type can be used to store up to $2^{30} - 1$ or approximately 1 billion characters using two times the number of characters of storage space in bytes.

Datatype	Type	Description
binary	Binary	The binary datatype is used to store fixed length binary data up to 8,000 bytes long. You should use this datatype when the entries in the table are going to be consistently close to the same length.
varbinary	Binary	The varbinary datatype is used to store variable length binary data up to 8,000 bytes long. You should use this datatype when the entries in the table are going to vary in size.
image	Binary	The image datatype is used to store variable length binary data up to 2^21-1 or about 2 billion bytes in length.

Nullability

Another decision you must make when creating your tables is whether you will allow NULL values to be inserted into specific columns in the table. NULL is a special value that represents an unknown value. NULL is not the same as a blank or 0; rather, it is a value that means unknown. When you define a column as NOT NULL, a row cannot be inserted into the table with a NULL value in that column.

Creating Tables

Two basic ways to create tables in SQL Server exist. You can either create them using SQL Enterprise Manager or through SQL Query Analyzer. In this section, I will cover both of these methods of table creation.

Creating Tables with SQL Enterprise Manager

Of the methods available to you for creating tables in your databases, using SQL Enterprise Manager is probably the easiest. This method allows you to create all your tables through a GUI. The following steps will walk you through setting up Table 7.2 in the OrderCenter database that you created earlier. Create the Customers table as outlined in Table 7.2.

TABLE 7.2   Customer Table Data

Column Name	Datatype	Nullable
CustomerID	INT	No
FirstName	VARCHAR(32)	No
LastName	VARCHAR(64)	No

7

continues

TABLE 7.2   continued

Column Name	Datatype	Nullable
Address	VARCHAR(128)	No
City	VARCHAR(32)	No
State	CHAR(2)	No
ZipCode	CHAR(10)	No
Phone	VARCHAR(16)	No

1. Open SQL Server Enterprise Manager and connect to the server that contains the OrderCenter database. When you are connected, click the plus sign next to the server, the plus sign next to the database name, and then click the Tables option. Your screen should look like the one shown in Figure 7.1.

FIGURE 7.1

SQL Enterprise Manager.

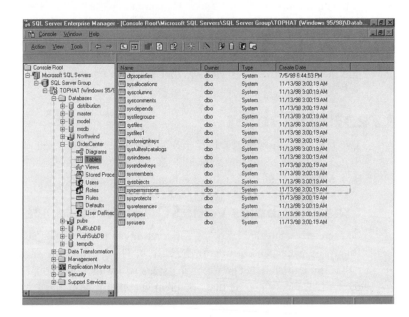

2. To begin creating the table, right-click in the right pane and select the New Table option, as shown in Figure 7.2.

FIGURE 7.2

The New Table option.

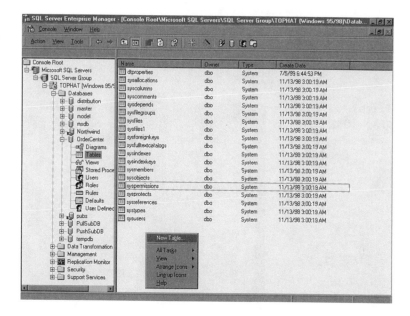

3. After you have selected the New Table option, SQL Server will open the table designer and prompt you to enter a name in the Choose Name dialog, as seen in Figure 7.3. In this dialog, enter Customers and then click on the OK button.

FIGURE 7.3

The Choose Name dialog.

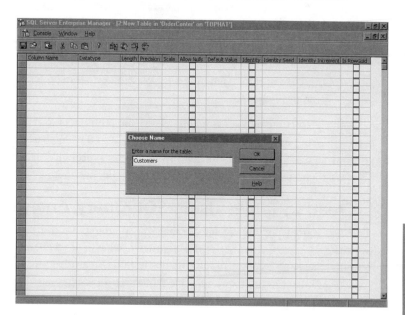

7

4. In the New Table window, you should begin filling out the options, as outlined in Table 7.2. When you are finished, the windows should look like the one in Figure 7.4. Make sure that you remove the checkmark from the `Allow Nulls` option, which is selected by default.

FIGURE 7.4

The New Table window.

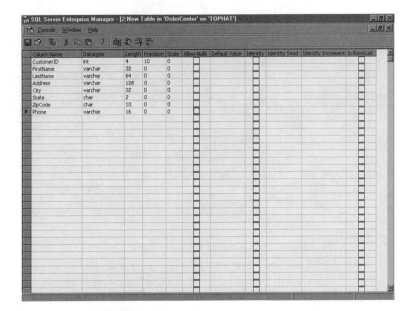

5. When you have completed filling in all of the columns, save your work, and then close the window.

6. Look at the right pane of the Tables window, and you will see the new table, as seen in Figure 7.5.

Although this method is extremely useful, the problem with it is that it is not very reproducible. In other words, if you are going to install this database on more than one server, always creating the tables by hand would be very difficult and time-consuming. The best way around this is to script out your tables and create them using SQL Query Analyzer.

Creating Tables Using SQL Query Analyzer

When you are creating a database that you are going to redistribute, the easiest way is to create the table using a script. Then, instead of having to walk any potential users of the system through creating all the columns in SQL Enterprise Manager, all you will have to do is tell them to run the script. One thing that you will notice throughout this book is that SQL commands are listed in all capital letters. There is no requirement for doing this, but it is frequently used to tell the difference between SQL commands and other words in your scripts.

FIGURE 7.5

*The new table is listed
in the right pane of the
Tables window.*

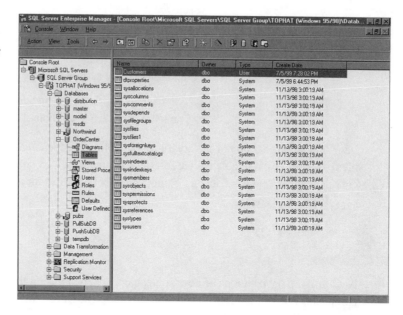

To create a table in SQL Query Analyzer, you will use the SQL command CREATE
TABLE. I will cover the basic syntax here. A lot more can be done with this command,
and if you want more information on it, you can look it up in Books Online. The syntax
of the command is as follows:

```
CREATE TABLE <table_name>
(
    <column_name> <datatype_definition> [NULL/NOT NULL],
    [...]
)
```

Where the options are

Option	Description
<table_name>	This is the name of the table that you are going to create. This must follow all the rules for identifiers as outlined earlier in this hour.
<column_name>	This is the name of the column you are going to create as part of the table. The column names must also follow the rules for identifiers as outlined earlier in this hour.
<datatype_definition>	This is the datatype of the column you are creating. You must always specify a datatype for every column you create.

7

Option	Description
[NULL/NOT NULL]	This is the nullability behavior of the column. If you do not specify this option, SQL Server will automatically assume that the column is nullable.
[...]	This signifies that you can add multiple columns to a table up to 1,024 columns.

Let's look at an example of the creation of a table using the CREATE TABLE command. In the following script, a table called TestTable is created with a column called col1 with a char datatype of length 16 and a column called col2 with an int datatype.

```
CREATE TABLE TestTable
(
    col1 CHAR(16),
    col2    INT
)
```

Now that you have an idea of how you can create a table using the CREATE TABLE command, you will use SQL statements and the SQL Query Analyzer to create the Products table as outlined in Table 7.3.

TABLE 7.3 Product Table Data

Column Name	Datatype	Nullable
ProductID	INT	No
ProductName	VARCHAR(32)	No
Description	VARCHAR(128)	Yes
Price	MONEY	No

The following tutorial will walk you through creating the preceding table using the SQL Query Analyzer and the CREATE TABLE statement:

1. Click the Start button, go to Programs, to Microsoft SQL Server 7.0, and then click SQL Server Query Analyzer. This opens the SQL Server Query Analyzer at the Connect to SQL Server dialog, as shown in Figure 7.6.

2. Log into SQL Server and type $I~SQL Query Analyzer;creating;tables>in the script required to create the Products table. The script is as follows:

```
CREATE TABLE Products
(
    ProductID     int NOT NULL ,
    ProductName     varchar(32) NOT NULL ,
    Description     varchar(128) NULL ,
    Price        money NOT NULL
)
```

FIGURE 7.6
The SQL Server Query Analyzer.

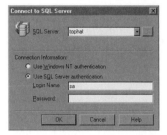

3. When you have completed typing in the preceding script, click the green play button. If you have typed in everything correctly, SQL Server will return the following message:

   `The command(s) completed successfully.`

4. After you have completed this, you can close SQL Query Analyzer.

Altering Tables

As we all know, project requirements change. Luckily, after you have your tables created, it is very easy for you to modify the tables. There are a few caveats to this, though, as outlined in the following:

- If at all possible, you should try to modify your tables while there is no data in them. This is especially true if you are changing the datatype of a column or adding a column that does not allow NULL values.

- If you are adding a column to a table that contains data, you must ensure that the column you are adding allows NULL values. This is because existing rows in the database will not contain values.

- If you are changing the datatype of a column in a table that already contains data, you should make sure that the datatypes are compatible. For example, if the existing data in the column is character data, you need to modify the column to a character datatype. If the datatype is not compatible, the alteration will fail. An example of what you cannot do is convert image data to character data. For more information on what you can and cannot convert, search for CAST and COVERT in Books Online.

As with creating tables, two ways to modify tables exist. You can either create the table using SQL Enterprise Manager or through the use of the ALTER TABLE command in SQL Server Query Analyzer. The following steps will walk you through modifying the previously created Customers table with the changes listed in Table 7.4.

7

TABLE 7.4   Modifying Customer Data

Column Name	Datatype	Nullable	Action
FirstName	VARCHAR(64)	No	Modify
Phone	VARCHAR(24)	No	Modify
LastOrderDate	DATETIME	Yes	Add

    1. Open SQL Server Enterprise Manager and connect to the server that contains the OrderCenter database. When you are connected, click the plus sign next to the server, the plus next to the database name, and then click on the Tables option. Your screen should look like the one shown in Figure 7.7.

FIGURE 7.7

SQL Enterprise Manager.

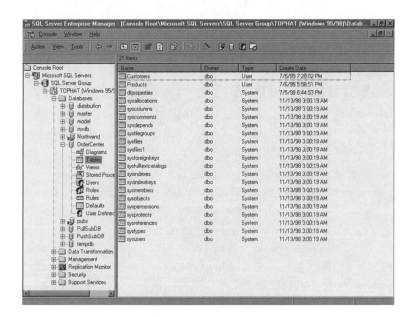

    2. Find the Customers table in the list of tables, and then right-click on the name to display the menu as shown in Figure 7.8. Click the Design Table option.

    3. After you have selected the Design Table option, the table designer opens up with the current design of the table.

FIGURE 7.8

Choose the Design Table option from the menu.

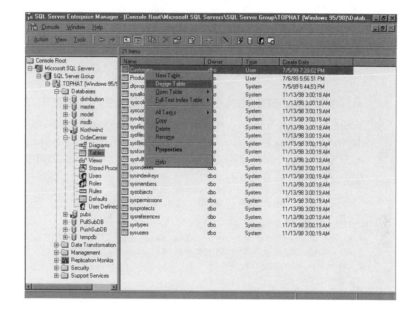

4. Make the changes, as shown in Table 7.4. The final version should look like that shown in Figure 7.9.

5. When you have completed all the changes, click the Save button, and then exit the table designer.

FIGURE 7.9

The table designer with the changes to the Customers table.

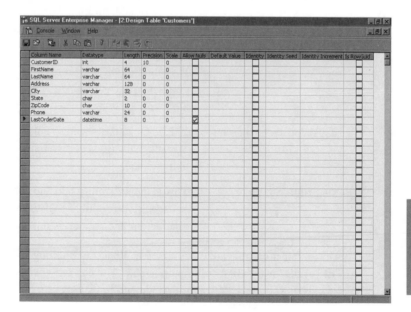

7

As with creating a table, it is much easier to modify a table using SQL Enterprise Manager, but the same shortcomings do apply. The main one being that the changes are not reproducible without having to connect to each server and modify the table manually. You can get around this through using the ALTER TABLE command.

Altering Tables Using SQL Query Analyzer

When modifying many servers that are using the same database, the easiest way to make the modifications is to write a script using the ALTER TABLE command that can be run in SQL Query Analyzer by the administrator of the system. All the rules for modifying table structures still apply.

The syntax of the ALTER TABLE command is as follows:

```
ALTER TABLE <table_name>
{ ALTER COLUMN <column_name> <new_datatype> [NULL/NOT NULL]}
{ ADD <column_name> <datatype_definition> [NULL/NOT NULL] }
{ DROP COLUMN <column_name> }
```

Where the options are

Option	Description
<table_name>	This is the name of the table that you are going to modify. Must be an existing table in the database.
<column_name>	This is the name of the column that you are going to modify or add during the operation. If you are creating a new column, the column names must follow the rules for identifiers as outlined earlier in this hour.
<new_datatype>	If you are modifying an existing column in the table, you will specify the new datatype that is to be associated with the column.
<datatype_definition>	This is the datatype of the column that you are adding. You must always specify a datatype for every column that you add.
[NULL/NOT NULL]	This is the nullability behavior of the column. If you do not specify this option, SQL Server will automatically assume that the column is nullable.

This looks rather complicated, but it is not. What this is telling you is that you can ALTER, ADD, or DROP a column on a table. You can only perform one of those commands in a single ALTER TABLE statement. Let's look at making some changes to the TestTable that you worked with earlier. This time, you want to add a column called col3 with a datatype of datetime, modify col1 to be varchar(32), and drop col2. The following will do that for you:

```
ALTER TABLE TestTable ADD col3 DATETIME
ALTER TABLE TestTable ALTER COLUMN col1 VARCHAR(32)
ALTER TABLE TestTable DROP COLUMN col2
```

Now that you have seen how this works, you are going to modify the Products table in the OrderCenter database to match the specification in Table 7.5.

TABLE 7.5 Modifying the Product Data

Column Name	Datatype	Nullable	Action
Price	SMALLMONEY	No	Modify
InStock	BIT	Yes(Default)	Add

The following tutorial walks you through modifying the preceding table using SQL Query Analyzer and the ALTER TABLE statement:

1. Click the Start button, go to Programs, to Microsoft SQL Server 7.0, and then click SQL Server Query Analyzer. This opens the SQL Server Query Analyzer at the Connect to SQL Server dialog.

2. Log into SQL Server and type in the script required to alter the Products table. The script is as follows:

   ```
   ALTER TABLE Products ALTER COLUMN Price SMALLMONEY NOT NULL
   ALTER TABLE Products ADD InStock BIT
   ```

3. When you have completed typing in the preceding script, click the green play button. If you have typed in everything correctly, SQL Server will return the following message:

   ```
   The command(s) completed successfully.
   ```

4. After you have completed this, you can close SQL Query Analyzer.

Now that you can create and modify tables, the last thing that you have to learn before you have truly mastered the art of tables is how to drop tables you no longer need.

Dropping Tables

7

At some point, you will have to drop a table that is no longer in use. One very important thing you have to remember is that there is no Undo command after you have dropped a table. The only way to get the table back is to restore the database, assuming that you have made good backups. As with creating and modifying tables, you can either do it through SQL Enterprise Manager or SQL Query Analyzer.

Dropping Tables Using SQL Enterprise Manager

Dropping tables using SQL Enterprise Manager is extremely simple. You need to be very careful when you do this because it is very easy to drop tables that you do not want to. If you should do this, you will need to restore the database from the last known good backup. The following walks you through dropping a table:

1. Open SQL Server Enterprise Manager and connect to the server that contains the OrderCenter database. When you are connected, click the plus sign next to the server, click on the plus sign next to the database name, and then click on the Tables option.

2. Find the Customers table in the list of tables, and then right-click on the name to display the menu as shown in Figure 7.10. Click the Delete option.

FIGURE 7.10

Choose the Delete option from the menu.

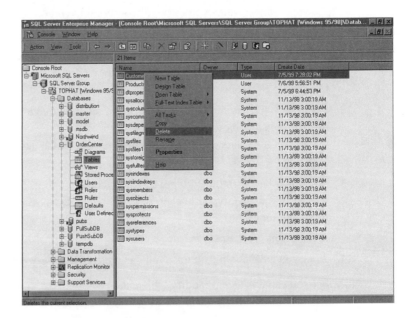

3. After you have selected the Delete option, the Drop Objects dialog opens, as shown in Figure 7.11. The name of the table that you are going to drop is listed in the dialog.

FIGURE 7.11

The Delete Objects dialog.

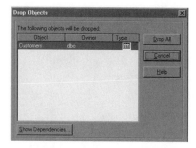

4. If you were going to actually drop this table, you would click the Drop All button. You are going to need this table later, so don't drop it. If you want to see what happens, drop it and then go back and recreate it as you did earlier in the hour.

As you probably guessed, you can also perform your table drops through scripts.

Dropping Tables Using SQL Query Analyzer

You will probably not want to go to every server and drop old tables by hand. Like the earlier discussions, the easiest way to drop old tables on many servers is to use the DROP TABLE command. The syntax of this command is very easy and is outlined as follows:

```
DROP TABLE <table_name>
```

Where <table_name> is the name of the table that you are going to drop. An example of this would be to drop the TestTable that I have been referring to throughout this chapter. The following does that for you:

```
DROP TABLE TestTable
```

The following tutorial walks you through dropping a table using the DROP TABLE command using SQL Query Analyzer:

1. Click the Start button, go to Programs, to Microsoft SQL Server 7.0, and then click SQL Server Query Analyzer. This opens the SQL Server Query Analyzer at the Connect to SQL Server dialog.

2. Log into SQL Server and type in the script required to create the Products table. The script is as follows:

```
DROP TABLE Products
```

3. When you have completed typing in the preceding script, click the green play button. If you have typed in everything correctly, SQL Server returns the following message:

```
The command(s) completed successfully.
```

4. After you have completed this, you can close SQL Query Analyzer.

7

Summary

In this hour I have covered SQL Server tables. You learned that the table is where all data storage takes place. Then you learned how to create, modify, and drop tables using both SQL Enterprise Manager and SQL Query Analyzer.

Q&A

Q I have a table with a column called OrderNumber that is currently defined as VARCHAR(32). My company has decided to go to a completely numeric order number. Can I change this directly?

A If all of the data in that column is currently numeric, you should be able to make the conversion. If there is currently alphanumeric data in that column, you will have to clean up that data by hand and then make the conversion.

Q Is it better to use SQL Enterprise Manager or SQL Query Analyzer when creating tables?

A This is really a matter of personal preference. If you are more comfortable creating tables in SQL Enterprise Manager, use that. Most developers will use some sort of tool to create their databases and then generate the scripts from that design. That way you have the best of both worlds.

Workshop

The quiz and the exercises are provided for your further understanding. The answers can be found in Appendix A, "Answers."

Quiz

1. What is a table?
2. What is a column?
3. Is the column name &Column 1 a valid column name? Why or why not?
4. What are datatypes used for?
5. What does the CREATE TABLE statement do?
6. If you do not specify NULL or NOT NULL when creating a table, what will SQL Server use as the default?
7. What is the command for altering a table called Table1 and adding a column called Column3 with a datatype of int?
8. If you mistakenly drop a table from a database, what must you do to get it back?

Exercises

1. Create the following table in the OrderCenter database using SQL Enterprise Manager:

Table Name: Products

Column Name	Datatype	Nullable
ProductID	INT	No
ProductName	VARCHAR(32)	No
Description	VARCHAR(128)	Yes
Price	SMALLMONEY	No
InStock	BIT	Yes

2. Create the following using the CREATE TABLE statement in SQL Query Analyzer:

Table Name: Sales

Column Name	Datatype	Nullable
OrderID	INT	No
CustomerID	INT	No
OrderTotal	MONEY	No
ShipMethod	VARCHAR(32)	No
Shipped	BIT	Yes

Table Name: SalesDetail

Column Name	Datatype	Nullable
OrderID	INT	No
ProductID	INT	No
Quantity	SMALLINT	No
ExtendedPrice	SMALLMONEY	No

7

HOUR 8

Logins and Security

There comes a time when you should realize something about your databases. That something is they contain a huge amount of data that can be extremely damaging to your company and the people in your company if the data falls into the wrong hands. This data can be anything from personnel information, to client lists, to confidential product information. You want to keep all of this away from competitors and, in general, people who really do not need to see it. SQL Server has a pretty robust security system that allows you to lock the server down to a level where you can control access to the server and access in the database down to specific columns on a table.

The highlights of this hour include

- The Need for Security
- SQL Server Security Basics
- Security Modes
- Server Logins and Database Users
- Roles

The Need for Security

Before we jump too far into setting up SQL Server security, you need to be properly impressed with the need for security. A security threat can come from three areas. These are outside intruders into your system, people within your own company, and accidental intrusion.

Outside intruders are people who try to gain access to your systems from outside your company. These people can do this for any number of reasons. For example, it is possible that these people are doing it just for kicks, to sell the information to another company, or it might simply be someone from another company. This type of intrusion is somewhat rare because most companies take basic and rather simple steps to deter this type of intrusion. Nevertheless, this type of intrusion still does happen. An example of this type of intrusion I have seen is a person gaining access to a company's intranet site, as well as gaining access to that company's client lists. For most companies, that can be very damaging for business.

People within your own company are probably the most common type of intrusion into your system. These types of people usually have some ulterior motive for gaining access to data that they are not supposed to see. Some of this might be plain curiosity and some of it might be straight maliciousness. To stop this type of intrusion into your systems, you really have to take a paranoid look at all your systems and lock them down as far as you can. The problem is doing this after the corporate culture has allowed most users to do what they want, when they want. When you do this, some users will begin to complain about "Big Brother". It is important that you make sure all these users' concerns are addressed and they be told why you are locking things down. An example of this type of intrusion is at a client site for which I performed some work. They had an employee who was not happy with some decisions that had been made within the company, so this user gained access to the HR databases and got a list of everyone's salary, which was in turn emailed to specific people, as well as printed out and left laying near the printer. This caused a major rift in the company and some real moral problems.

Accidental intrusion into a system is also a fairly common type. What occurs in this type of intrusion is a user logs into a system and expects to get a certain result and they do not get that result. Instead, you will find that users end up getting much more than they were supposed to. An example of this is a company that relied on someone other than the administrator to create and modify user logins into the database. This person accidentally set up a user as the database owner in a specific database. What happened was that the user now had a whole new set of features he could access.

These three examples are included here, so you can realize the importance of securing your SQL Servers. They are not included to make you paranoid and have you always watching your back, although in some respects that can help. Instead, take this as a warning about how important security is and then move forward by taking the proper steps to ensure that your servers are properly locked down.

SQL Server Security Basics

SQL Server has a large number of terms and concepts you need to be familiar with. These concepts include the actual steps that SQL Server takes to allow a user into the database under the different security modes, which we will discuss in a minute. First, you will need to learn more terms. They are as follows:

- Login ID—The login ID is part of the user credentials that are passed in by the user in order to gain access to the SQL Server itself. Depending on the security mode that is being used on the server, the user might or might not have to supply this.

- Password—This might seem evident, but a password is simply a string of characters that are passed into the server to validate that the person who is logging in with a particular login ID is who he says he is. Most of you should know the rules of a good password, but we should make sure. Good passwords should be alphanumeric and at least six characters in length. You should not use passwords such as your spouse's name, your children's names, your dog's name, your cat's name, or your user name. This is because anyone who knows you could potentially guess what your password is. Some good examples of passwords are 10sne1, 14deroad, or f8fulday. These are good passwords for two reasons. First of all, they contain both letters and numbers and do not contain any real words out of the dictionary. Secondly, these password are rather easy to remember because they actually say something when you read them. Another option that you have is to use the first letter of a phrase and then put some numbers in as well. For example, the phrase SAMS Teach Yourself SQL Server 7.0 in 24 Hours would be styss7i24h.

- User ID—This is another step you must take in order to gain access to a specific database. The login ID and password that we previously discussed only get you into the server. If that is as far as you go, you cannot access any of the databases on that server. Every user who has access to a database has been assigned a user ID in that database. In most cases, the user ID and the login ID will be the same thing. After SQL Server has authenticated the login ID and has determined that the specific user (human) has access to the server, that user must choose a database to work in. SQL Server then checks the login ID against all the user IDs in that database to ensure that that user (human) does have access to the database. If there is not a user ID mapped to that login ID, SQL Server will not allow the user to progress any further.

- Role—A role is a way to group users into similar job functionality for ease of administration. In older versions of SQL Server, roles were known as groups. In function, they still work pretty much the same way. Instead of assigning permissions to individual users within the database, you can create a role, assign all the users to the role, and then assign permissions to the role. This saves administration time because when you hire a new person, all you need to do is add her into the role and she already has all the permissions that she needs. Because there are a lot of older SQL Server administrators out there, you will commonly hear this still referred to as a group.

- Application Role—This is a special type of role that allows only specific applications to access the data contained in the database. Most SQL Server administrators have been begging for this type of functionality for years. What it does is force users to access data contained in the databases through the application only. This is important because most users will be able to use certain applications such as Microsoft Access, which can connect to the database and give the users direct access to the tables contained in it. This forces the users to use the application that was specifically written to access the data and disallows all other applications from doing so.

- Windows NT Groups—SQL Server security is based heavily on Windows NT security. Windows NT Groups can be directly mapped to SQL Server Roles, thus allowing any user who is assigned to that group to automatically gain access to the SQL Server.

Authentication Process

Now that you have an idea of the different terminology that will be thrown in your direction during the next few minutes, we need to look at the actual authentication process. Four checks are made against the user as he attempts to access the server. At each point, the users are checked to see if they have the proper access. If they do, they are allowed to pass on. If not, the user will receive an error message and his progress is halted.

The first level of this security is at the network level. In most cases, the users will be logging into a Windows NT network, but they can log into any network that can coexist with Windows NT. The user must provide a valid network login ID and password, or her progress will be halted at this level. There seems to be a few ways around this security level, but not really. The main one is in the case of when a user is using an Internet application, such as a Web page, to query data from a database. Although the user might or might not have to supply login credentials in order to access the network, the broker account, or the account that the application is running under on the server, still has to log into the network.

The second level of security occurs at the server itself. When the user gets to this level, he must provide a valid login ID and password to progress any further. Depending on which security mode that you are using on the server, SQL Server might be able to determine which login ID you logged into Windows NT with.

The third level of security is an interesting one. When a user has progressed past the second level, it is usually assumed that she has the correct permissions to access the databases on that server, but that is not true. Instead, what occurs is the user must also have been assigned a user ID in the databases she wants to access. No password is involved at this level; instead, the login ID is mapped to the user ID by the administrator of the system. If the user has not been mapped in any database, there is little that she can do, except in one situation. It is possible to have a guest user ID in a database. In this case, what occurs is that the user has gained access to the server through a valid login ID, but she does not have access into a database and that database contains a guest user ID. Permissions can be assigned to the guest user ID, just as you would assign them to any other user. By default, new databases do not contain a guest user ID.

The last and final level of SQL Server security deals with permissions. What occurs at this level is that SQL Server checks to see if the user ID that the user is accessing the server through actually has permissions to access specific objects within the server. It is possible to give access only to specific objects within the database and not to others, which is usually the way things work.

As you can tell, the levels of security can make it very difficult for unauthorized users to gain access to your server. Because of the many layers of security, Microsoft has added features that allow you to set up security with much less difficulty. We will cover these in a few minutes. Before we get into that, you must know about the different ways that SQL Server security can work.

Security Modes

SQL Server provides two different methods for authenticating users into the server. Depending on how your network is set up, you might end up using one or the other. The first method, Windows NT Authentication, relies on Windows NT to perform all the authentication. The second method, SQL Server Mixed Authentication, allows Windows NT to validate the users as well as allowing SQL Server to perform its own authentication based on credentials that the user passes in.

Windows NT Authentication

Windows NT Authentication is the preferred method of authentication for SQL Server 7.0. This is because Windows NT can enforce a great deal more features with its security system, including minimum password lengths, password expiration, auditing, secure validation, and account lockout after several unsuccessful login attempts. Windows NT Authentication is only available on servers that are running Windows NT. With Windows NT Authentication, SQL Server does not require that the user supply a login ID and password to access the server. Instead, SQL Server will query Windows NT for the name of the user and then compares the user name that it gets back to a list of allowed user names. With Windows NT Authentication, password checking is not performed. This is because SQL Server trusts Windows NT, and if it says that the user has logged in, SQL Server believes it.

The following will walk you through setting up SQL Server to run under Windows NT Authentication:

1. Open SQL Enterprise Manager and connect to the server that you are going to change the security mode on.

2. Right-click on the name of the server that you are going to change and select the Properties option. This opens the SQL Server Properties dialog box.

3. Find the tab that says Security and click on it. This displays the Security Dialog, as seen in Figure 8.1.

FIGURE 8.1

The Security tab of the SQL Server Properties dialog box.

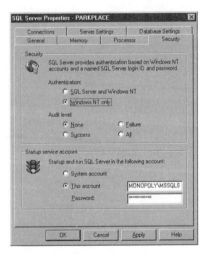

4. To change the server to run under Windows NT Authentication, select that option.

5. In order to get these changes to take place, you must stop and restart SQL Server. After you have restarted, SQL Server will not be running in the new security mode.

The other option for authenticating users is known as Mixed Authentication.

SQL Server Mixed Authentication

SQL Server Mixed Authentication, although not the preferred method of authenticating users, is often the only choice you have. This is because, as we mentioned before, Windows NT Authentication requires that the user connecting to the server must be logged into a Windows NT domain. For mixed environments, this is not an option because some clients cannot log into Windows NT at all. Mixed Authentication combines the strengths of Windows NT Authentication as outlined a few minutes ago. The major difference is that it also builds in an authentication method through SQL Server. Because it has more layers, it also becomes more complicated. Remember that SQL Server Authentication is the only method available to you when you are running SQL Server on a Windows 95/98 computer.

In a Mixed Authentication setting, if a client connects to a server without passing in a login ID and password, SQL Server will automatically assume that the user wants to use Windows NT validation and uses that method to validate the user. If the user actually passes in a login ID and password, SQL Server assumes that the user is connecting via SQL Server Authentication. In the SQL Server Authentication process, the login information the user passes in to the server is compared against a system table. If there is a match between the two passwords, the SQL Server allows the user access to the server. If there is not a match, the SQL Server disallows access, and the user will receive an error message back from the server.

The following will walk you through setting up the server to run on SQL Server Mixed Authentication:

1. Open SQL Enterprise Manager and connect to the server on which you are going to change the security mode.

2. Right-click the name of the server you are going to change and select the Properties option. This opens the SQL Server Properties dialog box.

3. Find the tab that says Security and click on it. This displays the Security Dialog, as seen in Figure 8.2.

4. To change the server to run under SQL Server Mixed Authentication, select the SQL Server and Windows NT option.

5. In order to get these changes to take place, you must stop and restart SQL Server. After you have restarted, SQL Server will not be running in the new security mode.

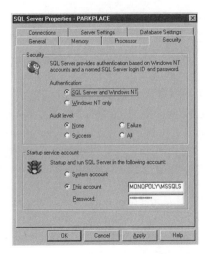

FIGURE 8.2

The Security tab of the SQL Server Properties dialog box.

Server Logins and Database Users

As with every other task that you will perform in SQL Server, there are several different ways to create login IDs and user IDs on your server. The first way to perform this task is through a wizard in SQL Enterprise Manager. This wizard will talk you through, step-by-step, creating a login ID and user ID. They have been clumped together because they are actually performed in concert with each other. The second option is to create the IDs using system stored procedures. If you choose this option, you will be able to recreate the same user logins on all servers you have, if needed. The final option is to create the login IDs and user IDs individually in SQL Enterprise Manager. We will not go over the last way of performing this, but you can get more information on this in Books Online.

Creating Login IDs and User IDs with SQL Enterprise Manager

The best thing about using SQL Enterprise Manager to create your login IDs and user IDs is that it is easy. This is because Microsoft has included a wizard that will walk you through setting up everything. This is useful because it will not let you forget any of the important steps. The following will walk you through setting up a login ID and user ID on your system:

1. Open SQL Server Enterprise Manager and connect to the server where you are going to create the login ID.

2. From the Tools menu, select Wizards. This opens the Select Wizard dialog, as seen in Figure 8.3.

FIGURE 8.3

The Select Wizard dialog.

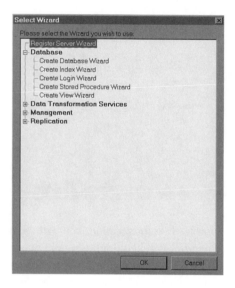

8

3. Expand the Database tree, select the Create Login Wizard, and click on the OK button. This opens the Create Login Wizard, as seen in Figure 8.4.

FIGURE 8.4

The Create Login Wizard.

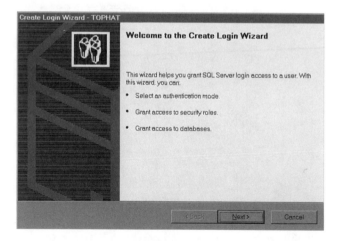

4. The next screen, as seen in Figure 8.5, allows you to choose the authentication mode for the login that you are going to create. If you have selected Windows NT Authentication Mode, SQL Server will only allow you to pick that option. Otherwise, both options will be available to you.

FIGURE 8.5

*The Select
Authentication Method
screen.*

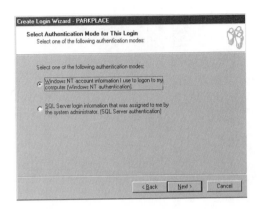

5. If you selected Windows NT Authentication, you will see the screen shown in
   Figure 8.6. In this screen, you are required to supply two pieces of information.
   The first is the Windows NT username for this user. You cannot browse for the
   user, so you must know the name of both the user and the domain in which
   the user resides. You must type the username in the DOMAIN\USER format. The
   other option that you must select is to deny or allow access to the server for this user.

FIGURE 8.6

*The Authentication
with Windows NT
screen.*

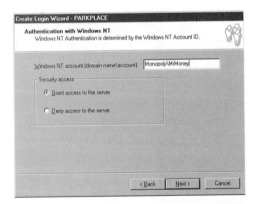

6. If you selected that you are going to use SQL Server Authentication for this login,
   you will see the screen shown in Figure 8.7. In this screen, you will be required to
   supply a login ID and the password for the user ID.

7. After you have defined the login ID, the next screen that you are presented with is
   the Grant Access to Security Roles screen, as seen in Figure 8.8. This screen is
   used to tell SQL Server if this user can perform any type of administrative functions. These functions can be used to offload some of these types of tasks to you.

FIGURE 8.7

The Authentication with SQL Server screen.

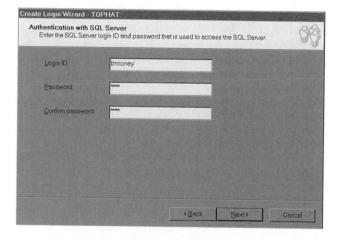

FIGURE 8.8

The Grant Access to Security Roles screen.

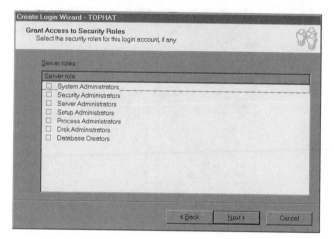

8. The next screen, called the Grant Access to Databases screen as seen in Figure 8.9, allows you to select which databases the new user will be able to access.

9. The final screen, as shown in Figure 8.10, is a summarization screen that describes all the actions that SQL Server is going to take in creating this login and user ID. After you click on the Next button, SQL Server will perform all these tasks and create the login ID.

FIGURE **8.9**

The Grant Access to Databases screen.

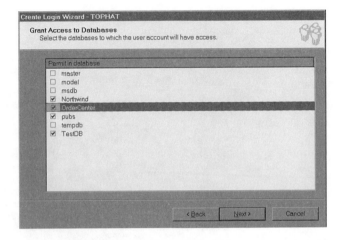

FIGURE **8.10**

The final summarization screen.

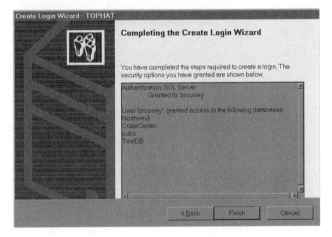

The other option that you have in adding a user ID to the server is to use system stored procedures and run the SQL Query Analyzer. For Windows NT Authentication, you will use the sp_grantlogin stored procedure. When using SQL Server Authentication, you will use the sp_addlogin stored procedure. The syntax of the sp_grantlogin is as follows:

```
sp_grantlogin [@loginame =] 'login'
```

where the option is the name of the Windows NT User, plus the domain in which the user is contained. For example, to add the user MrMoney from the Monopoly domain to the SQL Server, you would execute the following:

```
sp_grantlogin 'Monopoly\MrMoney'
```

This will grant that user access to the database, but will not allow her any further access. We will look at adding a user into a database after you see the sp_addlogin procedure. The syntax of this procedure is as follows:

```
sp_addlogin [@loginame =] 'login'
    [,[@passwd =] 'password']
    [,[@defdb =] 'database']
    [,[@deflanguage =] 'language']
    [,[@sid =] 'sid']
    [,[@encryptopt =] 'encryption_option']
```

where the options are as follows:

Option	Description
@loginame = 'login'	This is the name of the login ID that you are going to add to the server.
@passwd = 'password'	This is the password for the login ID that you are adding.
@defdb = 'database'	This is the default database for the user you are adding. A default database is one that the user will automatically use when he logs into the server. Even if you set this, you still must assign the user permission to use that database.
@deflanguage = 'language'	This is the default language for the user. It is possible to have multiple languages installed on the server, allowing the user to receive error and informational messages from SQL Server in his own language.
@sid = 'sid'	This is a security ID number that can be assigned to the user. This option is not normally used.
@encryptopt = 'encryption_option'	This option is used to tell SQL Server whether to encrypt the password that you pass into it. It is not a good plan to not encrypt the passwords. This option is not normally used.

Using this stored procedure, you can add a user to the server named mdavis with a password of initial and a default database of pubs using the following:

```
sp_addlogin 'mdavis', 'initial', 'pubs'
```

After you have added the login to the server, you must add the user ID to the databases they are going to be able to access. Without this, the users will not be able to access the databases. You will use the sp_grantdbaccess stored procedure. The syntax of this stored procedure is as follows:

```
sp_grantdbaccess [@loginame =] 'login'
    [,[@name_in_db =] 'name_in_db'
```

where the options are as follows:

Option	Description
@loginame = 'login'	This is the name of the login ID that you have added to the server. This ID must already be added to the server.
@name_in_db = 'name_in_db'	This is the name that this user will be added to the server as.

Roles

As you read earlier, roles are basically groups that you can use to group users who have similar access needs. A couple of different types of roles that you can use are as follows:

- Predefined server roles
- Predefined user roles
- The public role
- Custom database roles

Each of these different types of roles allows you to perform different functionality within the database.

Predefined Server Roles

The server roles are available to allow you to offload some of the administration of the server to other people. One of the things you can do is to allow certain users the ability to create and modify databases. Seven predefined server roles are available on the server. They are

- sysadmin—Members of the sysadmin server role are allowed to perform any action in the server. This is the most powerful of all the server roles and is analogous to the sa account in previous versions of SQL Server.

8

- serveradmin—Members of the serveradmin role are allowed to perform any configuration to server-wide settings.

- setupadmin—Members of the setupadmin server role are allowed to add and remove linked servers and execute some system stored procedures, such as sp_serveroption.

- securityadmin—Members of the securityadmin group can manage SQL Server logins.

- processadmin—Members of the processadmin group can manage any process that is running on the SQL Server. Membership in this group allows users to run commands like the KILL command.

- dbcreator—The dbcreator server group has the rights to create databases on the server.

- diskadmin—The diskadmin server group has the rights to create and manage disk files.

Predefined Database Roles

The predefined database roles are used to allow users to perform various functions in the database. Like the predefined server roles, the predefined database roles can be used to offload some of the administrative functions to other users. Nine predefined database roles are available for your use, and they are

- db_owner—Members of this group are considered to be the owner of the database. These users can perform the activities of all database roles, as well as other maintenance and configuration activities in the database.

- db_accessadmin—Membership in the group allows the user to add and remove Windows NT and SQL Server users in the database.

- db_datareader—The members of this group can see all data from all user tables in the database.

- db_datawriter—The members of this group have permission to add, change, or delete data from all user tables in the database.

- db_ddladmin—Membership in the group allows a user to add, modify, or drop objects in the database.

- db_securityadmin—The members of this group can manage roles and members of SQL Server database roles, and can manage statement and object permissions in the database.

- db_backupoperator—The members in this roll have permissions to back up the database.
- db_denydatareader—Members in this group cannot see any data in the database at all.
- db_denydatawriter—Members in this group have no permissions whatsoever to change data in the database.

The Public Role

The public role is a special database role that every user in the database is a part of. This role is created in every database when it is first created. As an administrator, you cannot make any changes to the properties of the public role, and you cannot add or remove users from that role. The usefulness of the public role comes when you need to supply a default set of permissions that all users have. For example, if you want every user in the database to have SELECT permissions on a specific table, assign those permissions to the public role and all users will have that permission.

Custom Database Roles

Custom database roles are database roles created by the administrator for special purposes. Custom database roles provide the ability to assign to users special permissions not provided by the built-in roles. Several rules that you need to keep in mind when using custom database roles are as follows:

- Custom database roles are created within the context of a database and cannot span across multiple databases.
- Users cannot belong to more than one custom database role at a time.
- Custom roles can contain Windows NT login IDs, SQL Server login IDs, and other SQL Server roles.

Summary

In this hour, we have covered information about SQL Server security and SQL Server security modes. One important thing you need to remember when setting up security is that you must be slightly paranoid. After that, we introduced login IDs, user IDs, and roles. These are important for you to know how to manage because they are how you will control access to your server.

8

Q&A

Q I am the database administrator at a small company, and I know and trust all the employees who work at the company. Is security really all that important?

A Unquestionably yes. Even though you trust **all** the employees who work for you, it is still an extremely good idea for you to maintain a fairly high level of security on your systems. Even if you trust your users, you still need to ensure that you have an adequately secure environment for outside users.

Q I do not want to have a public group in my database. Can I remove it?

A There is no way to remove the public group from any database. It must remain.

Workshop

The quiz and the exercise are provided for your further understanding. The answers can be found in Appendix A, "Answers."

Quiz

1. Why is security important?
2. What is a login ID?
3. What is a user ID?
4. What are roles used for?
5. What are application roles used for?
6. What is the difference between SQL Server Authentication and Windows NT Mixed Authentication?
7. What is the public role used for?

Exercise

Create a login ID on your SQL Server using SQL Enterprise Manager that uses SQL Server Authentication which has access to the pubs database.

HOUR 9

Permissions

In the last hour, you were introduced to the concept of security. In that hour, you saw how to secure your servers and disallow unwanted users from getting into the server. The problem that you will face, though, is after the users get into the databases on the server, then what? It is not uncommon to have data in a database that some users should not be able to see. For example, in a database that contains human resources data, you probably would not want all your users to see all the salary and tax information, but you might want to allow all your users access to name and phone number information. To allow for this type of functionality, you will need to assign permissions to certain users and revoke access to others.

The highlights of this hour include

- What Are Permissions?
- Types of Permissions
- Permission States
- Assigning Permissions
- Ownership Chains

What Are Permissions?

To put it succinctly, permissions control the ability for users to perform specific tasks in SQL Server. They allow your users access to objects within the database and what the users can do with those objects. If users have not explicitly been given permissions to access an object within the database, they will not be able to access anything within the database.

It is possible to assign permissions at several different levels within a database. You can assign permissions to individual users, to custom roles you have created, and to Windows NT groups you have added to the server. When you are assigning permissions, keep in mind that it is much easier to assign permissions to a role or group than it is to assign permissions to an individual user. The actual implementation of assigning permissions is the same; the difference comes in the amount of work. It is much easier to assign permissions to a single role or group that contains 100 people than it is to assign permissions 100 times to all 100 users.

Before you assign permissions to any user, you need to ensure that you have explored their needs. Some users will need only to look at data that is contained in the database, some users will need to be able to add and modify data, and yet others will need to actually make objects within a database. One of the major responsibilities of the DBA is to ensure that the proper permissions have been assigned to the users who need them.

Types of Permissions

Three types of permissions are available in SQL Server. Two of them can be delegated to other users. The third type of permissions is only available to people who belong to a certain role. The three types of permissions are known as statement, object, and implied permissions.

Statement Permissions

Statement permissions are usually given only to users who need the ability to create or modify objects within the database or to perform database or transaction log backups. These types of permissions are some of the most powerful permissions available in SQL Server and, under normal circumstances, very few people will need these permissions assigned to them. Usually, only database developers and other users who will be assisting with the administration of the server will require these types of permissions. It is important to realize that all these permissions are assigned on a per-database level, and it is not possible to have permissions that cross databases.

When you assign statement permissions to users, you are giving them the ability to create objects, usually referred to by their SQL command counterparts. The statement permissions include the following:

- CREATE DATABASE—Users who have been assigned this permission can create new databases on the server. This permission is set on the master database only.
- CREATE DEFAULT—Users who have been assigned this permission can create defaults in the current database.
- CREATE PROCEDURE—This permission allows users to create stored procedures in the current database.
- CREATE RULE—This permission allows users to create rules in the current database.
- CREATE TABLE—Users who have this permission are allowed to create tables in the current database.
- CREATE VIEW—This permission allows users to create views in the current database.
- BACKUP DATABASE—This permission allows users to create backups of the database on which they have been given the permission.
- BACKUP LOG—This permission allows users to create backups of the transaction log of the database on which they have been given the permission.

One note about statement permissions is that you will rarely actually assign them to your users. This is because you will more than likely assign your users to one or more of the predefined server roles that give them these permissions.

Object Permissions

Object permissions are assigned to objects at a database level and allow users to access and work with preexisting objects in the database itself. Without these permissions, your users will not be able to access any of the objects in the database. These permissions, like the statement permissions, are actually giving the users the ability to run specific SQL commands and are usually referred to by those commands. The available object permissions are as follows:

- SELECT—This permission is assigned to a user on a specific table in the database. When the user has been assigned this permission, he can access data that is being stored in the tables.
- INSERT—This permission is assigned to a user on a specific table in the database. If the user has been assigned this permission, he is able to add new data to the table.

- UPDATE—This permission is assigned to a user on a specific table in the database. When the user has this permission, she is able to modify existing data in the database.

- DELETE—This permission is assigned to a user on a specific table in the database. If a user has been assigned this permission, he is able to delete data from the table.

- EXECUTE—This permission is assigned to a user on a stored procedure. A user who has been assigned this permission has the ability to execute the stored procedure.

- REFERENCES—This special type of permission allows a user to link two tables together using a primary key/foreign key relationship. Under most normal circumstances, your users will not need to have this type of permission to a table.

The problem with assigning object permissions is that they must be assigned to each user or role one object at a time. This can be time-consuming when assigning permissions if you are assigning them to individual users. A better way to do this would be to assign the permissions to roles and then assign the users to the roles.

Permission States

When working with SQL Server permissions, there are three states that a permission can be in for a specific user. These states determine if a user can perform the specific function. It is important to note that when permissions are granted or revoked to a role, the users in that role inherit those permissions. Even if a user has been granted or revoked a permission directly, and she is a member of a role that has been revoked or granted that same permission, the role permission will override the direct permission.

The three states that a permission can be in are denied, revoked, and granted.

Deny

A denied permission is the strongest permission level. A permission that has been denied to a user, no matter the level, denies the user access to it even if they are granted access at a different level. For example, Mark is a member of the Editors role. The Editors role has been granted SELECT permissions on the authors table and Mark has been expressly denied SELECT permissions on the authors table. In this case, Mark will not be able to access the authors table. The converse of this also applies.

Revoke

When a permission is revoked, it simply removes the deny or grant that had been previously applied to that permission for that user. If that same permission is granted or denied at another level, it still applies. For example, Mark is a member of the Editors role. The Editors role has been granted SELECT permissions on the authors table and Mark has been expressly revoked SELECT permissions on the authors table. In this case, Mark will still be able to access the authors table. In order to completely cancel the permission, you must explicitly revoke or deny the permission on the Editors role or deny the permission from Mark.

Grant

A granted permission removes the previous denied or revoked permission and allows the user to perform the function. If the same permission is denied at any other level, the user will not be able to perform the function. If the permission has been revoked at another level, the user will be able to perform the function. For example, if Mark has been granted permissions to perform a SELECT on the authors table and the Editors role has been revoked permissions to SELECT on the authors table, Mark will still be able to access the table.

Assigning Permissions

Now that you know about the permissions you can assign and the levels at which you can assign them, it is time to look at how to actually assign the permissions. You can assign permissions through both SQL Enterprise Manager and by running SQL command in SQL Query Analyzer. You must be the database owner, be the objectowner, or belong to the db_securityadmin database role to assign permissions.

Assigning Permissions with SQL Enterprise Manager

Assigning permissions using SQL Enterprise Manager is the easiest way to assign permissions. All the work is done through the graphical interface, and you do not need to know about any of the underlying SQL commands that are actually running. The following walks you through assigning permissions to the user named TestUser, which you created in the pubs database in the last hour.

1. Open SQL Enterprise Manager and connect to the server on which you are going to work with the permissions.

2. Expand the tree next to the server name to show all the object categories on the server.

3. Expand the tree next to the databases folder to show all the databases on the server.

4. Click on the plus sign next to the name of the pubs database. This shows all the object categories in the pubs database.

5. Click on the Tables folder. Find the Authors table in the right pane, right-click on it, select the All Tasks option, and then click on the Manage Permissions option. This opens the Object Properties window, as seen in Figure 9.1.

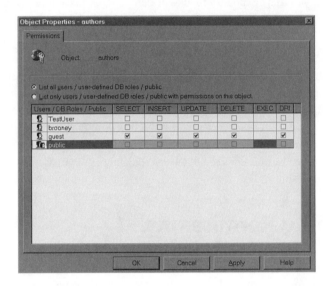

6. You will want to assign the TestUser user the ability to SELECT and INSERT data in this table, but to deny permissions to UPDATE and DELETE from the table. To do this, click in the box associated with the permission on the same line to assign the permissions. To grant permissions, click in the box once, until you see a checkmark. To deny permissions, click in the box twice, until you see a red X in the box. To revoke permissions, click in the box until there is nothing in the box. After you have assigned the permissions listed previously, the screen should look like the one in Figure 9.2.

7. When you have completed the assignment of permissions, click the OK button, and SQL Server will assign all the permissions.

Assigning Permissions with SQL Commands

The other option that you have in assigning permissions is to use SQL commands and run them in SQL Query Analyzer. This is done through using the GRANT, DENY, and REVOKE commands. The syntax of these commands is as follows.

FIGURE 9.2

The Object Properties dialog box after the permissions have been assigned.

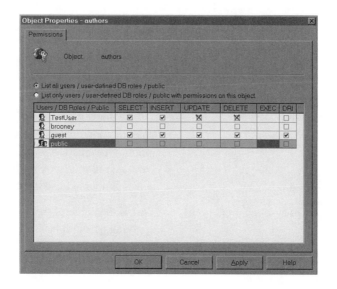

For statement permissions:

```
GRANT/REVOKE/DENY {ALL ¦ statement[,...n]}
TO/FROM security_account[,...n]
```

For object permissions:

```
GRANT/REVOKE/DENY
{ALL ¦ permission[,...n]}
{
[(column[,...n])] ON {table ¦ view}
¦ ON {table ¦ view}[(column[,...n])]
¦ ON {stored_procedure}
}
TO/FROM security_account[,...n]
[WITH GRANT OPTION]
[CASCADE]
```

Where the options are as follows:

Option	Description
ALL	This specifies that all permissions are being granted, revoked, or denied, depending on which command you are executing.

continues

Option	Description
statement[,...n]	This is the statement permission that you are applying. The list of statement permissions can be found in the previous section called "Statement Permissions."
TO/FROM	This is the keyword specifying to which account you are going to apply permissions. If you are granting permissions, you would use the TO keyword and if you are revoking or denying permissions, you would use the FROM keyword.
security_account[,...n]	This is the name of the account to which you are applying permissions.
permission[,...n]	This is the name of the object permission that you are going to be applying. The list of applicable object permissions can be found in the previous section titled "Object Permissions."
column[,...n]	It is possible to assign object permissions at a column level, if your need is as such. To do so, you would list the names of the columns here.
ON	This is the keyword that tells SQL Server to which table, view, or stored procedure to assign permissions.
table ¦ view	This is the name of the table or view to which you are going to apply permissions.
stored_procedure	This is the name of a stored procedure to which you are going to assign execute permissions.
[WITH GRANT OPTION]	When applying object permissions, it is possible to allow other users the ability to further grant permissions to other users if you specify this key phrase.
[CASCADE]	When you REVOKE or DENY permissions to a user, if you specify this option, SQL Server will also REVOKE or DENY permissions for any user to whom the original user granted permissions.

The code example in Listing 9.1 grants SELECT, UPDATE, and INSERT permissions to the authors table to a user named TestUser.

LISTING 9.1   Assignment of Permissions

```
GRANT SELECT, UPDATE, INSERT ON authors TO TestUser
```

9

Ownership Chains

This might seem to be an odd thing to throw in when you are learning about permissions, but it will have a definite impact on how you create objects in later chapters, as well as in later projects that you work on. Stored procedures and views will depend on other objects in the database, such as tables, views, or other stored procedures. These dependencies are sometimes referred to as an ownership chain.

In most situations, the user who owns the stored procedure or view will own the underlying objects as well and, in most cases, all the underlying objects will reside in the same database as the new object.

When a user accesses a view or a stored procedure, SQL Server will not check the permissions on the underlying objects if all the objects are owned by the same user and all the objects reside in the same database. If any of the objects are owned by different users or they reside in different databases, you have to deal with what is known as a broken ownership chain. If a broken ownership chain occurs, SQL Server will check the permissions on each object in the chain whose next link is not owned by the same user. The major problem with this is that the owner of the objects is the person who assigns the permissions on that object. This means that every time permissions are changed on the upper-level object, the owners of all the other objects will have to adjust the permissions on their objects. If they are not changed, the new user will not be able to access the underlying objects because of permissions issues.

The moral to this story is you need to ensure that all the objects in the database are owned by the same person when they are created. The easiest way to do this is to ensure that users who are going to be creating objects in the database are creating them as the database owner. You should also ensure that all other users have been denied permissions to create objects in the database.

Summary

In this hour, you have learned about permissions and how to assign them. You learned there are three basic types of permissions—only two of which can be assigned to users.

Next, you learned there are two different ways to assign your permissions, through SQL Server Enterprise Manager and by using SQL commands in SQL Query Analyzer. Last, you saw what an ownership chain is and how to avoid broken ownership chains.

Q & A

Q All the permissions dealing with data access are handled by the application my users use to access the data. Is it still important for me to assign object permissions in the database?

A Yes. You still need to assign permissions to the objects within your database because it is possible for your users to access the data in your database in other ways, such as SQL Server Query Analyzer.

Q I have had a user who has created an object in the database and that user has since left the company. What do I need to do before I remove that user from the server?

A You need to either drop the object that the user owned or change the owner of the object to another user through the use of the sp_changeobjectowner system stored procedure.

Workshop

The quiz and the exercise are provided for your further understanding. The answers can be found in Appendix A, "Answers."

Quiz

1. What are permissions used for?
2. What are statement permissions?
3. What are object permissions?
4. What are implied permissions?
5. What command would you use to allow a user SELECT permissions on a table?
6. What is an ownership chain?
7. What is a broken ownership chain?

Exercise

Write the statement required to allow the user named TestUser the ability to create tables within the pubs database.

HOUR 10

Implementing Backups

By now, you should have a pretty good feel for how important the data that you are storing in your SQL Server is. If you have not reached this point yet, read the following few sentences very carefully. The most important reason to back up your databases is for disaster recovery. Having a crashed database without a recent backup is not a situation that anyone needs to be in. In the end, it can boil down to whether you will have a job after a failure. If you are not backing up your SQL Server frequently, the best advice you should heed is to keep your resume updated.

The highlights of this hour include

- Why and When You Should Back Up
- How SQL Server Backups Work
- Other Backup Considerations
- Types of Backup Devices
- Backing Up User Databases
- Backing Up the System Databases

Why and When You Should Back Up

If you are not sufficiently impressed about the need to back up your databases, go back and reread the first section of this hour. This is a very important topic that should not be taken lightly. As I discussed, disaster recovery is the most important reason that you should back up your databases on a regular basis. Backing up gives you the ability to get production databases back online quickly and efficiently after the server has crashed. Nevertheless, the following lists a number of reasons besides disaster recovery why backups are useful:

- Accidental or malicious updates or deletion of data
- Natural disasters such as fires, floods, or tornadoes
- Theft or destruction of equipment
- Hardware failure
- Transportation of data from one machine to another
- Permanent archival of data

 You will frequently hear the terms backup and dump being used interchangeably by DBAs who have been around a while. This is because in previous versions of SQL Server, and in many other RDBMSs, backing up a database was known as dumping a database. With the release of SQL Server 7.0, Microsoft determined that the term dump be replaced with the more descriptive (and politically correct) term backup.

Now that you realize how important it is to back up the data in your databases, the next step is to decide when and how often to perform backups. SQL Server provides many efficient and reliable ways to back up your data, most with little impact on users.

The decision of when to back up is partially answered by determining what the acceptable loss is. An acceptable loss is the amount of data that can be lost without having an extremely detrimental impact on the business. This is a difficult concept to fathom, and you will need to invest a lot of time explaining what acceptable data loss is to management and, with their help, determine how much it is. Realize that most managers, when you first approach them, will immediately tell you that they want zero data loss at all times. Although this is conceptually possible, it is going to cost a lot of money and be difficult to reach, but sometimes it is worth striving for. In online transaction processing (OLTP) environments, for instance, an hour's worth of data loss could result in millions of dollars of lost business. You will need to balance these requirements with budgetary and reality requirements to come up with an acceptable solution.

The other factor in determining the frequency of backups is the degree in which the data is changed. If the data in your database does not change frequently, it is safe to back it up only after those changes have been made. If your database is updated daily, you should make backups daily. In a way, this factor plays directly back into the acceptable loss issue. The more data that is being changed will result in more data to lose if it is not frequently backed up.

How SQL Server Backups Work

SQL Server 7.0 has made several advancements over previous versions in the backup arena. SQL Server now has three different ways to back up data contained in your databases. When used in conjunction with each other, these methods can come close to achieving an environment in which you lose no data if your database crashes. These three methods are full database backups, transaction log backups, and differential backups.

Full Database Backups

Full database backups are favored on some systems because of their ease of implementation. Let's face it, very little thought has to go into backing up a full database at scheduled points during the day or week. The problem with this type of backup scheme is that you have very little flexibility, and you have the potential to lose a very large amount of data if the server crashes. For example, imagine that you are backing up your database every day at midnight. If the server were to crash at 11:00 PM, you would lose every modification that was made during the previous 23 hours. For most systems, this is unacceptable. A few, limited, exceptions to the rule are

- The importance of the data contained within the system is very low. A good example of this is a development server. On these types of servers, developers usually have old or bogus data loaded for testing applications. A daily backup of this type of database would be acceptable to pick up any database schema changes.

- The data contained within the system can be easily recreated. An example of this type of server would be a reporting server in which all of the data contained on it is loaded via a batch process. If this database crashes, all you have to do is rerun the batch process, and the data will be back.

- A remote site where there is little or no database administrator support. In this type of situation, you are frequently relying on people who are not adequately trained to maintain the backup scheme, and who frequently have other job functions. It is usually best to ensure that the backup scheme you implement is very simple, so as not to have to force these users to monitor and maintain it.

10

- Database changes are infrequent. An example of this would be historic data that is gathered and placed in a data mart or data warehouse. Usually, this data is queried to identify trends, but is rarely modified.

Transaction Log Backups

A transaction log backup is, as the name implies, only a backup of the information that is contained in the transaction log. Transaction log backups must be made in conjunction with at least one full database backup because you must have a starting point if you should have to restore the database. Transaction log backups take a great deal less resources than full database backups, making it easier to run them more frequently. This actually serves a twofold purpose. The first is that you reduce the amount of time between a server failure and the last backup, thus reducing the amount of data that is lost. Transaction log backups also allow you to perform a special type of recovery, known as point-in-time recovery. This type of recovery allows you to restore the database up until a specific point in time, such as five minutes before an actual failure took place. This is especially useful when someone performs accidental mass data updates or deletes that need to be removed. You simply recover the database up to about the time the action took place. The types of situations in which transaction log backups are useful are as follows:

- Situations where losing large amounts of data is unacceptable. In this type of situation, you might make a full database backup on a daily basis and perform transaction log backups on an hourly, or more frequent, basis. This reduces the overall amount of data that could conceivably be lost.

- The size of the database makes performing frequent full database backups difficult. For example, very large data warehouses can easily grow to measure in the terabyte size range. In this situation, you could make one full database backup and then perform transaction log backups whenever changes are made to the data.

- You want to take advantage of point-in-time recovery. Like I outlined previously, point-in-time recovery is a very important and useful feature that is available to you when you make transaction log backups.

- Changes are being made to the database at a high rate. When there are a large number of database changes, database backups can get out of date very quickly. If you take transaction log backups in conjunction with the full database backups, you can keep these changes in check.

Differential Backups

Differential backups are the newest technology that you can use to assist your backup scheme. These backups, like the transaction log backups, only back up the changes that have been made since the last full database backup. Unlike the transaction log, these backups do not allow for point-in-time recovery. They will only allow you to restore up to the point in which the backup was actually made. Therefore, these types of backups are often supplemented with transaction log backups. Some examples of situations where differential backups could be useful are

- Systems containing data that is not extremely important, so any changes that have been made can be lost without catastrophic effects. With these types of systems, it is often easier to recreate the data by hand than it is to create a transaction log backup scheme.

- A remote site where there is little or no database administrator support. In this type of situation, you are frequently relying on people who are not adequately trained to maintain the backup scheme and who frequently have other job functions. It is usually best to ensure that the backup scheme you implement is very simple, so as not to have to force these users to monitor and maintain it.

- The size of the database makes performing frequent full database backups difficult. For example, very large data warehouses can easily grow to measure in the terabyte size range. In this situation, you could make one full database backup and then perform transaction log backups whenever changes are made to the data.

- Systems in which you want to minimize down time by combining full database, differential backups, and transaction log backups.

Other Backup Considerations

Now that you know the different types of backup schemes and when they might be used, several other factors need to be taken into account when you are determining how to back up your SQL Servers. These points might not seem extremely important by themselves, but when you put them all together, they are.

What Medium (Disk or Tape) Will You Back Up To?

This question is an interesting one forseveral reasons. The first point that you have to think about when determining the answer to this question is performance. If you are backing up a large amount of data, you have to take into account the speed difference between backing up to tape and backing up to disk. Of course, backing up to tape is going to be much slower than backing up to disk. The next point that you have to consider is recoverability. The disk drives in a computer are usually the first piece of hardware to fail. If you are only backing up to disk, you are leaving yourself open for data loss. Usually, what most people determine to be a good mix is to back up your databases to disk and then back up the files on the disk to tape. Although this still leaves you open for some data loss between the point that you make the SQL Server backup and the time that you back up to tape, this is still safer than simply leaving the backups on the disk.

What Time of Day Will Backups Run?

When you are dealing with heavily updated databases, any performance hit on the computer can make life difficult for the users of that database. Although backing up the databases does not cause a huge performance hit, it can cause some slow downs. On large OLTPs, even the smallest slowdown can be unacceptable. So what is the answer? Most often, you will back up during the slowest period of data entry by your users. This time is usually known as your maintenance window. Although most DBAs get to experience a very large maintenance window, such as 5:00 p.m. until 7:00 a.m. the following morning, some DBAs get very small or no maintenance windows. When determining what time your databases will be backed up, be sure to take into account the fact that even though your users will experience some slow downs, it is much better than having a crashed database with no backup at all.

The great thing about SQL Server is that you do not have to be there to manually run the backups. Through the use of the SQL Server Agent, you can schedule backups to run at any time on any day that you want them to. This makes answering the previous question much easier because you do not have to rely on having a person there to take care of the backup.

Where Will Backups Be Stored?

A two-part answer to this question exists. The first part is it is best that your backups are not stored on the same machine as the data itself. For performance reasons, you will often dump data to the drives of the local machine because it is much faster than dumping to tape. After that, it is imperative that you copy the data through the network to another server or copy it to tape.

The second part of this is you should look into offsite storage for your backup tapes. This can be as simple as taking the tapes home with you at night, or as complex as having an offsite storage facility that comes and picks up the tapes on a daily basis.

How Long Will You Keep the Backups?

A frequently used backup strategy to help you answer this question is the grandfather—father—son, or generational, backup scheme. In this strategy, a monthly backup is made on either the first or last day of the month. This is the grandfather generation and should be kept offsite and retained indefinitely. The second generation is a weekly backup. This is the father generation and should also be kept offsite and retained for a definite period of time, perhaps a year. The son generation is made on a daily basis and is retained for a month before overwriting. This generation of backup tapes should be kept onsite in a safe place, such as a fireproof safe.

How Will Backups Be Verified?

This is a really important part to maintaining frequent backups of your databases. I have assisted companies trying to recover databases that they had been religiously backing up only to find out after a database had crashed that their tape drive had not been working properly. What could they have done to find out if everything had been working OK? First and foremost, check to make sure that everything is working before the database crashes. When you first set up a server, before you go into production, run backups and restore them to the same server to make sure that the hardware works. Other options that you have are to take your backups and restore them onto a development or Quality Assurance server to make sure that they work, or to look into one of the many companies that will verify your backup tapes for you. All you have to do is send them off to the company, and they will send it back to you with a letter telling you whether the tape was good.

10

Who Is Responsible for the Backups?

As I discussed in the section about the different types of backups you can make with SQL Server, this question can play a big role in how you set up your backups. If all your servers reside in a single data center with a support staff who will be responsible for making sure that your backup tapes are changed out and everything runs properly, having a rather complex backup scheme is not going to be a problem. If your servers are distributed across a large geographic region with a very limited support staff at each site, you might want to look into creating a less complex backup scheme.

Types of Backup Devices

A backup device is a location where SQL Server can store backup copies of databases or transaction logs. Backup devices can be disk files on the local machine, disk files on remote servers, tapes, or named pipes. When you create a backup device, you will give it both a logical name and a physical name. The logical name can be up to 120 characters in length and must follow the SQL Server naming convention for identifiers. It is usually a good idea to make these names as descriptive as possible without making them too long. This way, you can look at the logical name and have a good idea what backups will be contained on that device.

The physical name is a file system name that includes the path or the Universal Naming Convention (UNC) for network devices. Physical names can be up to 260 characters long. For example, if the share resides on the server called BackupServ, the UNC to this would look something like \\BackupServ\BackupShare. Table 10.1 shows examples of the logical and physical names of all the types of backup devices.

TABLE 10.1 Types of Backup Devices

Device Type	Logical Name	Physical Name
Local Disk	DB_BACKUP_DISK	D:\BACKUPS\DBBACKUP01.DAT
Network Disk	TL_BACKUP_SQLBACK	\\SQLBACK\BACKUPS\TLBACKUP.DAT
Tape	TAPE_BACKUP	\\.\TAPE0
Named Pipe	NP_BACKUP	\\SQLBACK\PIPE\SQL\BACKUP

Disk Backup Devices

Disk backup devices can reside either on the local machine or on a networked server. The advantage to using a disk backup device to back up your database is that the backup process is extremely fast. When using a disk device on the local machine, it is important to copy the backup device to tape or to a network server to protect it from disk crashes. When using a disk device on a network share, you must first check to see if the service account that SQL Server is running under has the correct permissions to write to the machine.

Tape Backup Devices

SQL Server currently only supports local tape devices. This release of SQL Server does not support the use of networked tape drives. Before SQL Server will recognize a tape drive, it must first be installed using Windows NT. When you create a tape device in SQL Server, you must specify the physical name that Windows NT assigned it. The first tape drive installed in the computer will be assigned the name \\.\TAPE0. Other drives installed will be given incrementing names.

Named Pipe Backup Device

Microsoft provides named pipe backup devices as a way for third-party software vendors to back up and restore SQL Server. Named pipe backup devices cannot be created or administered via SQL Enterprise Manager. To back up to a named pipe, you must provide the name of the pipe when you invoke the backup command.

Creating a Backup Device

Before I get into backing up your databases, you need to look at creating the backup devices that you are going to need. In the following steps, I am going to walk through creating three disk backup devices that you will use when you are backing up databases later this hour.

1. Click the Start button, go to Programs, Microsoft SQL Server 7.0, and then choose SQL Server Enterprise Manager.

2. When Enterprise Manager starts, double-click the name of the server that you are going to be working with. After you have connected to the server, click the plus (+)next to the Management folder and choose the Backup item. In the right-hand pane, right-click and choose the New Backup Device... option, as shown in Figure 10.1.

FIGURE 10.1

Select the New Backup Device... from the Backup item within SQL Enterprise Manager.

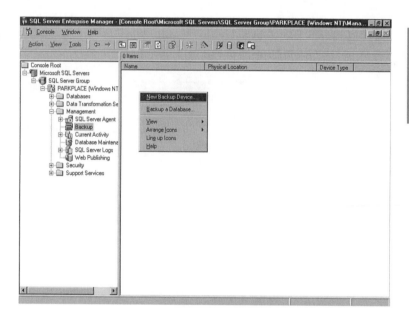

3. After you have selected the New Backup Device... option, the Backup Device Properties—New Device dialog opens up, as shown in Figure 10.2.

4. For the first backup device, enter Northwind_Full_Database in the Name box. Note that the File Name box is immediately filled in with what you type in the Name box. If you want, you can change the filename, but for these purposes, leave it as it is.

5. After you have filled in this information, click the OK button to create the backup device.

6. Repeat steps 2–5, using the name Northwind_Transaction_Log for the name.

FIGURE 10.2

The Backup Device Properties dialog.

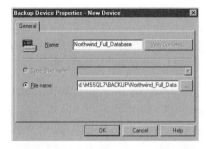

7. Repeat steps 2–5, using the name `Northwind_Differential` for the name.

8. After you have completed the previous steps, your Backup items folder should look similar to the one st provide the name of the pipe when you invoke the backup command shown in Figure 10.3.

FIGURE 10.3

The Backup folder after the backup devices have been created.

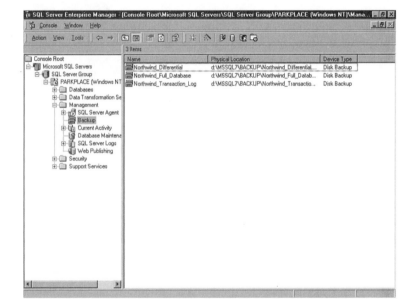

Backing Up User Databases

Now that you have gotten past all the theory and preparation, you are going to set up the backup scheme for a company known as Northwind Traders. As I have mentioned in previous hours, Northwind Traders is a fictitious company that imports and exports specialty food items from around the world. They currently do a lot of business, but they are getting worried because they do not have any backups implemented at this point. After discussing their needs for recoverability, you have decided to go with the following backup scheme:

- Full Database Backups—Northwind Traders has determined that they take the least amount of orders from midnight until 2:30 a.m. This is their maintenance window. As a starting point for all other backups you are going to run, you should run a full database backup during this time.

- Differential Backups—Because Northwind Traders would need to recover as quickly as possible, you have decided that you should perform differential backups every 6 hours. This provides the ability to recover the full database backup, and then the last differential backup taken, followed by any transaction log backups. This will greatly speed the recovery process.

- Transaction Log Backups—Northwind Traders are constantly taking orders from customers who are wanting products shipped to them. If they lose any of this data, the least that they are going to have are some very upset customers because they did not get their products. They have determined that the most data they can lose is 15 minutes worth. So, every 15 minutes between the differential backups, you will need to take transaction log backups.

Now that you know what and when you are going to back up the Northwind Database, the following section will walk you through setting up the full database backup. You will set up the other two in the exercises at the end of this hour. In order for this to work, you must first open the SQL Server Query Analyzer and run the code that is listed in Listing 10.1. This will turn off the truncate log on checkpoint option.

LISTING 10.1 Turn off Truncate Log on Checkpoint Database Option

```
1: sp_dboption Northwind, 'trunc. log on chkpt.', false
2: go
```

1. Click the Start button, go to Programs, Microsoft SQL Server 7.0, and then choose SQL Server Enterprise Manager.

2. When Enterprise Manager starts, double-click the name of the server that you are going to be working with. After you have connected to the server, click the plus sign (+) next to the Management folder and choose the Backup item. In the right-hand pane, right-click and choose the Backup a Database option, as shown in Figure 10.4.

FIGURE 10.4

Select the Backup a Database option from the Backup item within SQL Enterprise Manager.

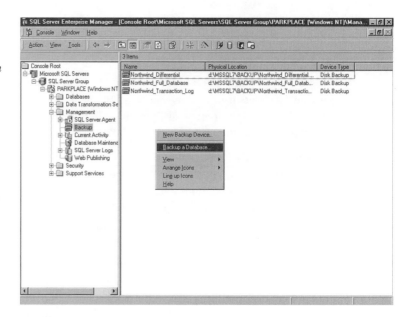

3. After you have selected this option, the SQL Server Backup dialog box opens, as seen in Figure 10.5.

FIGURE 10.5

The SQL Server Backup dialog.

4. This first backup that you will create is the full database backup of the Northwind database. From the Database drop-down box, select Northwind.

5. In the Name option, type in a name that best describes the backup you are creating. For the purposes of this exercise, type `Northwind Database—Full Backup`.

6. In the description box, you can type in any information that will help you remember what this backup job is going to do.

7. In the Backup section, make sure that the correct backup type is selected, in this case Database—Complete.

8. In the Destination Area, click the Add button. This opens the Choose Destination Device dialog. Click the Backup Device option button, select the correct Backup Device from the drop-down list, and then click the OK button.

9. In the Overwrite section, for these purposes, select the Overwrite Existing Media option.

10. Place a checkmark in the Schedule box and then click the button that contains the ellipses (…). This will open the Edit Schedule Box, as seen in Figure 10.6.

FIGURE 10.6

The Edit Schedule dialog box.

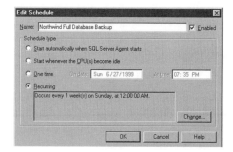

11. In the Name box, type in a name that will be descriptive to you. For these purposes, type in `Northwind Full Database Backup`.

12. From the Schedule Type box, select Recurring and then click the Change button. This opens the Edit Recurring Job Schedule dialog box, as seen in Figure 10.7.

FIGURE 10.7

The Edit Recurring Job Schedule dialog box.

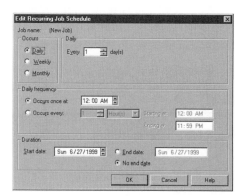

13. Select the schedule on which you want this backup to run, and then click the OK button. For these purposes, select Daily in the Occurs box and Occurs once at: 12:00 a.m. in the Daily Frequency box.

14. At the Edit Schedule box, click the OK button.

15. At the SQL Server Backup dialog, click the OK button.

16. After you have been returned to the Backups item, you can make sure that the backup task has been scheduled by clicking on the SQL Server Agent item and then selecting Jobs. The backup job that you just created will be listed in the right-hand pane.

Backing Up the System Databases

As with the user databases, you should also make periodic backups of certain system databases, specifically the master and msdb databases. You should make backups of the model database whenever you make changes to it. These changes are rare. You should also back up the distribution database if your server participates in replication.

Backing Up the Master Database

The master database contains information about the configuration of the SQL Server as well as information about all the other databases on the server. You should make frequent backups of this database, especially after making any configuration changes to the SQL Server or changes to the databases contained on it. These changes include adding or modifying a database, creating logins, or adding backup devices.

Backing Up the msdb Database

The SQL Server Agent uses the msdb database. This database is a storage area for all scheduled tasks as well as the history of those tasks. The database is changed whenever you add or modify tasks, add or modify automatic backup tasks, or change alerts. By default, the Truncate Log on Checkpoint database option is turned on when SQL Server is installed. In order to perform transaction log backups, you must turn off this option. You can back up this database as you would any user database.

Backing Up the Model Database

The model database is used whenever SQL Server creates a new database. It contains all the default objects that are in all databases. If you have added anything to the model database, you will need to back up this database.

Backing Up the Distribution Database

If the SQL Server is set up to participate as a remote distribution server or a publisher/distributor in the replication process, you will have a database dedicated to the distribution process. By default, the name of this database is distribution, but this can be changed when setting up replication. The distribution database holds all transactions waiting to be replicated and then forwards them on to subscription servers. The distribution database can be backed up as you would any user database and should be backed up frequently.

Summary

In this hour, I have gone over SQL Server backups. When determining how your databases will be backed up, several things must be taken into account, including the amount of data contained in the database, how much that data is changed, and how much data can be lost. After you have determined this information, you can set up and schedule the backups.

Q&A

Q **The transaction log gives me a great deal of recoverability. Because this is the case, why do I need to worry about backing up my databases frequently?**

A The transaction log gives you the ability to recover from partially completed transactions only. It does not allow you to recover after hardware failure.

Q **I am trying to make a transaction log backup on one of my databases and it keeps telling me that I can't. Why not?**

A Most likely the reason that you can't make transaction log backups on a user database is that the Truncate Log on Checkpoint database option is turned on. You can turn this off by running the following:

```
sp_dboption YourDatabaseName, 'trunc. log on chkpt.', false
```

Workshop

The quiz and the exercises are provided for your further understanding. The answers can be found in Appendix A, "Answers."

Quiz

1. Why should you back up your databases?
2. What is acceptable loss?

3. What are two situations in which running only a full database backup might be a good idea?

4. What is a transaction log backup?

5. What is point-in-time recovery?

6. What is a differential backup?

7. Why is it a good idea to verify your backups?

8. What is a backup device?

9. Why should you back up the master database?

10. Besides the master database, which other system databases should you backup?

Exercises

1. Create a backup job that performs a differential backup on the Northwind database at 6:00 a.m., Noon, and 6 p.m. Point the backup at the backup device called Northwind_Differential.

2. Create a backup job that performs a transaction log backup on the Northwind database every 15 minutes from 12:15 a.m. until 5:59 a.m. Point the backup at the backup device called Northwind_Transaction_Log. Do not worry about creating other backup jobs for the other times, I will go over a different way of scheduling the other runs in Hour 16, "Scheduling Tasks and Alerts."

HOUR 11

Restoring Databases

Under normal circumstances, no database administrator looks forward to restoring a database. This is not because the actual restoration process is difficult. Instead, it is because there is usually a lot of other stress associated with restoring the database. No users can be using the database when it is being restored and the database is usually being restored because of some sort of corruption in the database. Hopefully, you will never have to perform a database restore, but in the event you do, you should be familiar with the steps of the process and the limitations as well. You need to be aware that it is inevitable that your databases will fail at some point. You must realize that this is a fact of life and live with it.

The highlights of this chapter include

- Restore Overview
- Automatic Recovery
- Restoring Databases
- Restoring User Databases
- Restoring System Databases

Restore Overview

There are really two different scenarios in which you are going to have to perform a database restore. The main reason that you would need to perform a database restoration is because of database or data corruption. This can be anything from a user deleting vital data in the database, to actual corruption of the database files, to the loss of hard disk drives in the server. The second reason would be to copy a database from server to server for maintenance tasks or remote processing of data.

Restoring a database is the process of loading a backup and then applying the transaction logs to recreate the database. After applying the transaction logs, the database will be at the state it was at prior to the last transaction log backup.

In the event that files on which the database resides fails because of media failure, all you have to do is replace the hard disk drives and then restore the data. If you have corrupt or incorrect data in the database as a result of malicious or unintentional INSERTs, UPDATEs, or DELETEs, you can simply restore the database to the state it was at before the data corruption took place.

Users cannot be in the database that is being restored during the restoration process. All data in a database is replaced when a database is restored.

When restoring transaction log backups, you must keep in mind several key factors. First is that transaction logs must be loaded in the same order as they were taken. When the log is backed up, SQL Server places a timestamp in the file. When you start the restore process, SQL Server will check the timestamps to see if the sequence is correct. The changes in the transaction log are then re-executed. All other transactions are then rolled back.

Transaction logs can be restored to a specific time and date. This is called *point-in-time* recovery. All transactions committed after that time are rolled back. Point-in-time recovery applies only to transaction log backups and cannot be done with full database or differential restores.

The actual database restoration process has been improved a great deal in SQL Server 7.0. The biggest leap that has been made is when you restore a database, you do not have to recreate the database using the same steps with which it was created previously. In earlier versions of SQL Server, you had a database that had been created and then expanded several times, and you had to perform those same steps before the restore is done. If you did not, eventually your database would end up being corrupt. In SQL Server 7.0, all you have to do is restore the backup, and the database will be created for you.

Types of Database Restores

When it comes time for you to actually restore a database, you will have several options to choose from. These options depend on the types of database backups you have made. The following are the types of restores that you can make:

- Full Database Backups—A full database backup is a copy of the entire database at the time that the backup was made that is copied into a single file.

- Transaction Log Backups—A transaction log backup contains a copy of the transaction log, which contains a before and after image of every data modification that was made in the database.

- Differential Database Backups—A differential database backup contains a copy of all the changes in the database since the last full database backup was made.

Depending on the types of database backups you have made, the restoration process will change. Usually, you will start with the latest full database backup and then restore any transaction log backups or differential backups that you have made.

Automatic Recovery

Before we venture too far into restoring user backups, we need to discuss the automatic recovery feature of SQL Server. Automatic recovery happens every time SQL Server is started, and it is designed to check to see if any recovery needs to take place.

As we mentioned previously, not all changes to the database are written at the time they are made. The data that has been changed is stored in a cache and is written to the disk during the checkpoint process, which occurs about every 60 seconds. If the system crashes, or loses power, before a checkpoint has occurred, the automatic recovery process will examine the transaction log to make sure that all transactions have or have not been completed.

When a transaction begins, and before any actual data is modified, a row is written to the transaction log showing the beginning of the transaction. All changes made are then logged into the transaction log. When the transaction has completed, an end transaction row is written to the log. The begin and end records are how SQL Server delimitates the beginning and end of a transaction.

The automatic recovery process goes through the transaction logs of each database and searches for the begin and end records of transactions and compares that to the data in the database. Transactions that have not been committed at the time of the system crash are cancelled, or rolled back. When both begin and end transaction records are found in the transaction log, the transactions are re-executed, or rolled forward.

11

The automatic recovery process begins with the master database, and then moves on to the model database. The model database is what SQL Server uses as a template when it creates new databases. After the model database has been recovered, the automatic recovery process clears tempdb of all objects in it. The tempdb database is where SQL Server formats query results, creates temporary tables, and other temporary working storage needs. Next, msdb is recovered, and then pubs is recovered. The msdb database is where SQL Server stores information about scheduled tasks and completion of those tasks. The pubs database is a small database that can be used for testing and experimentation. If the server is set up as a distribution server, the distribution database is recovered next. After all the system databases have been recovered, the user databases are recovered. Users can log into the server after the system databases have been recovered, but they cannot use any user database until it has completed recovering.

The automatic recovery process cannot be turned off, but there are two configuration options that affect automatic recovery. During the automatic recovery process, the databases that are being recovered are grayed out in SQL Enterprise Manager with the word "Recovering" next to it. The recovery flags option determines what information SQL Server displays during the recovery process. The recovery interval option controls the maximum amount of time that SQL Server should take to recover the database. The value that you set here is used by SQL Server to determine the frequency of the CHECKPOINT process. These options can be set using SQL Enterprise Manager or the sp_configure stored procedure.

Restoring Databases

As we went over previously, when you need to recover your databases, you have to recover them in the same order in which they were taken. The first step that you will have to perform is to restore the most frequent database backup. After you have restored the full database backup, your second step will be to restore the transaction log backups in the order that they were made. If you have also made differential backups, you can restore these to take the place of the transaction log backups. It is important to remember that transaction log backups must be restored in the same order that they were made.

Backup Considerations

You should take several things into consideration when you are restoring a database. These considerations are as follows:

- If the hard drive that contains the database itself has crashed, and SQL Server is still running, it is possible to back up the transaction log for that database using the WITH NO_TRUNCATE option. This will make a copy of the transaction log without letting SQL Server look at the database itself. Then, after the hard drive has been replaced, it is possible for you to restore the database and then the transaction logs that you acquired from the previous backup process.

- If the hard drive that contains the transaction log for a particular database has crashed, SQL Server will stop any of your users from making any data modifications to that database. To recreate the transaction log, all you have to do is stop and restart the SQL Server, which will cause SQL Server to recreate a new transaction log.

- The database cannot be in use when you attempt to restore it.

- Transactions that are active and incomplete in the database when the database is backed up will be rolled back when the restore has completed. Transactions that had been completed but had not been written out will be rolled forward when the restore has completed.

- Transaction logs must be restored to the server in the same order they were taken. For example, in the event that you have taken a full database backup at midnight and then taken transaction log backups every hour after that, you will have to first restore the full database backup and then every transaction log backup you have taken. If you have lost a transaction log backup because of overwriting it or because of a bad tape, you will have to stop at that point.

- Most database options, such as READONLY, will have to be reset if the database was not present when the restore operation took place.

- When you are restoring a database that does not currently exist on the server, you must select the Restore as Database option and supply the name for the new database. We will go over this more in a minute.

- When restoring a database to a different server than the database was backed up on, you must ensure that both servers have the same or similar charactersets and sort orders.

- It is possible to restore a database's files to a different location than they were originally taken. To do this, you must select the Restore Database Files As option and type in the new path and name for the files. We will look at this option more in a minute.

- If a database restore operation was stopped before it had a chance to complete, you can continue the restore operation where it left off using the RESTART command.

- When SQL Server starts up and it cannot access a database because of hardware problems or corruption of the files, it will mark the database as suspect. This means that no user can access the database. In most cases, you will have to drop the database and restore from a backup.

11

Restoring User Databases

Now that you have seen some of the theory behind restoring databases, it is time to take a look at actually doing it. There are two main ways to restore a SQL Server database. The one you will learn about here is through SQL Enterprise Manager. The other option is to use the RESTORE DATABASE command from within SQL Query Analyzer. For more information on this option, search for RESTORE DATABASE in SQL Server Books Online. The following walks you through restoring a user database from within SQL Enterprise Manager:

1. Open SQL Enterprise Manager and connect to the server on which you are going to create the job.

2. Click on the plus sign (+) next to the databases folder. Right-click on the database that you are going to restore, choose All Tasks, and then click on the Restore Database option. In this case, choose the Northwind database. This opens the General tab of the Restore Database dialog, as seen in Figure 11.1.

FIGURE 11.1

The General tab of the Restore Database Dialog.

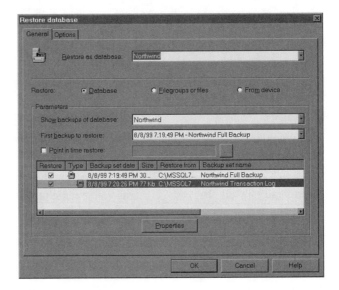

3. From the General tab, you can delete which database to restore and any options you have. The main option you have from this screen is to perform a point-in-time restore. To perform this, click in the box next to that option. This allows you to select the date and time that you are going to use for the point-in-time restore.

4. From the Options tab, as seen in Figure 11.2, you can select the options for which SQL Server is going to perform after the restore has taken place, as well as

optional new locations and names for the database files. It is sometimes useful to restore the database files to a different location than they originally were if you are trying to move the database files onto different hard drives.

FIGURE 11.2

The Options tab of the Restore Database Dialog.

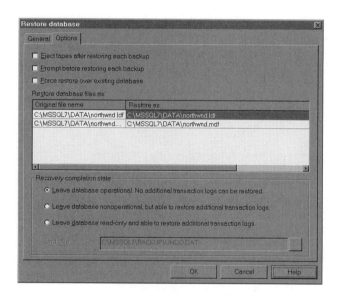

5. When you have finished filling out these options, click on the OK button to restore the database. This starts the restore process. You can track the progress of the restore as seen in Figure 11.3.

FIGURE 11.3

The progress of the restoration can be checked during the restoration.

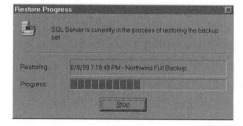

6. When the restoration has completed, SQL Server pops up a dialog telling you that the restore has been completed and the database is ready for use.

Now that you have an idea of how to restore a user database, you should have an understanding of how to restore system databases should they crash.

Restoring System Databases

The process for restoring system databases is very similar to restoring user databases except for the master database. If the master database is lost, you will not be able to start the SQL Server to restore any other databases. For any other system database, you will be able to follow the same restoration processes that we went over a few minutes ago. You have two options if the master database has crashed. The first option that you have is when you have made a backup of the master database. This is really the best thing to do if you have actually made a backup. If you do not have a backup of the master database, the only option that you have is to recreate the master database and then attempt to recreate the data about the databases.

Restoring the Master Database

Like we mentioned previously, SQL Server will not start if the master database is missing or corrupt. To get around this, you will have to rebuild a new master database and then restore the master database from a backup that you have made. The following walks you through creating a new master database. It is important to note that all other system databases, including model, msdb, and the distribution databases, will be rebuilt as well.

1. Start the SQL Server setup program from the SQL Server installation CD-ROM or from the BINN directory in the MSSQL installation directory. After the setup program has started, click on the Continue button.

2. When the rebuild process starts, choose the Character Set, Sort Order, and Unicode collation that you used when you originally set up the server. If you do not choose the same Sort Order that you used when you set up the original server, you will not be able to restore the master database. You must also make sure that you configure the new master database to be the size of the original master database.

3. When SQL Server completes rebuilding the master database, start the MSSQLServer service, open up the SQL Enterprise Manager, and connect to the server using the sa account with no password.

4. Add a backup device that corresponds to whatever type of device and name where your last backup of the master device resides.

5. Restore the master database from the most recent backup. After the master database has been restored, you must stop and restart the SQL Server.

6. Re-apply any changes that have been made since the most recent backup was made.

7. Restore the msdb database or recreate all the tasks and alerts that you had. You must do this because the process of rebuilding the master database destroys and rebuilds the msdb database.

Recovering the Master Database

If you do not have a good copy, or any copy at all, of the master database, you will have to recover the master database instead of restore it. This process is slightly more involved than a simple restore. During this process, you will have to recreate the master database and then reattach all the user databases. After you have recreated the master database, you will have to recreate all the user logins, database options, and backup devices. In most cases, you will want to keep this information either scripted or printed out for cases like this. If you do not have this information, the only option that you will have is to recreate all this information from memory, which is not the best option. The following walks you through recovering the master database and all the user databases on the server:

1. Run the SQL Server setup application and recreate the master database as outlined previously.
2. Recreate all the backup devices.
3. Restore msdb, model, and the distribution databases.
4. Reattach all your user databases using the sp_attach_db system stored procedure. For more information on the sp_attach_db stored procedure, search for sp_attach_db in Books Online.
5. Re-associate the database users with the server login IDs using SQL Enterprise Manager.
6. Reset the database options such as Select Into/Bulk Copy.
7. All your SQL Server configuration information will have to be re-entered, including the SQL Mail configuration, Security configuration, and Memory configuration.

Summary

In this hour, we have gone over restoring databases. First, we went over all the requirements for the actual restoration process. Then we went over the automatic recovery process. Next we went over restoring user databases. Lastly, we went over restoring and recovering the master database.

Q&A

Q **In previous versions of SQL Server, it was possible to recover individual tables in the database. Is this possible in SQL Server 7.0?**

A SQL Server 7.0 does not allow you to restore single tables. You must restore the entire database.

Q **After I have backed up a database, is there anything that I should do before I restore the database?**

A You should attempt to restore the database to another server or database to ensure that your backups actually worked.

Workshop

The quiz and the exercise are provided for your further understanding. The answers can be found in Appendix A, "Answers."

Quiz

1. What does it mean to restore a database?

2. Is it possible for users to actively be using the database when you restore it?

3. When you are restoring transaction logs, what is the major limitation that you have?

4. Do you have to recreate the database in the same way that it was created previously before you actually restore it?

5. What is automatic recovery?

6. What happens to transactions that are incomplete in the database after the database is restored?

7. What must you do to get SQL Server to start before you restore the master database?

Exercise

Restore the Northwind database and its transaction log from the backups that you made in Hour 10, "Implementing Backups."

HOUR 12

Importing and Exporting Data

One of the biggest hurdles that a database administrator will face is the fact that most companies will have more than one type of database management system in use. Although actually using the different systems is not usually difficult, the problem that you will have is trying to share data between systems. In older systems, you had to figure out a way to export data from one system and import it into another through manual processes. This usually meant that a person who knew the requirements of both systems and how to operate both systems would have to work to determine how data is moved and loaded. The actual interoperability issues have not been solved with SQL Server 7.0, but the implementation of interoperability has become much easier.

The highlights of this hour include

- Interoperability
- Data Transformation Services Overview
- Bulk Copy Program
- BULK INSERT

Interoperability

You might be wondering why interoperability between different systems is so important. It all comes down to the amount of work that your users are going to have to do. In a large number of organizations, there is still a major dependency on mainframes. Many of these companies have huge numbers of applications that still reside on their mainframes. What is more, these companies are also frequently running other client/server database platforms. If you imagine that there is information such as human relations data stored in both places and that the systems are not talking to each other, your users will have to enter the same data into both platforms, thus doubling their overall workload. When things like this occur, the users who have to perform all the double entry usually begin to grumble and express their overall concern about having to perform all this extra work. This is the perfect time for the friendly DBA to step in and create a solution that solves all their problems.

Aside from custom applications that move data between different database platforms, two major technologies are available in SQL Server to assist you in moving data. The first technology that I will go into is the Data Transformation Service, or DTS. This service allows you to write powerful applications, called packages, that can involve multiple steps and conditional execution of those steps. The second technology that I will go over is the Bulk Copy Program, or BCP. BCP is a tool that has been around since the earliest versions of SQL Server. This tool, although it is an older technology, is still quite powerful. BCP is used to extract data out of a SQL Server to a file and then to load those files into a SQL Server table.

Data Transformation Services Overview

The Data Transformation Services is a powerful technology provided in SQL Server that allows users to import, export, and transform data from multiple sources. These sources can be SQL Server, any ODBC-compliant data source, OLE DB-complaint data sources, and text files. Some of the functionality provided in DTS are as follows:

- Builds data warehouses and data marts by importing and transforming data from multiple heterogeneous sources either interactively or on a scheduled basis.
- Creates custom transformation packages that can be integrated into third-party applications.
- Accesses databases using third-party OLE DB drivers, thus giving those applications the capability to be used as sources and destinations for data.
- Accesses native application drivers such as SQL Server, Access, Excel, and Oracle.

- Accesses fixed length and delimited flat files using the built-in data pump.

- Adds high-speed, nonlogged inserts into the database.

- Transfers data between multiple SQL Server 7.0 databases, including all the data and the structures in the database. This can be used to move entire databases between services.

Data Transformation Services

When working with Data Transformation Services, or DTS, two steps usually are involved. The first step is the actual movement of data from one location to another. The second step involved in this usually occurs between the two locations. This step is the transformation of the data. When these two operations are combined, this makes DTS an extremely powerful application.

The transformation of data is used to separate operational data into a format that is appropriate for the specific application. Data transformation usually also involves some sort of formatting or modifying the extracted data into merged or derived values. Some examples of transformation include the following:

- Calculating new values based on values that are stored in the existing database. This type of transformation can include aggregation and summarization of values.

- Breaking columns that contain single values into separate columns. For example, you might want to break a column that contains a date into several different columns that contain a month, a day, and a year.

- Merging data from several columns into a single column. For example, combining the product ID and description for a particular product.

- Changing the format of the data that is contained in the column. For example changing all the alphabetic characters into all uppercase or converting all the numbers contained in a column into words.

Now that you have an idea of what you can do with DTS, you actually need to know how to set it up. SQL Server will allow the user to interactively create objects using the import and export wizards. These wizards allow you to create DTS packages, which are the main DTS objects. The following walks you through setting up a DTS package that will export data from the Northwind database and copy it into the OrderCenter database.

1. Open SQL Enterprise Manager and connect to the server on which you are going to run the DTS wizard.

2. After you have connected, click on the Tools menu and choose the Wizards option. This opens the Select Wizard dialog, as seen in Figure 12.1.

12

FIGURE **12.1**

The Select Wizard dialog.

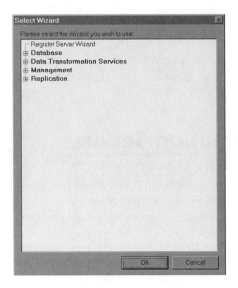

3. Click on the plus sign (+) next to the Data Transformation Services option, click on the DTS Export Wizard, and then click on the OK button. This opens the Data Transformation Services Export Wizard, as seen in Figure 12.2.

FIGURE **12.2**

The Data Transformation Services Export Wizard.

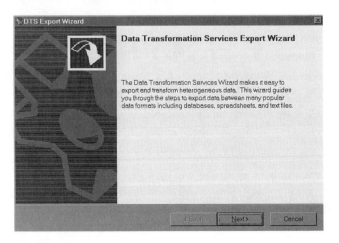

4. From the introduction screen, click on the Next button. This opens the Choose a Data Source dialog, as seen in Figure 12.3. From this screen, you can choose the database from which you are going to export. In the Source box, you can select the driver you are going to use to export the data. For these purposes, select the Microsoft OLE DB Provider for SQL Server. In the server box, the current server

will be selected. Click on the Refresh button next to the Database drop-down box. This forces SQL Server to fill the drop-down with the names of all the databases on the server. Choose the Northwind database from this box. When you have completed the login information, select the Next button.

FIGURE 12.3

The Choose Data Source Dialog.

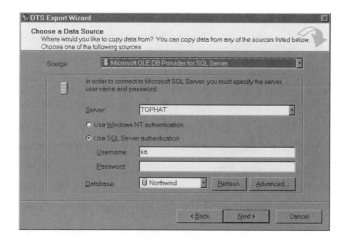

5. The next screen is the Choose a Destination screen, as seen in Figure 12.4. From this screen, you can choose the information about the database to which you are going to export. From the Database drop down, select the OrderCenter database and then fill out the login information. When you have completed this, select the Next button.

12

FIGURE 12.4

The Choose a Destination dialog.

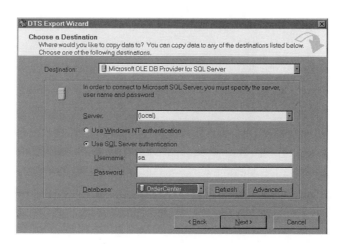

6. The next dialog, the Specify Table Copy or Query, as seen in Figure 12.5, allows you to choose the actual action that you are going to take. You can choose to either copy tables, specify a query that will be used to choose the data, or transfer the objects between the databases themselves. For these purposes, select the Copy Tables from the source database.

FIGURE 12.5

The Specify Table Copy or Query dialog.

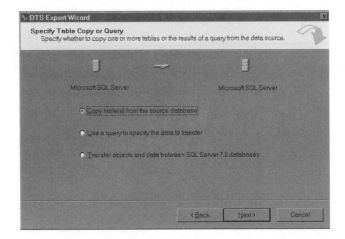

7. The next screen, the Select Source Tables dialog, as seen in Figure 12.6, allows you to choose the tables that you are going to copy from the source database. For these purposes, choose the Products table.

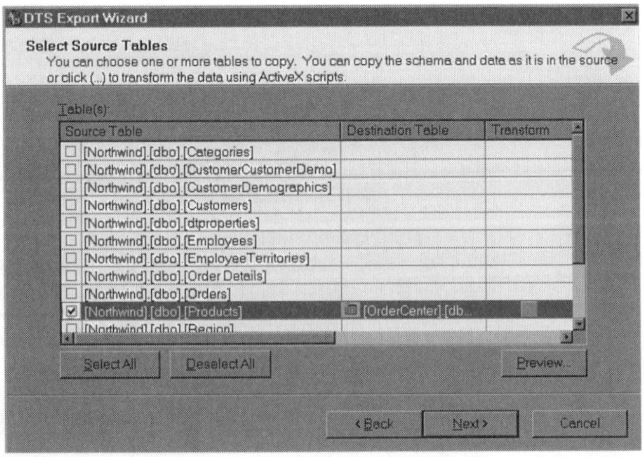

FIGURE 12.6

The Select Source Tables dialog.

8. If you want to make any transformations during the movement of the data, click on the button that has the ellipses. This opens the Data Mappings and Transformations Dialog, allowing you to make changes.

9. The next screen, the Save, Schedule and Replicate Package, as seen in Figure 12.7, allows you to run the package that you are creating, schedule it to run at a later time, or save the package. If you select to save the package, you can choose where you would like to save it: to SQL Server, Repository, or a file.

FIGURE 12.7

The Save, Schedule and Replicate Package dialog.

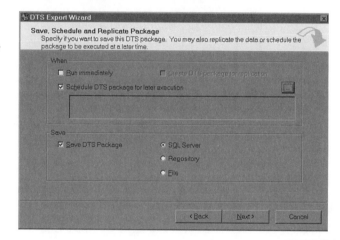

10. If you have selected to save the package, the next screen will be the Save DTS Package, as seen in Figure 12.8. SQL Server will supply a default name, which you can change for your purposes.

12

FIGURE 12.8

The Save DTS Package dialog.

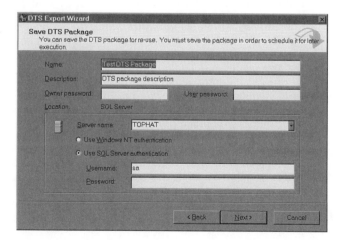

11. The final screen outlines all the steps that SQL Server takes in creating the DTS package. After you have reviewed this data, click on the Finish button, and SQL Server completes the package, as seen in Figure 12.9.

FIGURE 12.9

The DTS Package Wizard creating the package.

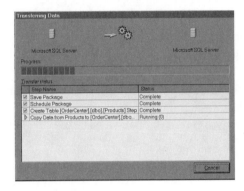

The other option that you have in exporting and importing data from a SQL Server is the Bulk Copy Program, or BCP.

Bulk Copy Program

The Bulk Copy Program, or BCP, is an older tool used to import and export data to and from SQL Server. This tool, although it is an older technology, has yet to and will probably never outlive its usefulness. BCP is a command-line utility that can be used to pull data out of a SQL Server table or view into a file on the computer in which BCP is being run. That file can then be transferred to another computer or location and can be imported back into another computer. The other option you can use is to take data that has been exported from a mainframe or other database application and import it into SQL Server using BCP.

Using BCP

As I mentioned before, BCP is a command-line utility, which means that a large number of switches can be passed in to get SQL Server to perform the functions you need. The following is the syntax of the command:

```
bcp {{table_name | view_name} | "query"}
{in | out | queryout | format} data_file
[-m max_errors] [-f format_file] [-e err_file]
[-F first_row] [-L last_row] [-b batch_size]
[-n] [-c] [-w] [-N] [-6] [-q] [-C code_page]
[-t field_term] [-r row_term]
```

```
[-i input_file] [-o output_file] [-a packet_size]
[-S server_name] [-U login_id] [-P password]
[-T] [-v] [-R] [-k] [-E] [-h "hint [,...n]"]
```

Where the possible options are

Option	Description
table_name	This is the name of the table that you are going to copy out of or in to during the BCP operation.
view_name	This is the name of the view that you are going to copy out of or in to during a BCP operation. If you are going to BCP data into a view, you have to abide by the same rules as you would when inserting data into a view.
"query"	This is a SQL query that you can use to specify specific rows and columns out of different tables. If you specify this option, you must also specify the queryout option as well.
in	This keyword is used to tell SQL Server to copy the contents of a file into the specified table or view.
out	This keyword is used to tell SQL Server to copy the contents of the specified table or view out to a file.
queryout	This keyword is used in conjunction with an SQL query to tell SQL Server that it is supposed to run a query and return the results to the specified file.
format	This option is used to force SQL Server to create a format file based on the table or view, the specified code page, and the delimiters that you choose. If you specify this option, you must also specify the -f option as well.

12

continues

Option	Description
data_file	This is the file that you are either going to copy data into or copy data out of.
-m max_errors	The option is used to specify a number of errors that can occur before the entire operation is cancelled. Any row that fails to be copied into the database is counted as one error. If this value is not specified, SQL Server will use the default of 10.
-f format_file	This option is used to specify the location of a format file that SQL Server uses to determine how the data will be formatted when it is either copied into or out of the database. It is not a requirement to create a format file. You will learn more about the usage of the format file in a few minutes.
-e err_file	This option is used to specify the location of a file that will be used to store any errors that occur during the BCP process. If you do not specify this option, SQL Server will return all errors that occur to the screen.
-F first_row	This option is used to specify the first row of data that is to be BCPed. The default for this is 1, which indicates the first row in the data file that you are copying up to the server.
-L last_row	This option is used to specify the last row of data that is to be BCPed. The default for this is 0, which indicates that all rows are to be processed.

Option	Description
`-b batch_size`	This option is used to specify the number of rows per batch to be copied. Each batch is copied to the SQL Server as a single batch. Do not use this option in conjunction with the -h "ROWS_PER_BATCH =bb" option. If you do not specify a batch, the entire process is treated as a single transaction. If this fails for any reason, SQL Server will cancel the whole thing.
`-n`	This option is used to specify a that the bulk copy is to be performed using native database format. If this option is specified, SQL Server does not prompt for any field information.
`-c`	This option is used to specify that the bulk copy is to be performed using character format. With this, SQL Server uses the char datatype for the storage type, \t (tab) for field delimiters, and \n (new line) for the row terminators.
`-w`	This option is used to specify that the BULK COPY operation is to be performed using the Unicode characterset. This option does not prompt for the field types, it uses the nchar datatype for the storage type, \t (tab) for the field delimiter, and \n (new line) for the row terminators.

12

continues

Option	Description
-N	This option is used to specify that the bulk copy is to be performed using the native database format. This is different from the -n option in that it allows the Unicode character types to be used. This option is not available when BCPing in or out of earlier versions of SQL Server.
-6	This option is used to force SQL Server to BCP data using SQL Server 6.5 datatypes. You must use the -n or -c option in conjunction with this option.
-q	This option is used to tell SQL Server that quoted identifiers should be used. If your table or view names contain characters that are not ANSI characters, you must enclose them in quotes.
-C code_page	This option is used to specify the code page that will be used in the data file. For more information on this option, search for Copying Data between Different Code Pages in Books Online.
-t field_term	This option is used to specify a field terminator that you want used in the data file. The default for this option is /t, which produces a tab.
-r row_term	This option is used to specify the row terminator that you want used in the data file. The default for this option is /n, which produces a new line.
-i input_file	This option is used to specify a file that contains the answers that must be provided when you are running BCP in interactive mode.

Option	Description
-o output_file	This option is used to specify a file that receives the output from BCP. If this option is not specified, this information is sent to the screen.
-a packet_size	This option is used to specify the number of bytes that SQL Server will send through the network. In large BCP operations, increased packet sizes can increase the performance of the process. Valid values for this option range from 512 bytes to 65,536 bytes. Windows NT and SQL Server both default to 4,096 bytes.
-S server_name	This option is used to specify the name of the server that you are going to connect to when performing the BCP operation.
-U login_id	This option is used to specify the login ID with which you are going to login to the server.
-P password	This option is used to specify the password associated with the login ID that you are passing in.
-T	This option is used to tell BCP that you are going to connect to the server using a trusted connection.
-v	This forces SQL Server to return the version information and copyright for the BCP utility.
-R	This specifies that the currency, date, and time data is copied into the SQL Server using the client local information.

12

continues

Option	Description
-k	This option specifies that any empty columns retain a NULL value when the data is copied into the tables that contain a default value for a particular column. If you do not specify this value, SQL Server will put the default value in the column instead.
-E	Specifies the values for any identity columns present in the file. If the -E option is not specified, SQL Server will ignore the identity values and create new values.
-h "hint [,...n]"	This option specifies any hints to be used during a bulk copy operation into a table or view. For more information on this subject, search for BCP Utility in Books Online.

Admittedly, a very large number of options are available to you when using BCP, but you will use very few of them. The following will use BCP to copy all the rows out of the authors table in the pubs database on the server tophat. You will have to replace that value with the name of your server.

```
bcp pubs..authors out authors.txt -c -r \n -t, -U sa -P -S tophat
```

If you look at the file, the preceding command will produce the following output:

```
172-32-1176,White,Johnson,408 496-7223,10932 Bigge Rd.,
➥Menlo Park,CA,94025,1
213-46-8915,Green,Marjorie,415 986-7020,309 63rd St. #411,Oakland,
➥CA,94618,1
238-95-7766,Carson,Cheryl,415 548-7723,589 Darwin Ln.,Berkeley,
➥CA,94705,1
267-41-2394,O'Leary,Michael,408 286-2428,22 Cleveland Av. #14,
➥San Jose,CA,95128,1
274-80-9391,Straight,Dean,415 834-2919,5420 College Av.,Oakland,
➥CA,94609,1
```

BULK INSERT

The last option that you have in dealing with the migration of data is the BULK INSERT command. This command is a new one that was introduced in SQL Server 7.0. It is used only to insert data into the database and is executed directly from within SQL Server. The syntax of this command is as follows:

```
BULK INSERT [['database_name'.]['owner'].]{'table_name'
FROM data_file}
[WITH
(
[ BATCHSIZE [= batch_size]]
[[,] CHECK_CONSTRAINTS]
[[,] CODEPAGE [= 'ACP' ¦ 'OEM' ¦ 'RAW' ¦ 'code_page']]
[[,] DATAFILETYPE [=
{'char' ¦ 'native'¦ 'widechar' ¦ 'widenative'}]]
[[,] FIELDTERMINATOR [= 'field_terminator']]
[[,] FIRSTROW [= first_row]]
[[,] FORMATFILE [= 'format_file_path']]
[[,] KEEPIDENTITY]
[[,] KEEPNULLS]
[[,] KILOBYTES_PER_BATCH [= kilobytes_per_batch]]
[[,] LASTROW [= last_row]]
[[,] MAXERRORS [= max_errors]]
[[,] ORDER ({column [ASC ¦ DESC]} [,...n])]
[[,] ROWS_PER_BATCH [= rows_per_batch]]
[[,] ROWTERMINATOR [= 'row_terminator']]
[[,] TABLOCK]
)
]
```

As you can tell, most of the options you have are the same that are available with BCP. To load the file that we created earlier using the BCP command, you would run the following command within SQL Server Query Analyzer:

```
BULK INSERT pubs..authors
FROM C:\TEMP\authors.txt
WITH( DATAFILETYPE = char,
      FIELDTERMINATOR = ',',
      ROWTERMINATOR = '\n')
```

Summary

In this hour, we have covered some of the options you have available to you when you are importing and exporting data. The first and newest option that you have is the Data Transformation Services, or DTS. This technology is very involved and a great deal of options are available to you when implementing it. I have barely scratched the surface of

12

what you can do with it here. The other technologies that you can utilize for importing and exporting data are BCP and the BULK INSERT command.

Q&A

Q I am trying to move data between a SQL Server and a DB2 system running on a mainframe. How should I do this?

A You have two options. The more in-depth option would be to create a DTS package that would perform the required steps. The other option you have is to export the data from the DB2 system and import it into the SQL Server using BCP.

Q I have heard that you cannot recover the database if you are performing a bulk copy and the database fails. Is this true?

A Actually, it is not true. There are times when you will force BCP to perform a non-logged operation. In this case, SQL Server does not log all the inserts into the table. This speeds up the inserts into the table. SQL Server will still log all space allocation operations, though. If the operation does fail, SQL Server can roll back the space allocation to make the database consistent again.

Workshop

The quiz and the exercise are provided for your further understanding. The answers can be found in Appendix A, "Answers."

Quiz

1. Why is interoperability between systems important?
2. What is DTS?
3. What is a DTS application called?
4. What are the three main functions that can be performed with DTS?
5. What is the bulk copy program used for?
6. What database objects can you use the BCP command with?
7. What is the BULK INSERT command used for?

Exercise

Create a DTS package using the Import and Export Wizard that pulls all of the data out of the titles table in the pubs database and export it out to a text file.

HOUR 13

Introducing Replication

In this section, you will cover the basics of SQL Server Replication. This powerful tool can help you move data between different locations. In order to understand replication, you must first understand the terminology and methodologies of replication.

The highlights of this hour include

- What Is Replication?
- The Publisher/Subscriber Metaphor
- How Replication Works
- Replication Agents
- Factors in Replicated Data
- Distribution Methodologies

What Is Replication?

Today's business world is about data. In other words, who has the data and who controls where it is going. Every day, all businesses are collecting data on customers, sales, inventory, transactions, and just about any other category you can think of. The problem that can arise is making sure that everyone has the data they need at the exact time at which they need it. In a simple explanation, imagine you are the CEO of a company, and you are attempting to make a decision that could make or break your company. All you need is a phone call from one person to supply that last little piece of information before you make your decision, and the person is late in calling you. Imagine your frustration as you wait and wait for the call.

Although SQL Server Replication cannot make sure that you get the phone calls you need, it can ensure that data stored in SQL Server is where you need it when you need it. Replication allows you to move data closer to the clients who need it.

SQL Server Replication can provide several other benefits to you. One of the biggest benefits is, as mentioned previously, the data can be delivered to different locations. This can help eliminate network traffic and spread data access across several servers, thus reducing load. For example, you could move data that is important for reporting off a busy transaction processing server. Another benefit for moving data off of a single server and onto different servers is for availability. You could use replication to create a mirror of your main database, so if one server crashes, the users could continue with very little downtime. Although this is not a perfect solution to data availability, many people do rely on it.

In order to get replication to work properly, you should be familiar with all the terms that are associated with it. Over the next several sections, I will cover the important terms and other needed information.

The Publisher/Subscriber Metaphor

SQL Server Replication follows what is known as the publisher/subscriber metaphor when describing all the major players in the scenario. This includes all the server roles and the individual portions of data that will be replicated. As the name implies, all these terms come from the publishing business.

Publisher

The publisher is the server that makes data available to other servers. The publisher specifies which data is to be replicated and determines which data has been changed since the last synchronization has taken place. The publisher maintains the only master copy of the replicated data. The other servers in the replication scenario can modify the data, but only the publisher has the master copy.

Distributor

The distributor is the server that takes the data from the publisher and moves it out to the subscribing servers. A single distribution server can service multiple publishers and subscribers. The actual role of this server can vary depending on the methodology that you choose to perform replication. The distribution server contains a special database known as the distribution database. The distribution database is a database that is stored on the Distribution server. This database is also known as the store-and-forward database, and all data modifications are stored in this database before they are moved to the subscribing servers.

Subscriber

The subscriber is the server that receives data from the publisher through the distributor. Unlike previous versions of SQL Server where the replicated data was treated as read-only, replicated data in SQL Server 7.0 can be modified without the changes being lost. These changes can then, if the servers are configured to do so, be sent back to the publisher for redistribution to any other subscribers.

Publication

A publication is a group of one or more articles. A publication is the smallest unit in which a subscriber can subscribe. Security is also provided at the publication level. This security is provided in the form of a Publication Access List, or PAL. The PAL contains a list of all logins that are allowed to have access to the publication.

Article

An article is a grouping of data that is provided for replication as a part of a publication. An article contains either all the data in a table, a subset of the columns in a table, a subset of the rows in the table, or a combination of both. These subsets of data are created through a process known as filtering. Three types of filtering are vertical, horizontal, and combination.

Vertical Filtering

Vertical filtering, as seen in Figure 13.1, is the process of narrowing down the number of columns that you want to send to the client. This can be for one of many reasons. First of all, it reduces the overhead on all servers involved because you reduce the amount of data that is processed. Secondly, there might be a security reason for not sending out all the data.

13

FIGURE **13.1**

Vertical filtering.

au id	au lname	au fname	phone	city
172-82-1176	White	Johnson	408-796-7223	Menlo Park
213-46-8915	Green	Marjorie	415-986-7020	Oakland
296-95-7766	Carson	Cheryl	415-548-7723	Berkeley
267-41-2394	O'Leary	Michael	408-286-7428	San Jose
274-00-9091	Straight	Dean	415-004-2919	Oakland
341-22-1782	Smith	Meander	913-843-0462	Lawrence
409-56-7008	Bennel	Abraham	415-658-9932	Berkeley
427-17-2019	Dull	Ann	415-006-7120	Palo Alto

Publishing Server

Subscription Server

au lname	au fname	city
White	Johnson	Menlo Park
Green	Marjorie	Oakland
Carson	Cheryl	Berkeley
O'Leary	Michael	San Jose
Straight	Dean	Oakland
Smith	Meander	Lawrence
Bennel	Abraham	Berkeley
Dull	Ann	Palo Alto

For example, in some human resources databases, you might have a table that contains employee information such as name, address, phone number, and salary. All this information, except the salary, needs to be sent out to the regional offices. Vertical filtering can solve this problem for you.

Horizontal Filtering

Horizontal filtering, as seen in Figure 13.2, is the process of narrowing down the number of rows that are sent to the subscribers. This process could be used when you are replicating data to different regions.

For example, you might have several different cold storage facilities, which are used for storing meat products after they are produced and before they are sent to the stores. Each cold storage facility needs to have product information for every product that it could possibly store. This product information can be modified at a single location, and then replicated out to the sites that need the data.

FIGURE 13.2

Horizontal filtering.

au id	au lname	au fname	phone	city
172-82-1176	White	Johnson	408-796-7223	Menlo Park
213-46-8915	Green	Marjorie	415-986-7020	Oakland
296-95-7766	Carson	Cheryl	415-548-7723	Berkeley
267-41-2394	O'Leary	Michael	408-286-7428	San Jose
274-00-9091	Straight	Dean	415-004-2919	Oakland
341-22-1782	Smith	Meander	913-843-0462	Lawrence
409-56-7008	Bennel	Abraham	415-658-9932	Berkeley
427-17-2019	Dull	Ann	415-006-7120	Palo Alto

Publishing Server

Subscription Server

au id	au lname	au fname	phone	city
296-95-7766	Carson	Cheryl	415-548-7723	Berkeley
267-41-2394	O'Leary	Michael	408-286-7428	San Jose
274-00-9091	Straight	Dean	415-004-2919	Oakland
409-56-7008	Bennel	Abraham	415-658-9932	Berkeley
427-17-2019	Dull	Ann	415-006-7120	Palo Alto

Combination Filtering

It is possible to combine vertical and horizontal filtering, as seen in Figure 13.3, to pare down the data that is being sent to the client even further. This type of filtering might be used to send phone information about certain client sites only to those sites.

FIGURE 13.3

Combination filtering.

au id	au lname	au fname	phone	city
172-82-1176	White	Johnson	408-796-7223	Menlo Park
213-46-8915	Green	Marjorie	415-986-7020	Oakland
296-95-7766	Carson	Cheryl	415-548-7723	Berkeley
267-41-2394	O'Leary	Michael	408-286-7428	San Jose
274-00-9091	Straight	Dean	415-004-2919	Oakland
341-22-1782	Smith	Meander	913-843-0462	Lawrence
409-56-7008	Bennel	Abraham	415-658-9932	Berkeley
427-17-2019	Dull	Ann	415-006-7120	Palo Alto

Publishing Server

13

Subscription Server

au lname	au fname	city
Carson	Cheryl	Berkeley
O'Leary	Michael	San Jose
Straight	Dean	Oakland
Bennel	Abraham	Berkeley
Dull	Ann	Palo Alto

Subscriptions

Subscription servers receive data from the publication server through subscriptions to publications. Two options that you have when setting up a subscription are push and pull subscriptions.

A *push* subscription is one that is created and managed by the publication server. The publication server pushes the publication to the subscription server with very little configuration occurring at the subscription server. The advantage of using push subscriptions is that all the administration takes place in a central location. Publishing and subscribing happens at the same time, and many subscribers can be set up at once.

A *pull* subscription is set up and managed at the subscription server. In this case, the subscription server connects to the publication server and pulls down the subscription and any subsequent data changes. The major advantage is that pull subscriptions allow the administrators of the subscription servers to choose which publications they want. With pull subscriptions, publishing and subscribing are separate acts and are not necessarily performed by the same user. Usually, pull subscriptions are best when the publication does not require high security.

How Replication Works

In its simplest form, the actual process of replication is rather simple. After the publication has been created, the subscriber database is synchronized with the publisher to ensure that both servers have a similar starting point. As changes are made to the publisher, they are read from the transaction log by the log reader process. This process moves the transactional information to the distribution server where it is sent to the subscribers. The transactions are then applied to the subscribing server's database.

Synchronization Process

As mentioned previously, before the actual replication process gets started, the subscription database must first be synchronized with the publisher. This includes table schema and data. SQL Server will automatically perform the synchronization process for you. It will create the schema scripts, run them on the remote server, and populate the data for you. This is known as automatic synchronization.

In some cases, though, you will not want SQL Server to automatically synchronize the data. For example, imagine attempting to automatically synchronize a publication of more than 5GB. Because all synchronization takes place over the network, this could cause an extreme bottleneck. In this case, you would want to perform a manual synchronization. Before you do this, you would need to determine how the database is to be synced.

This could be a backup or even a series of scripts that you make and then send out to the clients on tape. This will save hours of time and a great deal of network bandwidth.

Replication Agents

Along with the basic components of replication, processes known as replication agents are responsible for different actions during the replication process. Each replication scenario will contain at least two different replication agents. These include: snapshot, log reader, distribution, and merge.

Snapshot Agent

The snapshot agent is responsible for preparing the schema and initial data files of published tables and stored procedures, storing the snapshot on the distribution server, and recording information about the synchronization status in the distribution database. Each publication will have its own snapshot agent that runs on the distribution server. The snapshot agent runs within the SQL Server Agent and can be administered using SQL Server Enterprise Manager.

Log Reader Agent

The log reader agent is responsible for moving transactions marked for replication from the transaction log of the published database to the distribution database. Each database published using transactional replication has its own log reader agent that runs on the distribution server.

Distribution Agent

The distribution agent moves transactions and snapshot jobs held in the distribution database out to the subscribers. Transactional and snapshot publications set for immediate synchronization when a new push subscription is created will have their own individual distribution agent that runs on the distribution server. Those not set up for immediate synchronization share a distribution agent that runs on the distribution server. Pull subscriptions to either snapshot or transactional publications have a distribution agent that runs on the subscriber. Merge publications do not have a distribution agent at all. Rather, they rely on the merge agent, discussed next. The distribution agent usually runs within the SQL Server Agent and can be administered using SQL Server Enterprise Manager.

Merge Agent

When dealing with merge publications, the merge agent moves and reconciles incremental data changes that occurred after the initial snapshot was created. Each merge publication

13

has a merge agent that connects to the publishing server and the subscribing server and updates both as changes are made. In a full merge scenario, the agent first uploads all changes from the subscriber where the generation is 0 or the generation is greater than the last generation sent to the publisher. The agent gathers the rows in which changes were made, and those rows without conflicts are applied to the publishing database.

A *conflict* is a row in which changes were made at both the publishing server and the subscriber. The conflicts are handled by the conflict resolver that is associated with the article in the publication definition. The agent then reverses the process by downloading any changes from the publisher to the subscriber. Push subscriptions have merge agents that run on the publishing server, whereas pull subscriptions have merge agents that run on the subscriber. Snapshot and transactional publications do not use merge agents.

Factors in Replicated Data

When determining what and how you are going to replicate data, you need to determine several key factors. You have to determine how important each different factor is to you before you determine the distribution methodology that suits your needs. These factors are the latency of the data, the autonomy of each individual site, and the consistency of the data.

Data Latency

Data latency is simply the amount of time that it takes to get updated data sent to the subscribing servers. With most replication methods, it is normal to expect a certain amount of latency between the time that data is updated and the time that the subscribers get the changes. The important thing that must be taken into consideration is how critical it is for the clients to have the most up-to-date data. Two methodologies can be used depending on how latent the data can be. The method with the most data latency is SQL Server replication. Replication is sometimes called real-enough time data. In other words, the data is not always up-to-date, but it will be soon enough. The other method, known as distributed transactions, ensures that the data is always up-to-date. This method relies on two-phase commits in order to work. For two-phase commits to work, both servers have to be available whenever either one wants to make a data modification. This can be very overhead intensive for both the server and the network.

Site Autonomy

Site autonomy refers to the capability for each individual site to operate without interacting with any of the other sites. When a site can operate without talking to any of the other sites, it is highly autonomous. Replication allows for sites to remain highly autonomous because they do not have to be constantly connected to continue operation. On the other hand, distributed transactions rely on all servers always being connected. If even a single server is offline at any point, no other server can continue to work.

Transactional Consistency

Transactional consistency means that data at any participating site is the same data that would have resulted if all transactions had been performed at a single site. Although this sounds complicated, it really isn't. What this boils down to is that through the process of replication, no data should be changed in ways that it had not been changed on the publication server. The following two levels of transactional consistency are available in SQL Server:

- Immediate transactional consistency—All sites participating in replication have the same data at the same time. The only way that this can occur in SQL Server is through the use of distributed transactions.

- Latent transactional consistency—All sites are guaranteed to have the same data as the publishing site at some point. Unlike immediate transactional consistency, there can be a delay from when the actual update takes place to when the subscribing sites get the changes.

Methods of Data Distribution

After you have determined the acceptable amount of data latency, site autonomy, and transactional consistency, the next step is to select the data distribution method. As shown in Figure 13.4, each different type of distribution method has a different amount of site autonomy and data latency.

The different distribution methods have differing levels of site autonomy and data latency, as show here.

- Distributed transactions—Distributed transactions ensure that all sites have the exact same data at all times.

- Transactional replication with updating subscribers—Users can change data at the local location, and those changes are applied to the source database at the same time. The changes are then eventually replicated to other sites. This type of data distribution combines replication and distributed transactions. Because data is changed at both the local site and source database, conflicts do not occur.

- Transactional replication—With transactional replication, data is only changed at the source location and is sent out to the subscribers. Because data is only changed at a single location, conflicts cannot occur.

13

- Snapshot replication with updating subscribers—This method is much like transactional replication with updating subscribers, in which users can change data at the local location, and those changes are applied to the source database at the same time. The entire changed publication is then replicated to all subscribers. This type of replication provides a higher autonomy than transactional replication.

- Snapshot replication—An entire copy of publication is sent out to all subscribers. This includes both changed and unchanged data.

- Merge replication—All sites make changes to local data independently and then update the publisher. It is possible for conflicts to occur, but they are resolved.

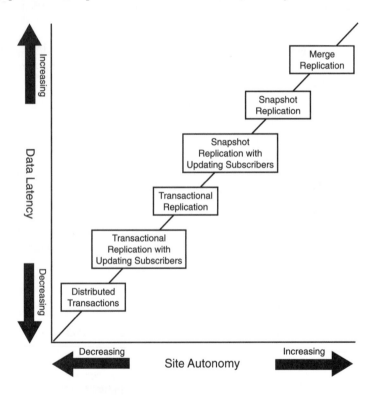

FIGURE 13.4
Each distribution method has a different amount of site autonomy and data latency.

Distribution Methodologies

The four basic methodologies for distributing data are snapshot, transactional, merge, and distributed. The method you choose depends on your business needs. Each type relies on different amounts of computer and network resources.

Snapshot Replication

As the name implies, snapshot replication makes a picture of all the articles in the publication at a moment in time, and then moves the entire picture to the subscribers. Very little overhead is involved in this method because this form of replication does not track any changes to the data. Instead, it merely copies all the data, changed or not, to the subscribers. The biggest drawback to snapshot replication is that there can be a huge amount of network bandwidth involved, especially if the articles contained in the publications are very large. This type of replication is extremely easy to set up and, for the most part, is ideal when you are working with smaller publications in which subscribers will not be performing updates to the data that they receive. For example, phone numbers and catalog information are good candidates for snapshot replication.

Snapshot replication is primarily designed as a one-way replication methodology. In other words, after the data is sent to the subscribers, it is not modified. In the event that you need to modify data at the subscriber, SQL Server 7.0 has built-in functionality to allow you to make changes without losing them. This functionality, known as immediate updating subscribers, uses two-phase commits to make the changes at the publication server as soon as the modifications are made. These changes are then replicated out to all the other subscribers.

Transactional Replication

Transactional replication captures transactions from the transaction log of the published database, and then applies them to the subscription database. Because all data modifications are already stored in the transaction log, half of the work required to make this type of replication is already done. This means that, although this sounds like it could cause a large amount of overhead on the server, it is not as much as you would think. The changes are read from the transaction log, forwarded on to the distribution server, and then sent out and applied to the subscription server in the same order that they were originally made.

With standard transactional replication, modifications to the data are made only at the publisher. The changes are propagated to the other sites in nearly real time and in the exact same order as they were made at the publisher. This keeps data conflicts from occurring. What this means is that multiple updates to the same data cannot occur at the same time, forcing SQL Server to decide which update is the one to keep.

As with Snapshot replication, there are times that you will need to enable transactional replication publications to support immediate updating subscribers. This process uses two-phase commits to send transactions to the publisher. In this setup, only the publisher needs to be available. After the change is made at the subscriber and sent to the publisher, it will eventually get sent to all other subscribers to the publication. Subscribers performing

13

updates do not have full autonomy because the publisher must be available at the time of the data modification, or no modification can be made at all.

Merge Replication

Merge replication is the most complicated of all the different replication methods. This new feature to SQL Server 7.0 tracks all the changes to the articles in the publication on all servers and then synchronizes those changes, so all copies of the database have identical data. Because any server can make changes to the data, there will always be some sort of conflict resolution. This resolution is based on criteria that is determined by the administrator. After any conflicts have been resolved, the changes are propagated back to the publishing server and then replicated out to all subscribers.

When you create a publication for merge replication, SQL Server performs three different schema changes to your database. First, SQL Server must either identify or create a unique column for every row that is going to be replicated. This column is used to identify the different rows across all the different copies of the table. If the table already contains a column with the ROWGUIDCOL property, SQL Server will automatically use that column for the row identifier. If not, SQL Server will add a column called rowguid to the table. SQL Server will also place an index on the rowguid column.

Next, SQL Server adds triggers to the table to track any changes that occur to the data in the table. The triggers track any changes and record them in the merge system tables. The triggers can track changes at either the row or the column level, depending on how you set it up. SQL Server 7.0 will support multiple triggers of the same type on a table, so merge triggers will not interfere with user-defined triggers on the table.

Last, SQL Server adds new system tables to the database that contains the replicated tables. The MSMerge_contents and MSMerge_tombstone tables track the updates, inserts, and deletes. These tables rely on the rowguid to track which rows have actually been changed.

The merge agent identifies conflicts using a special table called MSMerge_contents. In this table, a column called lineage is used to track the history of any changes that are made to a row. The replication process updates the lineage value whenever a user makes changes to the data in a row. The entry into this column is a combination of a site identifier and the last version of the row created at the site. As the replication process is merging all the changes that have occurred, it examines each site's information to see whether a conflict has occurred. If a conflict has occurred, the agent initiates conflict resolution based on the conflict resolution process determined by the administrator.

Distributed Transactions

Last but not least, there is distributed transactions. As mentioned previously, distributed transactions is not truly replication. Distributed transactions operates through a process known as a two-phase commit. A two-phase commit, also known as 2PC, ensures that a transaction is either committed on all servers or rolled back on all servers. This can be a very positive thing because this ensures that the data on all servers is always going to be up-to-date. The drawback to this sort of data distribution is that if, for any reason, any server is unavailable when it comes time for the transaction to be committed, the transaction will fail. For this type of solution to work, you must have a high-speed LAN. This type of solution is not always feasible for large environments with many servers because short-term network outages can occur.

Summary

This hour introduces the basics of replication and the different types of replication that can be used. These are just the basics of replication. Replication is a very powerful tool that can solve a great deal of business problems. In the next two hours, I will cover replication scenarios and how to set up and monitor replication.

Q&A

Q Can I replicate data between SQL Server 7.0 and previous versions of SQL Server?

A It is possible to set up certain types of replication between SQL Server 7.0 and previous versions of SQL Server. You can set up snapshot replication and transactional replication in this type of a scenario. You cannot set up merge replication. Previous versions of SQL Server do not have the technology required to maintain merge replication.

Q Can SQL Server replication solve all my data and server availability problems?

A Although SQL Server can assist you in keeping multiple copies of the data you need and moving them to the locations that you need, SQL Server replication cannot solve all your data and server availability problems. To correctly answer server availability issues, you should look into Windows NT Enterprise Server using SQL Server 7.0 Enterprise Edition. With the combination of these two powerful pieces of software, and a significant investment in hardware, you can create a server solution that is up to 99.99 percent available to your users.

13

Q Does replication cost extra to implement?

A In and of itself, SQL Server replication does not cost anything extra to implement. The functionality is built in to SQL Server. When implementing replication, though, you will normally have at least two copies of SQL Server and the operating system on top of which it is running. You will have to pay for each instance of SQL Server and the operating system, or you will be out of licensing compliance.

Workshop

The quiz and the exercise are provided for your further understanding. The answers can be found in Appendix A, "Answers."

Quiz

1. What is SQL Server replication?

2. When might you use SQL Server replication?

3. What are the four main methods for distributing data?

4. What is the purpose of the publishing server?

5. What is the purpose of the distribution server?

6. What is a publication?

7. What is contained in an article?

Exercise

Investigate your business situation and try to determine which distribution methodologies would be correct in your company. Remember to take into account any requirements that your clients have with updating replicated data.

HOUR 14

Replication Scenarios

By now, you should have a good idea of the major components of
SQL Server replication. In this hour, I will get into the different business
implementations in which you can use replication. This hour will not tell
you exactly how to solve your business problems. Instead, I will go over
different scenarios that you might run into and how they are implemented.

The highlights of this hour include

- Replication Scenarios
- Publishing Databases to the Internet
- Replication in Heterogeneous Environments
- Replication Security

Replication Scenarios

When you are getting ready to set up replication, several ways to get things
done exist. These are different replication scenarios: in other words, where

each server is going to reside and what each server's role is going to be. You can choose from several different replication scenarios, as follows:

- Central publisher
- Central publisher with a remote distributor
- Publishing subscriber
- Central subscriber
- Multiple publishers or multiple subscribers
- Publishing Subscriber

Central Publisher

The central publisher scenario, as seen in Figure 14.1, is the most common and easy to set up. This scenario provides a single server that performs the functions of both the publisher and the distributor. This server makes and manages all publications available to subscribers. This single server can service any number of subscribers. This is the default scenario for SQL Server replication.

FIGURE 14.1

The central publisher replication scenario.

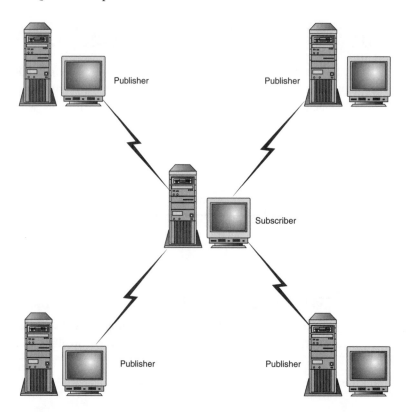

Publisher

Publisher

Subscriber

Publisher

Publisher

Several different business problems that this scenario can solve are

- Reporting—This is probably one of the most frequent business problems that you will work with. With large online transaction processing databases, such as those at large catalog order centers, performance is extremely important. When reporting queries are run against these databases, performance can be destroyed. The solution is to replicate this data off the main production server onto a reporting server. This allows your users to query the data without affecting the users who are taking orders.

- Localization of Data—Another business solution that can be solved with this type of replication scenario is localization of data. For example, most retail stores have several different locations. In order to keep these locations up-to-date with pricing changes, data can be replicated and localized. Without data replication, you can imagine the problems that you could have. One solution would be to send out all the changes and have the managers input all the new prices by hand, as if they do not have enough to do already. Another solution would be to have every transaction go back to one central server to get the most current price. Although this is a better solution than the first one, it still has several flaws. The first is the cost—you would need extremely high bandwidth connections between each site. Also, if someone cuts the wire, you can't make any more sales. This replication scenario allows you to move data out to each local store, so they will have a local copy of the important data.

- Redundancy—Another business solution that this replication scenario is used to solve is that of database availability. Although this is not the best solution for this problem, it is possible to use replication to make a duplicate of all the data in your database. If your server crashes, all your users need to do is point to the backup server and continue to work.

Central Publisher with Remote Distributor

The central publisher with a remote distributor, as seen in Figure 14.2, is very similar to the central publisher. The main change is that the distribution server functions are moved from the publishing server and to a separate server. This removes the overhead of distributing the data changes from the publication server.

Several different business problems that this scenario can solve are

- Reporting—Like the Central Publisher scenario, this scenario can be used to off load the overhead of ad hoc queries against the database to another server. This scenario also off loads the distribution process to another server. Although this whole process does not take a huge amount of overhead, on smaller and less powerful servers, this can help.

14

- Single Distribution Server—As I discussed in the last hour, it is possible for a single distribution server to handle the distribution process for several publishers. This allows you to set up a single distribution server to which all your subscribers connect in order to access all subscriptions in your enterprise.

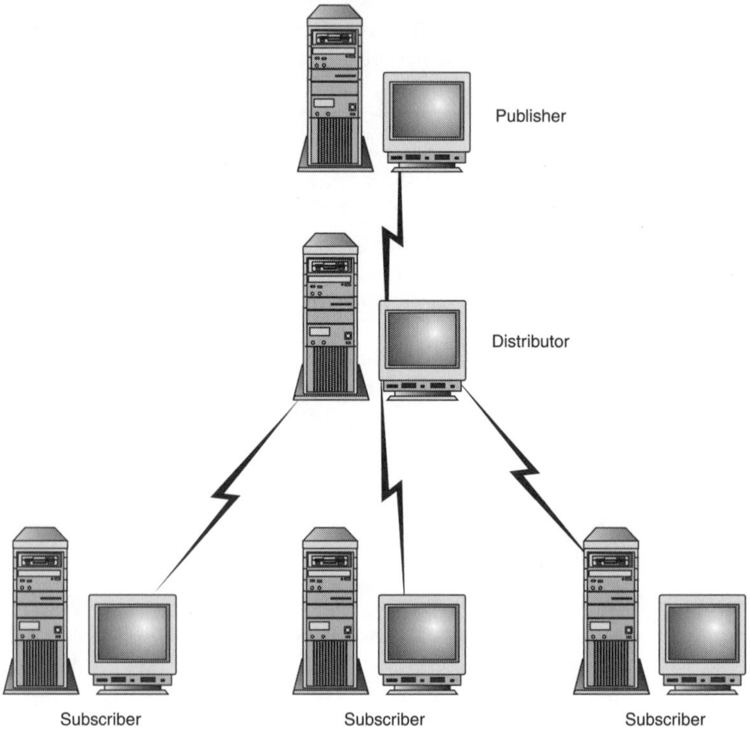

FIGURE **14.2**

The central publisher with remote distributor replication scenario.

Publisher

Distributor

Subscriber   Subscriber   Subscriber

Publishing Subscriber

The publishing subscriber replication scenario, as seen in Figure 14.3, allows a single subscriber to act as both a subscriber to the original publisher and then turn around and publish its local copy to other subscribers. Although this might sound strange, there is a very good reason that you would consider using this type of replication scenario. This scenario is best used when you have to replicate data across a slow or expensive WAN link. Instead of having all your subscribers connect to the main publishing server, a single subscriber connects to the main publishing server and, in turn, sends the replicated data out to the other servers.

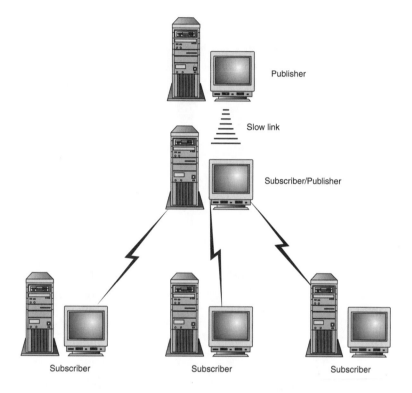

FIGURE 14.3
The publishing sub-scribers replication scenario.

Several different business problems that this scenario can solve are

- Slow WAN Link—As I discussed earlier, the best reason for using this type of replication scenario is a slow WAN link. For example, ABC Corp's main office is in San Diego and has several branch offices in Japan. Instead of replicating changes to all the branch offices in Japan, ABC Corp chooses to send all the updates to a server in Tokyo. The server in Tokyo then replicates the updates to all other subscriber servers in Japan. This allows for a reduction in network traffic and a reduction in communication costs.

- Dialup Remote Offices—This scenario is much like the previous business problem. Instead of operating over a WAN connection, this type of replication operates through dialup using a modem. The replication process operates only when the dial-up connection is active. This allows a single subscriber to pick up any changes that have occurred and then copy them out to any other subscribers.

14

Central Subscriber

The central subscriber scenario, as seen in Figure 14.4, creates a single central subscriber that receives data from several publishers. This scenario is best when you need to provide a central location that has all the data from the remote locations.

FIGURE **14.4**

*The central subscriber
replication scenario.*

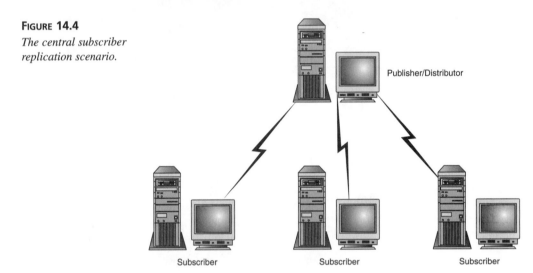

When you implement this scenario, you need to take several precautions to make sure that all the data remains synchronized and is not overwritten. These steps include

1. Create a column that contains a unique identifier of the datatype UNIQUEIDENTIFIER for the data that will be replicated from each site. You will then use this identifier to partition the rows.

2. Add the column that contains the unique identifier to the primary key.

3. Perform a manual synchronization of the table.

Several different business problems that this scenario can solve are as follows:

- Rollup Reporting—Rollup reporting is the process of bringing data from remote locations to one central server for the process of generating reports. The business problem that is solved in this scenario is similar to the ones that we looked at with retail stores. This might seem rather trivial, but imagine what could happen if all that data remained on the remote servers. You would have very few options for generating reports. One option would be to have the managers generate the reports and send them to the central office, which would be slow and possibly inaccurate. Another option would be to attempt to run the reports over the network, but this might not be an option when you have a large number of servers in very remote locations. With rollup reporting, sales data can be sent, or rolled up, to a central data server where reports can be generated.

- Inventory Reorder—Similar to the rollup reporting process, inventory reorder is another business problem that can be solved through the use of the central subscriber replication scenario. When products are sold, that data can be sent to the order department where the product is reordered and sent back to the store.

Multiple Publishers or Multiple Subscribers

In the multiple publishers or multiple subscribers scenario, as shown in Figure 14.5, a single, horizontally partitioned table is maintained on every server participating in the scenario. Each server publishes a particular set of rows that pertain to it and subscribe to the rows that all the other servers are publishing. You must be careful when implementing this scenario to ensure that all sites remain synchronized. When setting up this system, you should make sure that only local users can update local data. This check can be implemented through the use of stored procedures, restrictive views, or a check constraint.

FIGURE 14.5

The multiple publishers or multiple subscribers replication scenario.

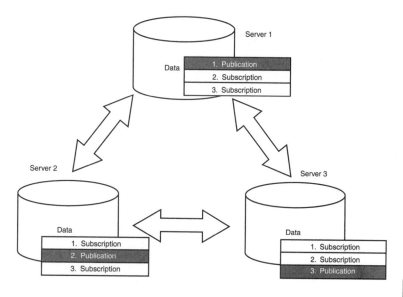

Several different business problems that this scenario can solve are

- Regional Order Processing—In many cases, when you call large volume catalog order centers, you will be routed into the least busy call center available. This means that from day-to-day, you might speak to people from different locations.

14

As a customer, this can be very frustrating if you were to call in and get one of the order centers that had no idea of what you had talked about. For example, imagine that you call and place an order and then decide the next day to change it. If this type of replication were not in use, you might or might not get someone who can access your order or change your order.

• Reservation Systems—Like the previous example, when making reservations for things like airline tickets, frequently several different places are taking reservations. In this case, it can be very frustrating for your clients if different places sell the same tickets. This type of replication allows all users at all locations to see which tickets have been sold.

Publishing Databases to the Internet

One of the newest advances in SQL Server 7.0 replication technology is the ability to publish data through the Internet. One of the first things that you have to do is configure the server to allow anonymous subscriptions.

Anonymous Subscriptions

In SQL Server 7.0, it is possible to add anonymous subscriptions. An anonymous subscription is a special type of pull subscription that is usually used when you are publishing databases to the Internet. Normally, information about all the subscribers, including performance data, is stored on the distribution server. In the event that you have a large number of subscribers, or you do not want to track detailed information about the subscribers, you might want to allow anonymous subscriptions to a publication.

Anonymous subscriptions are always created by the subscriber. The subscriber is responsible for ensuring that the subscription is synchronized. An anonymous subscription is created using the same steps used to create a pull subscription.

Configuring Internet Replication

Although I do not go completely into configuring replication to work with the Internet, I will go over the basics of the following steps to be implemented:

1. Configure the publisher or distributor to listen on TCP/IP.
2. Configure a publication to use FTP.
3. Create a subscription to use FTP.

Configuring a Publisher or Distributor to Listen on TCP/IP

Before you can set up replication to Internet subscribers, you must configure SQL Server to communicate on TCP/IP or the multiprotocol network library. You can configure this area using the SQL Server Network Utility. You must also have Internet Information Server set up on the distribution server because Internet replication relies on the FTP service to transfer the snapshots from the distribution server to the subscribers. You have to set up the FTP home directory to the snapshot folder and configure the FTP home directory as an FTP site.

Configuring a Publication to Use FTP

After you have configured the server to use FTP, the next step is to set up the publication to allow for Internet replication. You can do this using SQL Enterprise Manager. After it is configured, the distribution or merge agents will use FTP to download the snapshot files to the subscriber server. When the snapshot files are copied to the subscriber, the agent applies the files to the tables at the subscriber.

Configuring a Subscription to Use FTP

After the publication has been configured to use FTP, you must create a pull or anonymous subscription to the database. These subscriptions are created the same way that you would create any other subscription. The difference is that you need to configure the FTP options.

Replication in Heterogeneous Environments

SQL Server 7.0 allows for transactional and snapshot replication of data into and out of environments other than SQL Server. The easiest way to set up this replication is to use ODBC and create a push subscription to the subscriber. SQL Server can publish to the following database types:

- Microsoft Access
- Oracle
- Sybase
- IBM DB2/AS400
- IBM DB2/MVS

14

SQL Server can replicate data to any other type of database, providing that the ODBC driver supports the following:

- The driver must be ODBC Level-1 compliant.
- The driver must be 32-bit, thread-safe, and designed for the processor architecture on which the distribution process runs.
- The driver must support transactions.
- The driver and underlying database must support Data Definition Language (DDL).
- The underlying database cannot be read-only.

Replication Security

When setting up SQL Server replication, you should be mindful of how you are going to secure the replicated data. This security should keep people who should not have access to it from seeing it and ensure that data is not deleted or changed accidentally. Several methods can be employed in any combination that will allow you to help increase the security on your server. The following is a list of these:

- Role Requirements—If you ensure that all users are mapped to the correct user roles, you can greatly increase security on your server. The most important roles that you need to look at are the sysadmin fixed server role, the db_owner database role, the current user login, and the public role. Each of these roles has permissions that enable them to perform certain functions in setting up replication.
- Distributor Security—One of the ways that SQL Server provides internal security is by creating a secure link between the publisher and thedistributor. Publishers can be treated as trusted or untrusted. A trusted publisher will not have to log in to the distributor, whereas an untrusted publisher will have to log in to the distributor.
- Registered Subscribers—Along with distributor security, you can limit subscribers that are known to the publisher, anonymous, or subscribers that have a login in the publication access list, PAL.
- Publication Access Lists—A publication access list, or PAL, is a list of all logins that are allowed to access a publication. SQL Server automatically creates a PAL that contains the default login IDs and different logins can be added or deleted from within SQL Enterprise Manager.
- Snapshot Security—Windows NT will automatically limit access to files contained on the server's hard drives. Another way to limit access is to configure the permissions so that only certain users have access to those files.

- SQL Server Agent Login Security—Through the use of SQL Server Agent login security, SQL Server forces all agents to supply a valid login account when connecting to the SQL Server. All replication agents are required to supply a valid user login and password to the server in order to connect.
- Immediate Updating Subscriber Security—Immediate updating subscribers rely on stored procedures to apply changes back to the publication database. You can apply security to those stored procedures so that only specific users and agents can use them.

Summary

In this hour, we have covered several business problems and different solutions that can be used to solve them. We also looked at the process required to publish a publication through the Internet. Last, we looked at different ways of securing publications, so users who do not have the right to access your data do not get to it.

Q&A

Q Can every business problem that relies on distributed data be solved through replication?

A Probably not. Replication is usually known as real-enough time data. What this means is that the data is not required to be 100 percent up-to-date at all times. If you need your data to always be up-to-date, you should look into using distributed transactions.

Q What is the best form of replication security?

A The best form of replication security is to combine several of the different forms of security that were outlined in this hour.

Workshop

The quiz and the exercise are provided for your further understanding. The answers can be found in Appendix A, "Answers."

Quiz

1. What is the default replication scenario?
2. When setting up replication over a slow WAN link, what is the best replication scenario to use?

14

3. What type of replication scenario is best for roll-up reporting?

4. When setting up replication over the Internet, what protocol must you use?

5. Which replication scenario involves several servers that act as both publishers and subscribers to certain data?

6. What replication security method involves a list of login IDs and passwords that are allowed to access specific publications?

7. How are Internet publications transferred?

Exercise

Examine your current business requirements and determine which, if any, of the SQL Server Replication scenarios would work best in your business. Make sure to take into account the speed of your network links and the amount of security that can be allowed.

Hour **15**

Implementing Replication

Over the past few hours, I have discussed all the planning that goes into
setting up replication. In this hour, you will look at setting up all the components of replication. After you get replication set up, you will want to monitor
it and make sure that it is happening correctly. The last part of this hour goes
over monitoring replication.

The highlights of this hour include

- Setting Up Replication
- Monitoring Replication

Setting Up Replication

Luckily, SQL Server 7.0 replication is much easier to configure and get
running than SQL Server 6.5. This is because Microsoft has added a large
number of wizards to assist you in setting it all up. Before you get too far
into looking at the different wizards, you must first understand the order

and steps that you must go through to set up replication. These steps are outlined as follows:

1. Create or enable a distributor.
2. Create a publication and define articles within the publication.
3. Define subscribers and subscribe to a publication.

Enable Publishing

Before setting up a publisher, you must designate a distribution server to be used by the publishing server. As you have seen, you can either configure the local server as the distribution server or choose a remote server. You can create a distributor in one of two ways. First, you can configure the server as a distributor and publisher at the same time, or configure the server as a dedicated distributor. You can do this using the Configure Publishing and Subscribers Wizard. You must be a member of the sysadmin server role in order to use this wizard. Use the following steps to configure a server as a distributor.

1. Connect to the server that you are going to be setting up as a distributor within SQL Enterprise Manager. From the Tools menu, choose Replication, and then select Configure Publishing and Subscribers. This opens the Configure Publishing and Distribution Wizard, as seen in Figure 15.1.

FIGURE 15.1

The Configure Publishing and Distribution Wizard.

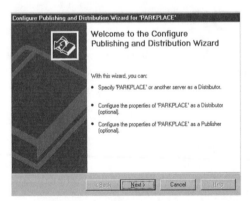

2. At the introduction screen, select the Next button.
3. From the Choose Distributor screen, as seen in Figure 15.2, you are prompted to either set up the local server as the distribution server or select a remote distributor. For these purposes, I will assume that you are configuring a new distributor on the local server. If you have already created a distributor, choose that server for use with the publisher that you are creating. After clicking the Next button, SQL Server

will verify the account context that it is currently running in. If SQL Server is running under the LocalSystem account, you will not be able to perform multisite replication. This is because the LocalSystem account does not have access to network resources.

FIGURE 15.2

The Choose Distributor screen.

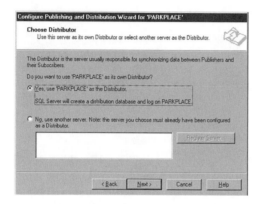

4. From the Use Default Configuration Screen, as seen in Figure 15.3, you can either choose to use the default settings or select to specify your own options. I will specify my own options in this numbered list.

FIGURE 15.3

The Use Default Configuration screen.

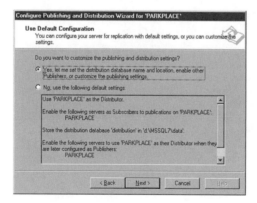

5. The next screen, the Provide Distribution Database Information screen, as seen in Figure 15.4, allows you to choose the name of the distribution database and the location of the files.

FIGURE 15.4

*The Provide
Distribution Database
Information screen.*

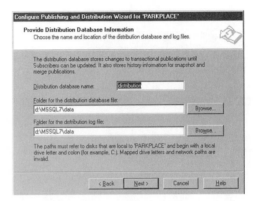

6. The Enable Publishers screen, as seen in Figure 15.5, allows you to configure which publishers are allowed to use the distributor that you are currently setting up. If you click on the button with the ellipses (…) after the publishers name, it will bring up the Server Properties screen, as seen in Figure 15.6, which allows you to choose specific options about that publisher. From this screen, you can also choose which accounts the distribution agents will use to log into the publisher.

FIGURE 15.5

*The Enable Publishers
screen.*

FIGURE 15.6

The Server Properties screen.

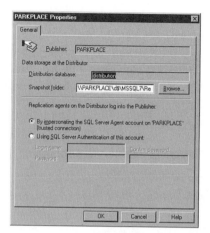

15

7. From the Enable Publication Databases, as seen in Figure 15.7, you can select any user database that is shown in the window for either transactional or merge replication. If you are setting up this server to act as a distribution server only, do not select any of these databases.

FIGURE 15.7

The Enable Publication Databases screen.

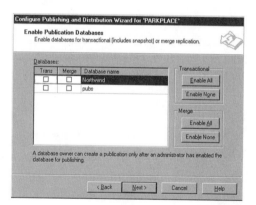

8. From the next screen, the Enable Subscribers dialog, as seen in Figure 15.8, you can select which servers are allowed to connect to this server. If you click the button with the ellipses (...) after the subscribers name, you can set up specific options about that subscriber. On the General tab, you can specify the account that will be used to connect to the subscriber. From the Schedules tab, you can select what times both the distribution and merge agent run. By default, they are both set to continuously.

FIGURE 15.8

The Enable Subscribers dialog.

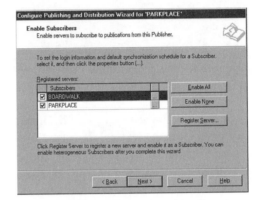

9. The last screen, as seen in Figure 15.9, is a summarization screen that provides you with a summarization of what steps the server is going to perform to set up the distributor and publisher.

FIGURE 15.9

The Final Summarization screen.

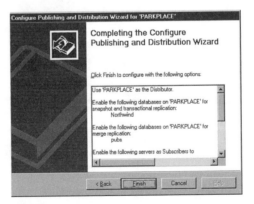

Create a Publication

Now that the distribution database has been created and publishing has been enabled on the server, the next step that you need to take is to create and configure a publication for

15

subscribers to connect to. You can use the Create and Manage Publications Wizard to do this. You must be a member of the sysadmin server role in order to use this wizard. The following steps will walk you through setting up a new publication:

1. Connect to the server that you are going to be setting up as a distributor within SQL Enterprise Manager. From the Tools menu, choose Replication and then select Create and Manage Publications. This opens the Create and Manage Publications Wizard, as seen in Figure 15.10.

FIGURE 15.10

The Create and Manage Publications Wizard.

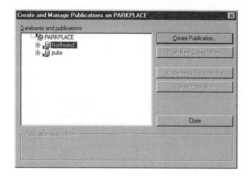

2. At the first screen, you are prompted to select on which database you are going to set up a publication. These were the databases that you selected while you were setting up replication. Choose the database and click the Create Publication button.

3. The next screen is an introduction screen that outlines what steps you will go through while setting up the publication. Click on the Next button.

4. The next screen, called the Choose Publication Type screen, as seen in Figure 15.11, allows you to choose which type of replication you will be using for this publication. The types that are presented to you are based on what you selected in the Configure Publishing and Subscribers Wizard.

FIGURE 15.11

The Choose Publication Type screen.

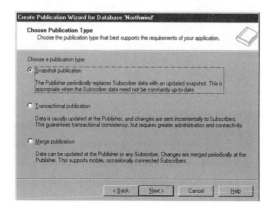

5. If you choose either snapshot or transactional replication, the next screen will be the Allow Immediate-Updating Subscribers screen, as seen in Figure 15.12, which allows you to configure whether you are going to allow immediate updating subscribers. Otherwise, you will skip to the next step.

FIGURE 15.12

The Allow Immediate-Updating Subscriptions screen.

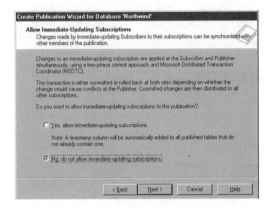

6. The next screen, the Specify Subscriber Types screen, as seen in Figure 15.13, allows you to choose what type of subscription server will be connecting to this server. If servers other than SQL Server will be connecting to this server, make sure you select that option.

FIGURE 15.13

The Specify Subscriber Types screen.

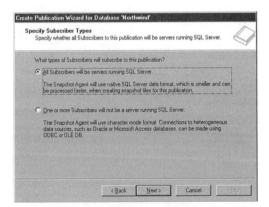

7. From the next screen, the Specify Articles screen, as seen in Figure 15.14, you are prompted to create articles in your publication. You must include at least one article in your publication. After you select an article, a button with ellipsis (...) appears after the article name. If you push this button, you are able to select options for your article. For snapshot and transactional replication, you can determine how the

snapshot portion of the replication will occur. If you have selected merge replication, you will be able to select the conflict resolver that you are going to use. You can either select the default SQL Server resolver or create your own stored procedure or COM objects. For more information on creating a custom conflict resolver, search for "Using a Custom Resolver" in SQL Server Books Online.

FIGURE 15.14

The Specify Articles screen.

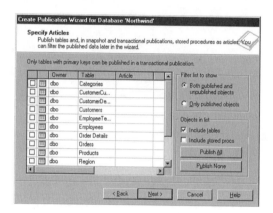

8. The next screen, the Choose Publication Name and Description screen, as seen in Figure 15.15, allows you to configure the name of your publication and provide a description of it.

FIGURE 15.15

The Choose Publication Name and Description screen.

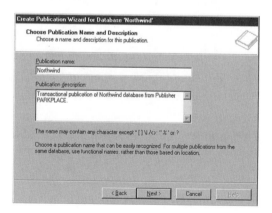

9. On the next screen, the Use Default Properties of the Publication screen, as seen in Figure 15.16, you are asked whether you want to define data filters, enable anonymous subscriptions, or customize other properties. If you select that you do not want to, the next screen will allow you to finish the publication.

FIGURE **15.16**

The Use Default Properties of the Publication screen.

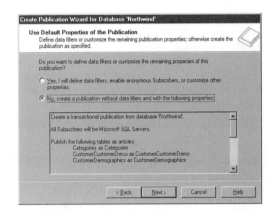

10. If you select that you do want to further customize your publication, on the next screen, the Filter Data screen, as seen in Figure 15.17, you are asked whether you want to filter data. If you select no, you will skip the next two steps.

FIGURE **15.17**

The Filter Data screen.

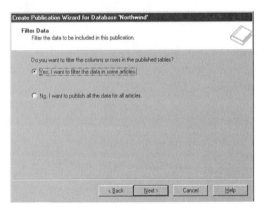

11. If you select that you want to filter the data, the next screen, the Filter Table Columns screen, as seen in Figure 15.18, presents you with a list of all the articles in your publication and the columns contained in them. You can select columns that you want to publish instead of the entire table.

FIGURE **15.18**

*The Filter Table
Columns screen.*

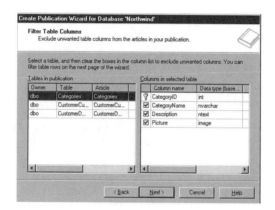

12. From the next screen, the Filter Table Rows, as seen in Figure 15.19, you are
prompted to filter individual rows for each article. If you push the button with the
ellipsis (...), you are asked for the criteria for the row filters. For example, if you
want to publish data out of a table that comes only from a single store, you would
place that criteria in the box.

FIGURE **15.19**

*The Filter Table Rows
screen.*

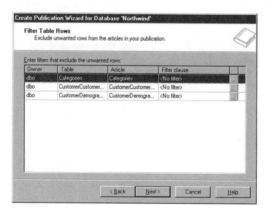

13. On the next screen, the Allow Anonymous Subscribers screen, as seen in Figure
15.20, you are asked if you want to allow anonymous subscribers. If you select that
you do want to create anonymous subscribers, SQL Server will allow any server
to connect to and receive data from your publication. SQL Server also does not
track all of the performance data that it normally does when you are not using
anonymous subscribers.

FIGURE **15.20**

*The Allow Anonymous
Subscribers screen.*

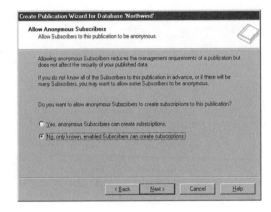

14. The next screen, the Set Snapshot Agent Schedule screen, as seen in Figure 15.21, allows you to choose the frequency that snapshots occur. Remember that creating the snapshots can be an intensive process and should be configured to happen during off hours of the day.

FIGURE **15.21**

*The Set Snapshot
Agent Schedule screen.*

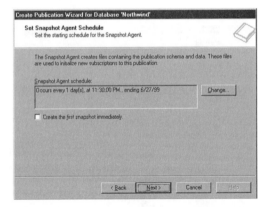

15. The last screen is a summary screen that outlines what steps and options you have selected. After you select the Finish button, SQL Server creates the publication for you.

Creating Subscriptions

Now that you have installed and configured replication and set up the publications, the next step is to create subscriptions. Remember that there are two different types of subscriptions that you can create: push and pull subscriptions. Push subscriptions are easier to create because the entire subscription process is performed and administered from one machine. Pull subscriptions allow remote sites to subscribe to any publication that they want, but you must be confident that the administrators at the other sites have properly configured the subscriptions at their sites. The following will walk you through creating a push subscription. The next section will assist you in creating a pull subscription.

1. Connect to the publishing server within SQL Enterprise Manager. From the Tools menu, choose Replication and then select Push Subscriptions to Others option. This opens the Create and Manage Publications Wizard, as seen in Figure 15.22.

FIGURE 15.22

The Create and Manage Publications Wizard.

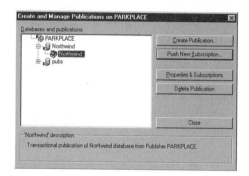

2. The Create and Manage Publication Wizard opens and allows you to select the publication that you will push out to the other sites. Select the publication and click the Push New Subscription button. This opens the Push Subscription Wizard, as seen in Figure 15.23.

FIGURE 15.23

The Push Subscription Wizard.

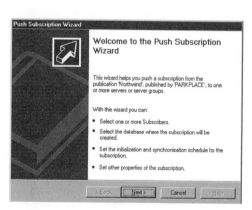

3. After the introductory screen, you are prompted to choose which servers you will publish to in the Choose Subscribers dialog, as seen in Figure 15.24.

FIGURE 15.24

*The Choose
Subscribers dialog.*

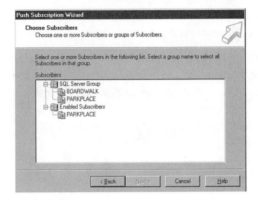

4. From the next screen, the Choose Destination Database screen, as seen in Figure 15.25, you are prompted to choose which database you will publish to. If you click the Browse Database button, you can see a list of all the databases that are on the destination server. If you want to create a new database on the destination server, click the Create New button.

FIGURE 15.25

*The Choose
Destination Database
screen.*

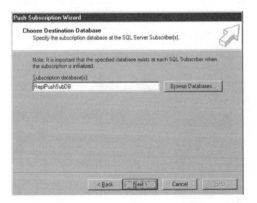

5. The Set Distribution Agent Schedule screen, as seen in Figure 15.26, allows you to configure how the distribution agent will run. If you want to provide the lowest latency, select the Run Continuously option. Otherwise, configure the distribution

agent to run at specific times during the day. By default, the distribution agent runs once an hour every day.

FIGURE 15.26

The Set Distribution Agent Schedule screen.

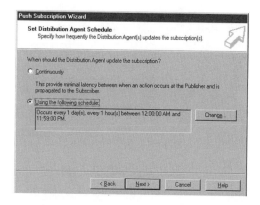

6. After you have configured when the distribution agent will run, you are prompted to configure the initialization of the database schema in the Initialize Subscription screen, as seen in Figure 15.27. This task is performed by the snapshot agent. The wizard will check the contents of the destination database and might force you to initialize if the table schema is not already there.

FIGURE 15.27

The Initialize Subscription screen.

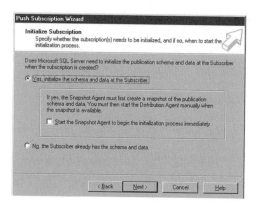

7. The Start Required Services screen, as seen in Figure 15.28, checks to see whether the required services are running on the destination server. These include the MSSQLServer Service and the SQLServerAgent service. If these are not running, they will need to be started before you go any further.

FIGURE **15.28**

*The Start Required
Services screen.*

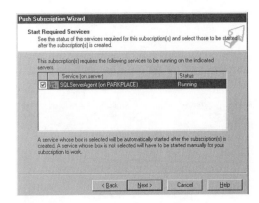

8. The last screen is a summarization screen that outlines the options you selected and the steps SQL Server will perform to create the subscription. When you click the Finish button, SQL Server will create the subscription.

The other option when creating new subscriptions is to create pull subscriptions from the subscribing servers. This allows the administrators of remote servers to subscribe only to the publications that they want to receive.

1. Connect to the publishing server within SQL Enterprise Manager. From the Tools menu, choose Replication and then select Pull Subscriptions to *'Server Name'*. This will open a window called Pull Subscription to *'Server Name'*, as seen in Figure 15.29. Click the Pull New Subscription button.

FIGURE **15.29**

*The Pull Subscription
to 'Server Name'
screen.*

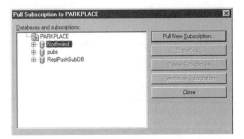

2. The Pull Subscription Wizard will open, as seen in Figure 15.30. An introductory screen will open detailing the actions that you will need to take to create a pull subscription.

FIGURE 15.30

*The Pull Subscription
Wizard.*

15

3. The next screen, the Choose Publication screen, as seen in Figure 15.31, allows
   you to select a publication from any server that you currently have registered in
   SQL Enterprise Manager on the server. If you need to connect to another server,
   select the Register Server button. After you select the server name, you will get a
   list of all the publications on that server. Select the publication that you want to
   pull and click the Next button.

FIGURE 15.31

*The Choose
Publication screen.*

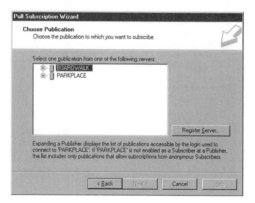

4. In the Specify Synchronization Agent Login screen, as seen in Figure 15.32, you
   will be prompted to enter the login that the synchronization agent will use to connect to the publisher and the distributor. Fill in the correct information and select
   the next button.

FIGURE 15.32
The Specify
Synchronization Agent
Login screen.

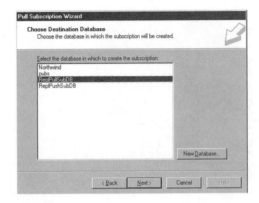

5. From the Choose Destination Database screen, as seen in Figure 15.33, you are
   prompted to choose which database you will publish to. If you click on the browse
   database button, you can see a list of all the databases that are on the destination
   server. If you want to create a new database on the destination server, click the
   Create New button.

FIGURE 15.33
The Choose
Destination Database
screen.

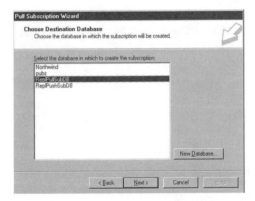

6. The Initialize Subscription screen, as seen in Figure 15.34, allows you to choose
   whether the database schema will be initialized. If you select yes, the distribution
   agent will make a copy of the schema and data of the subscriber.

FIGURE 15.34

The Initialize Subscription screen.

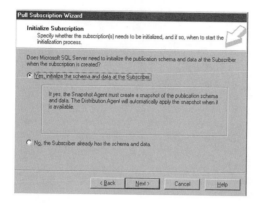

7. The next screen, the Set Distribution Agent Schedule, as seen in Figure 15.35, allows you to configure how the distribution agent will run. If you want to provide the lowest latency, select the Run Continuously option. Otherwise, you can configure the distribution agent to run at specific times during the day. A new option is available using pull subscription that allows you to synchronize the subscription on demand. By default, the distribution agent runs once an hour every day.

FIGURE 15.35

The Set Distribution Agent Schedule.

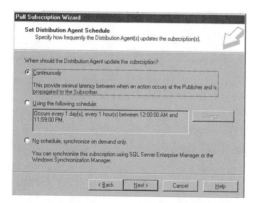

8. The Start Required Services screen, as seen in Figure 15.36, checks to see if the required services are running on the destination server. These include the MSSQLServer Service and the SQLServerAgent service. If these are not running, you will need to start them before going any further.

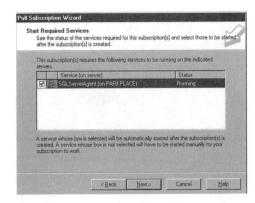

FIGURE 15.36

*The Start Required
Services screen.*

9. The last screen is a summarization screen that outlines the options you selected
   and the steps SQL Server will perform to create the subscription. After you click
   the Finish button, SQL Server will create the subscription.

Now that replication is set up, the only thing left to do is wait. If you have properly
configured replication, it will only be a matter of time before you begin to see replication
actions beginning to take place.

Monitoring Replication

After replication is up and running, it is important for you to monitor the replication and
see how things are running. Several ways to do this include using SQL Statements, SQL
Enterprise Monitor, or Windows NT Performance Monitor.

SQL Statements

The easiest way to monitor replication is to look at the actual data that is being replicated. To do this, simply run a select statement against the table in which data is being
replicated. Is the most current data available in the database? If you make a change to
the data in the published table, do the changes show up in the replicated tables? If not,
you might need to go back and investigate how replication was configured on the server.

SQL Enterprise Manager

SQL Enterprise Manager provides a great deal of information about the status of replication. This is done by selecting the Replication Monitor from within SQL Enterprise
Manager. In the replication monitor, folders can be used to find information about replication. These folders track information about publishers, agents, and any alerts that are
triggered by replications.

- Publishers—This folder contains information about publishers on the machine. By selecting any publisher on the machine, you can view information about any computers that have subscribed to the publication. This will tell you the current status and the last action taken by the subscriber.

- Agents—The agents folder contains information about the different agents that are on the machine. By choosing any agent's folder, you can see the current status of that agent. If you select an agent and double-click it, it will display the history of that agent.

- Replication Alerts—The replication alerts folder allows you to configure alerts to fire in response to events that occur during replication. These can activate when errors occur or in response to success messages.

Performance Monitor

If you are running SQL Server on a Windows NT computer, you have the ability to use Windows NT Performance Monitor to monitor the health of your replication scenario. When you install SQL Server, it adds several new objects and counters to Performance Monitor. These new objects are outlined as follows:

- SQLServer:Replication Agents—This object contains counters used to monitor the status for all replication agents, including the total number running.

- SQLServer:Replication Dist.—This object contains counters used to monitor the status for the distribution agents, including the latency and the number of transactions transferred per second.

- SQLServer:Replication Logreader—This object contains counters used to monitor the status of the logreader agent, including the latency and the number of transactions transferred per second.

- SQLServer:Replication Merge—This object contains counters used to monitor the status of the merge agents, including the number of transactions and the number of conflicts per second.

- SQLServer:Replication Snapshot—This object contains counters used to monitor the status of the snapshot agents, including the number of transactions per second.

Summary

In this hour, you looked at setting up replication. I went over installing the distribution database and setting up a server for publication. After that, you looked at setting up a publication and preparing it for subscription. Then you saw how to create push and pull subscriptions. Last, you looked at monitoring replication using a variety of tools.

Q&A

Q I have SQL Server set up on a Windows 98 computer. Can I create a transaction-based subscription?

A No. SQL Server Desktop Edition publishes full merge and snapshot replication. It can subscribe only to transactional replication.

Workshop

The quiz and the exercise are provided for your further understanding. The answers can be found in Appendix A, "Answers."

Quiz

1. When setting up replication, what is the first thing that you must have defined?

2. What role must you be a member of in order to install and configure replication?

3. When you install replication on a Windows NT computer, what ways are available to you to monitor the progress of replication?

4. When you install replication on a Windows 95/98 computer, what monitoring method is not available to you?

5. What type of subscription is created from the client computer?

6. What type of subscription is created from the server computer?

7. When configuring a subscription, what schedule should you set up for the replication agent to provide the lowest latency?

Exercise

Set up a transactional replication scenario that replicates the authors table in the pubs database to another database, either on the same server or to another. When setting this up, use the local server as the distribution server.

HOUR 16

Scheduling Tasks and Alerts

You will run many database tasks against your SQL Server that you will not want to run during normal production hours. This might be because these processes are heavily resource intensive, causing your users' operations to slow down, or the processes might affect a very large amount of data in the database, such as archival processes. Other issues that you have to get around are tasks that have to occur at a specific time every day. If there were no way to schedule the tasks to run at a specific time, you would have to rely on a human being to run the tasks, which means that the tasks might or might not run if the human being forgets. SQL Server allows you to schedule and run jobs using the SQL Server Agent, which is a separate service that controls tasks and alerts. A *job* is any task that runs against SQL Server, and an *alert* is how SQL Server will react if a certain event occurs, such as a database becomes full.

The highlights of this hour include

- The SQL Server Agent Service
- Managing Jobs

- Alerts and Operators
- SQL Mail

The SQL Server Agent Service

The SQL Server Agent is a very powerful helper application that comes with SQL Server 7.0. This application allows the administrator of a system to schedule periodic activities on the server and to notify certain users when an event, such as an error, occurs on the server. This allows the administrator to rely on the server, after the jobs and alerts have been created, to ensure that database maintenance has occurred correctly, and if it hasn't, to let the administrator know through a page or an email. Three main components that the SQL Server Agent uses are as follows:

- Jobs—A job is a series of at least one task, potentially many more, that is performed to reach a specific goal. An example of a job is a backup. Jobs can be scheduled to occur either at specific times during the day or on a recurring schedule, such as every hour. For the most part, creating and scheduling jobs will be your major interaction with the SQL Server Agent.

- Alerts—An alert is a set of actions that are taken when an event occurs on the server. Some examples of events that the SQL Server Agent can respond toare specific errors, errors of specific severity levels, databases reaching a specified amount free, or other user-defined errors occurring. SQL Server can then respond to the alert by paging one of the operators defined on the server, sending an email or running a task that will correct the problem.

- Operators—An operator is a person who is defined on the server as a target for an alert. When an alert occurs, these are the people who are emailed, paged, or notified through the network. Operators will usually be people who can address any problems that arise if the server has any problems.

Jobs, alerts, and operators are all defined in SQL Server using SQL Server Enterprise Manager and are stored in the msdb database on the SQL Server. When the SQL Server Agent first starts, it looks at the msdb database to see what jobs, alerts, and operators have been defined and which ones to enable for processing. When a specified runtime for a job occurs, SQL Server activates that job. If an error occurs anywhere in SQL Server, whether it is from a scheduled job or from SQL Server itself, the server passes that information on to the SQL Server Agent service, which will respond to the error if an alert has been defined for that error.

Managing Jobs

As I mentioned before, a job is simply a series of steps that SQL Server must perform to attain a certain goal. An example of a job that we have looked at before are backups. Under most circumstances, you will simply schedule your database backups to occur at specific times during the day. As the administrator of the system, you will not want to go back every day and ensure that the backups are run manually. Other examples of jobs that will need to be created are database maintenance tasks, batch processing, and archival processes. All these tasks are usually very resource intensive and will slow down your users if they are run during the middle of the day.

16

One of the most useful functions that you can perform when you are scheduling jobs is the ability to schedule them to run on multiple servers. This is known as *multiserver administration*. Multiserver administration allows you to manage jobs that will run on multiple servers from a single master server. The master server distributes jobs to the target servers and receives events from those servers. The master server contains the definitions for the jobs that will run on all target servers. The target servers periodically connect to the master server to receive any new jobs that have been created. After the target server has completed the job, it will connect to the master server and report the status of the job.

One example of this type of administration would be several SQL Servers that are located across a wide geographic area. You could create a single backup job with all the required steps, operators who are alerted when the job is completed, and an execution schedule. After you have set it all up and tested it, all you have to do is enlist all the remote servers as a target server. This saves you from having to define the job on all the servers.

Scheduling Jobs

The easiest way to create a job is within SQL Enterprise Manager. The other way that is available is to use system stored procedures from within SQL Query Analyzer. The following will walk you through setting up a job using SQL Enterprise Manager. This job will create a temporary table that contains all names and phone numbers of the people in the authors table, it will BCP the data out into a flat file in the c:\temp directory, and then it will drop the table.

1. Open SQL Enterprise Manager and connect to the server on which you are going to create the job.

2. Click on the plus sign (+) next to the management folder. Then click on the plus sign (+) next to the SQL Server Agent folder. Lastly, click on the Jobs folder. This displays any jobs that have been created, as seen in Figure 16.1.

FIGURE 16.1

The Jobs folder in SQL Enterprise Manager.

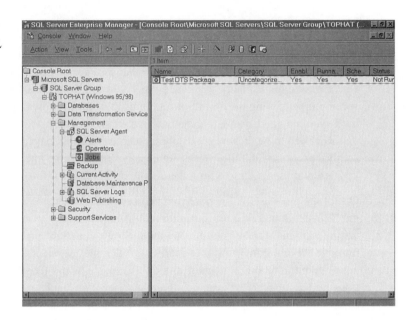

3. Right-click in the right pane and then click on the New Job option. This opens the New Job Properties dialog, as seen in Figure 16.2.

FIGURE 16.2

The New Job Properties dialog.

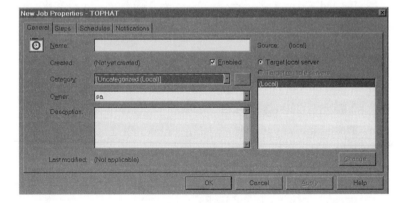

4. The first tab, the General Tab, allows you to fill out general information about the job itself. The name is the name that both you and SQL Server will use to refer to the job. The Category drop-down box is used to place similar jobs into different categories based on what they do. The owner of the job is the person who owns, and consequently will be allowed to run the job. The Description box allows you to type in a short description that explains the functionality of the job. In this case, name the job Test Job 1. In the category box, select Database Maintenance. In the description box, type Test Job for Hour 16.

5. The second tab, as seen in Figure 16.3, allows you to define steps for this job. In this tutorial, we will define three different steps. The first will create the table and populate it, the second will BCP the data out of the table, and the third will drop the table.

FIGURE 16.3

The Steps tab of the New Job Properties dialog.

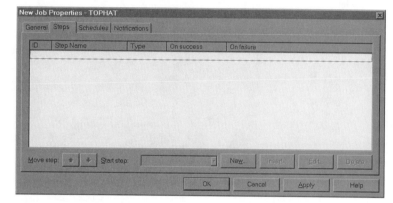

6. To define the first step, click on the New button. This opens the New Job Step dialog, as seen in Figure 16.4. In the Step Name box, type the name that you will use to refer to this step; in this case, put Populate Table in the dialog. The Type box allows you to determine which type of step this is going to be. In this case, select Transact-SQL Script (TSQL). Next, you will have to choose the database in which this will run. This script will run in the pubs database. In the command section, type the following:

```
SELECT au_lname + ', ' + au_fname AS Author_Names, phone
INTO phone_book
FROM authors
ORDER BY Author_Names
```

FIGURE 16.4

The General tab of the New Job Step dialog.

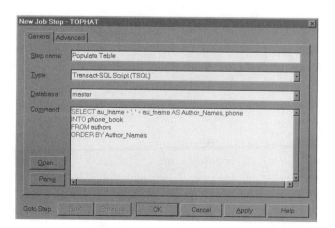

7. On the Advanced tab of the New Job Step dialog, as seen in Figure 16.5, you are able to set up how SQL Server will handle the failure of this job step, as well as the options of the SQL script command options.

FIGURE 16.5

The Advanced tab of the New Job Step dialog.

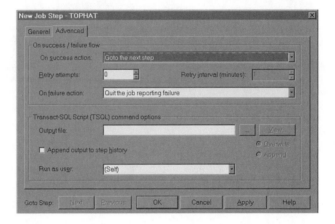

8. After you have completed the preceding steps, click on the OK button to save this step. Because there will be two more steps, click on the New button again. The options for the second step are shown in Figure 16.6.

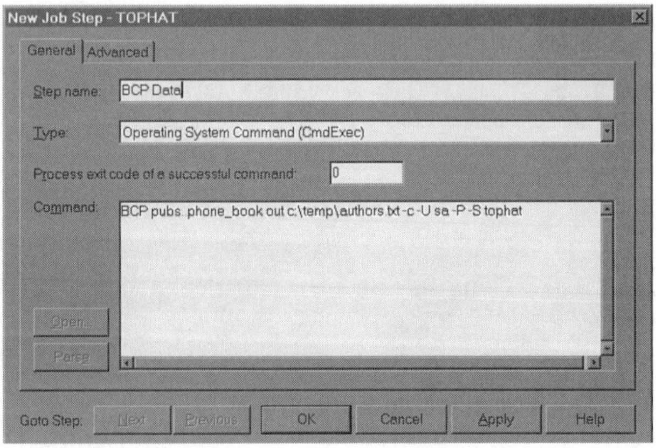

FIGURE 16.6

The General tab of the New Job Step for the second step.

9. The third step is another Transact-SQL Script (TSQL) that will drop the table from the system. The options for the third step are shown in Figure 16.7. Because the third step is the last step, change the On success action on the Advanced tab to Quit job reporting success.

FIGURE 16.7

The General tab of the New Job Step for the third step.

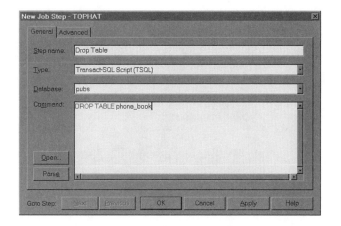

10. After you have completed filling out the steps, the New Job Properties screen should look like Figure 16.8.

FIGURE 16.8

The Steps tab of the New Job Properties dialog after all the steps have been created.

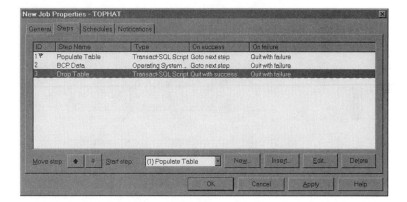

16

11. The third tab, the Schedule tab, as seen in Figure 16.9, allows you to create multiple schedules for when this task will run.

12. To create a new schedule, click on the New Schedule button. This opens the New Job Schedule dialog, as seen in Figure 16.10. In this dialog, you can determine how and when SQL Server will run this task. In the Name box, type in the name by which you will refer to this schedule. In this case, type Phone Book Schedule. Currently, this schedule is set to run at 12:00 a.m. every Sunday, which is actually what we want. Click on the OK button.

FIGURE **16.9**

*The Schedules tab of
the New Job
Properties dialog.*

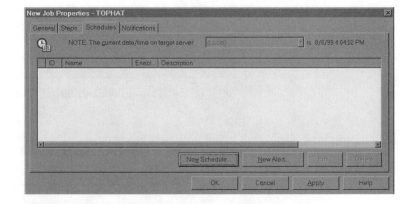

FIGURE **16.10**

*The New Job Schedule
dialog.*

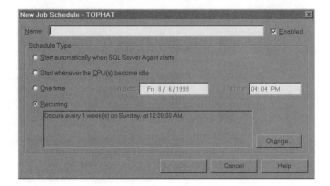

13. The last tab, the Notifications tab, as seen in Figure 16.11, allows you to determine
who and how users will be notified when the job succeeds or fails. You will find
out more about setting up alerts later in the hour.

FIGURE **16.11**

*The Notifications tab
of the Test Job
Properties dialog.*

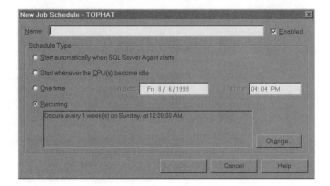

14. After you have completed all these steps, click on the OK button, and the task will be created.

15. You can test to see if this job will work by right-clicking on its name and choosing Start Job. This runs the job and allows you to see the results in the c:\temp directory on your hard drive.

Viewing Job History

After you have jobs set up and running, it is important for you to monitor and make sure that they are running correctly. This can be done by viewing the error log for that particular job. This will give you information about how the task ran, as well as the duration it took. The following will walk you through viewing the error log of a job:

1. Open SQL Enterprise Manager and connect to the server on which you are going to create the job.

2. Click on the plus sign (+) next to the management folder. Then click on the plus sign (+) next to the SQL Server Agent folder. Lastly, click on the Jobs folder. This displays any jobs that have been created.

3. Choose the name of the job that you want to get information on and right-click on it. This pops up a menu, allowing you to choose the View Job History option, as seen in Figure 16.12.

FIGURE 16.12

Choosing the View Job History option.

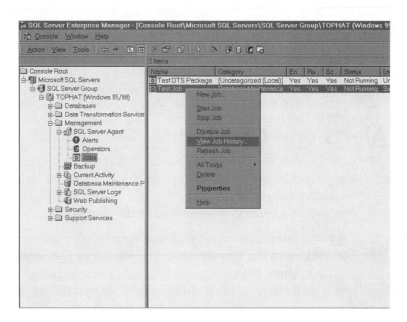

4. After you have selected the View Job History option, SQL Server will pop up the Job History dialog, as seen in Figure 16.13. From this dialog, you will be able to view all relevant information about how this job has been run.

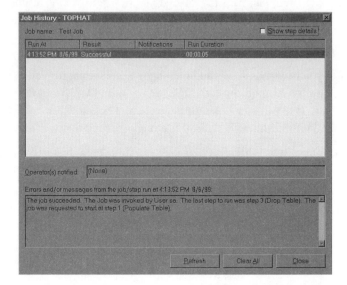

5. When you have completed viewing the job information, click on the Close button to exit.

As you can tell, you can do a large amount of things with SQL Server jobs. When you begin working with production SQL Server environments, you will find that you will have many jobs you will use to ensure that your tasks get done on the server.

Alerts and Operators

As I mentioned previously, it is possible for SQL Server to send a message to a user when something out of the ordinary occurs. This can be anything from when an error of a specific level occurs, when scheduled jobs fail to run properly, or when other SQL Server events occur. In order to do this, you must define two things.

The first is that you must determine what events you are going to send alerts on. Aside from error messages, there are other times when you might consider setting up alerts to fire. For example, in an online transaction processing scenario, you might want to send an alert when a certain customer places an order or when you are getting to a certain level of product in your warehouse. Granted, these two scenarios will also require that you write some extra SQL Server code to get this to work, but it is possible. You should also realize that when you are working with alerts, you can do more things than send someone a message when an error occurs. You can also set up tasks that can be run by the SQL Server when the alert is fired. For example, when the transaction log of a database becomes full, it is possible to define an alert that sends an email to the administrator telling him that it was full, as well as makes a backup of the transaction log.

The second decision that you will have to make is who is going to actually receive the alerts. Usually, these people are going to be able to take care of any problems that occur on the server. So, this means that you will be receiving the most alerts. The people who you send alerts to are called operators.

Creating Operators

Because you will need to have operators in place when you are going to create alerts, I will walk you through setting up operators first. You need to be aware of a couple of things when you are working with operators. First of all, an operator can be contacted three ways when an alert has been sent. The first is through email. This is done by setting up SQL Mail. This is a special part of SQL Server that allows it to communicate with a Microsoft Exchange Server and send email. The second option that you have is for SQL Server to page someone when the error occurs. Although this sounds like a great function, it is important to note that all the paging takes place through email gateways that are set up by your paging company. This means that you still need SQL Mail set up and working in order to receive pages. The last option you have is for SQL Server to send a net message to contact the user. This sends out a message to a person's computer that will be displayed on the user's screen. There are two issues with this, though. First of all, this option is only available to you if you are using a Windows NT computer. The second issue is that if your users are running Windows 95/98 as their desktop operating system, the user will have to keep an application running on his computer, called WinPopup, in order to get the messages.

The following will walk you through creating an operator in which you can send alerts.

1. Open SQL Enterprise Manager and connect to the server on which you are going to create the operator.

2. Click on the plus sign (+) next to the management folder. Then click on the plus sign (+) next to the SQL Server Agent folder. Lastly, click on the Operators folder. This displays any operators that have been created, as seen in Figure 16.14.

3. Right-click in the right pane and then click on the New Operator option. This opens the New Operator Properties dialog, as seen in Figure 16.15.

FIGURE **16.14**

*The Operators Folder
in SQL Enterprise
Manager.*

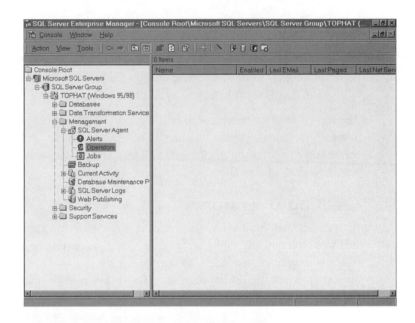

FIGURE **16.15**

*The New Operator
Properties dialog.*

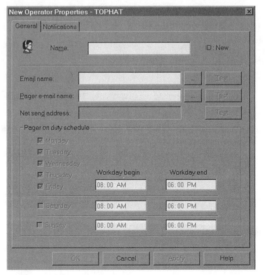

4. On the General tab, you will outline information about the user and that user's work hours. In the Name box, you will put the name of the operator. In this case, put your name in the box. As outlined previously, there are three different ways for you to alert a user that something has occurred. The first is to send an email. To configure this, put your email address in the Email name box. The second is to page the user. To do this, you must have a paging company that will send you a

page through an email gateway. To configure this, you will need to know what the email address of the pager is. The last option is to send a net message to the user's computer. To configure this, you must put the name of the computer that you are going to send the message to in the Net send address box.

5. After you have entered a pager address for this operator, you will be able to configure a work schedule. This will allow you to specify hours this operator can be paged.

6. On the Notifications tab, as seen Figure 16.16, you can configure this user to receive notifications from any already existing alerts.

16

FIGURE 16.16

The Notifications tab in the New Operator Properties dialog.

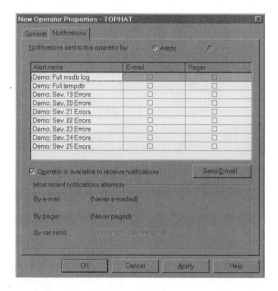

7. After you have configured all the options, click on the OK button to create the operator.

Now that you have created and configured operators, you can create new alerts that can be fired in response to server events.

Creating Alerts

Alerts are fired in response to SQL Server errors that are written to the Windows NT application log. The SQL Server Agent reads the application log and compares the events that are contained in it to alerts that you have defined. When the SQL Server Agent finds a match, the alert is fired. The following events are logged to the Windows NT application log:

- Errors that have a severity level of 19 or higher are always written to the Windows NT application log.

- Errors that are raised using the RAISERROR statement, which has been invoked using the WITH LOG option.

- Application events that are raised with the xp_logevent extended stored procedure.

The other option that you have in raising alerts is to base the alerts on SQL Server performance information. This allows you to alert when specific performance thresholds have been reached. For example, you might create an alert that informs an operator when the number of users logged into the server is more than 25, or some other threshold that you determine.

The following will walk you through setting up an alert that will inform the operator that you created earlier when an 1105 error occurs in any database on the server. An 1105 error indicates that the database files for a specific database has become full, thus keeping your users from adding any new data to the database.

1. Open SQL Enterprise Manager and connect to the server on which you are going to create the alert.

2. Click on the plus sign (+) next to the management folder. Then click on the plus sign (+) next to the SQL Server Agent folder. Lastly, click on the Alerts folder. This displays any alerts that have been created, as seen in Figure 16.17.

FIGURE 16.17

The Alerts Folder in SQL Enterprise Manager.

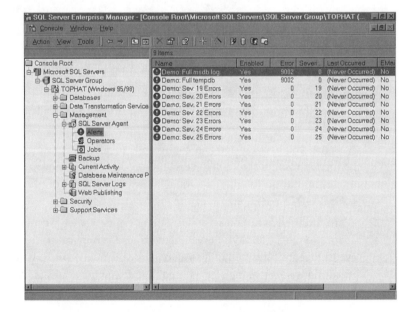

3. Right-click in the right pane and then click on the New Alert option. This opens the New Alert Properties dialog, as seen in Figure 16.18.

FIGURE 16.18

*The New Alert
Properties dialog.*

16

4. In the Name box, type in the name that you want to call this alert. In this case, call this alert Full Database .

5. To get SQL Server to alert on the 1105 errors, type 1105 in the Error Number box. If you do not know what the error number is, but you know some of the text of the error message, you can click on the button with the ellipses (…) on it. This opens a box that will allow you to search for error messages.

6. On the Response tab of the New Alerts Properties dialog, as seen in Figure 16.19, you can determine what actions will be taken when this alert occurs. This can be anything from sending an email or a page to an operator, or running a task that will correct the problem. In this case, the best option would be to page the operator. Click on the box below Pager on the same line as the operator that you are going to alert.

FIGURE **16.19**

The Response tab of the New Alert Properties dialog.

7. After you have completed filling out the options, click on the OK button to create the alert.

SQL Mail

As you can tell, it is possible for SQL Server to interact with the users through email. Before this can happen, though, you must configure SQL Server to utilize email. This process can be rather complicated to do. I have spoken with users who have fought with this process for several days before they got it to work properly. One important thing to remember is that SQL Mail will only work with Mail Application Programming Interface, or MAPI, compliant mail systems. For the most part, though, SQL Mail really only works well with Microsoft Exchange servers. SQL Server can send messages when the following conditions occur:

- When an SQL Server Alert is fired.
- When a Windows NT Performance Monitor threshold is reached or exceeded.
- After a scheduled job has completed or failed.
- From within custom stored procedures.

The process of setting up SQL Mail is rather complex with many different things for you to look at. We will cover the five basic steps in installing SQL Mail and then for more detailed steps, search for Using SQL Mail in SQL Server Books Online. The five basic steps for installing SQL Mail are as follows:

1. Create an account on your email system for SQL Server.
2. Configure SQL Server to log into the network using the account that owns the email account that you created in the first step.
3. Install the email client on the computer that is running SQL Server.
4. Configure SQL Mail with the appropriate logon account.
5. Start the SQL Mail client.

Summary

In this hour, we have gone over most of the things that deal with the SQL Server Agent. The SQL Server Agent is responsible for running scheduled tasks, firing alerts based on events that have occurred on the server, and notifying operators when events occur. Scheduled tasks are very important and useful for running tasks at different times of the day. Alerts and operators are good for notification purposes. Last, we looked at SQL Mail and the basic steps that are taken to set it up.

Q&A

Q Why is it important for me to run tasks like batch processing and archival during off production hours?

A The simple answer to this is to keep your users happy. When resource heavy processes are run on your server, this slows things down in general, including all your users.

Q Is it possible to monitor the server without setting up alerts and operators?

A It is possible to monitor the server manually by viewing error logs on a daily basis. If this does not work for you, the other option you have is to purchase a third-party application that performs the same type of functionality.

Workshop

The quiz and the exercise are provided for your further understanding. The answers can be found in Appendix A, "Answers."

Quiz

1. What is the SQL Server Agent?
2. What is a job?

3. What is an alert?

4. What two things can you configure an alert to fire from?

5. What is an operator?

6. How does SQL Server provide paging support?

7. What type of mail system is required for SQL Mail to work?

Exercise

Create an alert that fires when the transaction log in the pubs database gets full. When this occurs, run a job that backs up and truncates the transaction log in that database.

HOUR 17

Querying Data

Over the past several hours, we have discussed creating databases, creating tables, assigning permissions, and other administrative tasks. What we have not discussed yet is getting to the actual data that is stored in the databases. This is a rather important function that you will need to know how to do.

The highlights of this hour include

- Getting to the Data
- Overview of the pubs Database
- Using a Database
- The SELECT Statement
- Limit the Number of Rows
- Functions

Getting to the Data

As a part of day-to-day operations in your database, you will need to get the data out of the database. What good is storing all this data if you can't get to it? Most of the time, you and your users will be accessing the data contained in the databases using the application that was written to put the data in the database. Some times, though, you will have to access the data through other methods. The main method you will use is the SELECT statement.

Overview of the pubs Database

In most of the previous hours, we have used the OrderCenter database for most of our exercises. In this and the following few hours, we will use the pubs database. This is because we do not have any data in the OrderCenter database yet. In order for you to understand many of the SELECT statements we are going to cover in this section, you need to understand what the pubs database looks like and how the tables interact with each other. As we have mentioned before, the pubs database is a small database that is installed when SQL Server is installed. The pubs database is a model of what a publishing company's database might look like. This database tracks authors, publications, publishers, and other similar information. A diagram of what the pubs database looks like is shown in Figure 17.1.

FIGURE 17.1

The pubs database diagram.

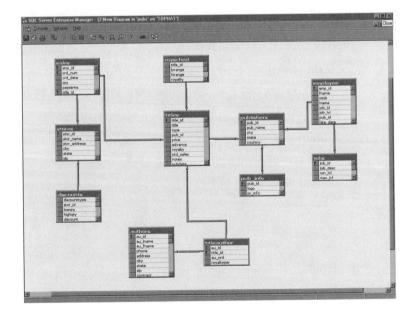

Using a Database

The concept of using a database means that you are logged into SQL Server and have told SQL Server that you are going to execute commands in a specific database. When you are working in SQL Query Analyzer, you will use a database in one of two ways. The first way is to choose the name of the database out of the drop-down list in the upper right corner, as seen in Figure 17.2.

FIGURE 17.2

The database box in SQL Query Analyzer.

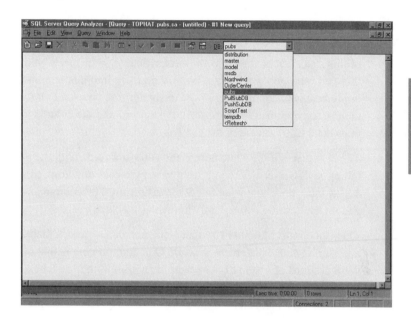

The other option you have is to use the SQL Server USE keyword in a SQL script. The following is the syntax of the command:

```
USE <database_name>
```

where <database_name> is the name of the database you want to use.

The SELECT Statement

The SELECT statement is the tool you will use to access and retrieve data out of the tables in your databases. This tool is one of the most powerful tools, and it has more options available than any other statement in SQL. The SELECT statement can be used to return all the columns and rows out of a table, or a subset of either. The most basic SELECT statement is the one that can be used to select all the rows and all the columns out of a table. For most of the examples in this hour, we are going to use the authors table. To select all the columns and all the rows out of the authors table, you would issue the command in Listing 17.1.

LISTING 17.1 Simple SELECT Statement

```
1: SELECT *
2: FROM authors
```

As you can see, four basic parts to the previous statement exist. The first part is the SELECT keyword. You are just telling SQL Server what you are going to do. The next part of this statement is known as the SELECT list. In some cases, you will list the columns that you want out of the table. We will go more into this later in the hour. What you are doing here is using the asterisk (*) to signify that you want all the columns out of the table. The combination of the SELECT keyword and the column list is sometimes referred to as the SELECT clause or SELECT list.

The next piece of this statement is the FROM keyword. With the FROM keyword, you are telling SQL Server where you want to get the columns from. Finally, you tell SQL Server what table you want to get the data from. The combination of the FROM keyword and the table name is frequently known as the FROM clause.

This is the most basic SELECT statement, and demonstrates the very minimum that you need for a SELECT statement to work. One thing to note is that placement and spacing of these portions of a SELECT statement are not important, as long as you have the order of the words right. For example, all of the following statements will produce the same results, but the placement of the words in Listing 17.1 is the preferred method.

```
SELECT * FROM authors
```

and

```
SELECT
*
FROM
authors
```

and

```
SELECT
* FROM
authors
```

and

```
SELECT
* FROM
authors
```

When you execute this statement, you will get a resultset similar to the one shown in Figure 17.3.

FIGURE 17.3

The resultset from Listing 17.1.

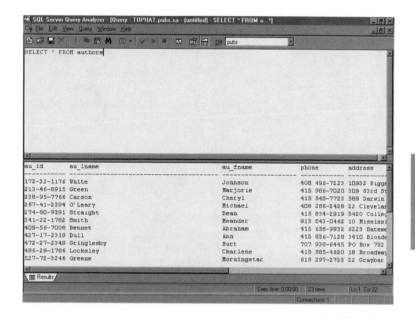

Limiting the Columns

As you can tell, this returns quite a bit of data. In very large tables, this can be more information than you want to sort through. For example, what happens if the vice president of your company tells you that he wants a list of every author's first name, last name, and phone number. You can find that data with the previous query, but it would be much easier if you could just see the information you require. To do this, you need to list the names of the columns that you want to see. If you look at the results from the previous query, the column names are listed above the returned information. In this case, you will want to query only the columns called au_fname, au_lname, and phone. Listing 17.2 outlines the query you will have to run.

LISTING 17.2   Limiting Columns

```
1: SELECT au_fname, au_lname, phone
2: FROM authors
```

As you can see, what we have done is replaced the asterisk (*) in the SELECT list with a listing of column names separated by commas. The rest of the SELECT statement is the same as we had outlined before. The resultset from this query is show in Figure 17.4.

FIGURE 17.4

The resultset from Listing 17.2.

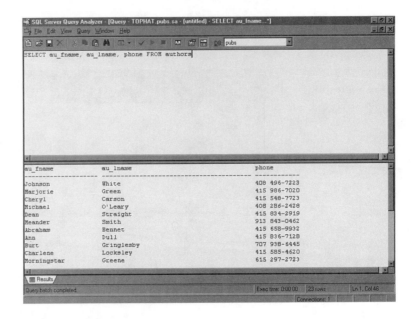

Changing Column Headings

The resultset from the query in Listing 17.2 is much more useful for users to look at without having to sort through a great deal of data to find what they are looking for. As is the case with most queries, people other than yourself will usually want to look at the data that you have queried. Remember, we are creating a phone list for the vice president of the company.

One of the limitations of this is that sometimes you will come across developers who name the columns in their tables names that are difficult to understand. For example, a very popular system called SAP uses six- to-eight letter German contractions for all its column names. Imagine someone who is not familiar with the system trying to make sense of that. One way around this is the ability to change the column name that is returned to make it more human readable. This is called *column aliasing*. Listing 17.3 shows how to do this.

LISTING 17.3   Changing Column Headings

```
1: SELECT 'First Name' = au_fname, 'Last Name' = au_lname, phone AS
2: ➥'Phone Number'
3: FROM authors
```

As you can see, there are two different ways to perform the same thing. The first is to put the alias in front of the column name separated by an equal sign, as seen with the au_fname and au_lname columns. The other option is to use the SQL AS keyword. To use this, you put the alias after the column name separated by the AS keyword. Both of these work the same way, but the AS approach to aliasing is the preferred method. The result from this query can be seen in Figure 17.5.

FIGURE 17.5

The resultset from Listing 17.3.

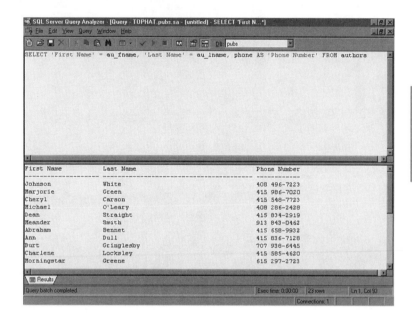

Adding Literals

Another option you have when writing SELECT statements is to add literal values into the resultset you are returning. A *literal* is simply a string value that you add to the returned results. This value does not change from row to row. An example of this would be to add the word "Phone:" in front of every phone number that is returned from the server. Listing 17.4 shows the query required to perform this.

LISTING 17.4 Adding Literals

```
1: SELECT 'First Name' = au_fname, 'Last Name' = au_lname, 'Phone:  ' +
2: ➥phone AS 'Phone Number'
3: FROM authors
```

What we have done is added the word "Phone"—called a literal expression—to the resultset, as seen in Figure 17.6, using the SQL string concatenation function: the plus sign. What you are telling SQL Server to do is add the two strings together to form one string.

FIGURE 17.6

The resultset from Listing 17.4.

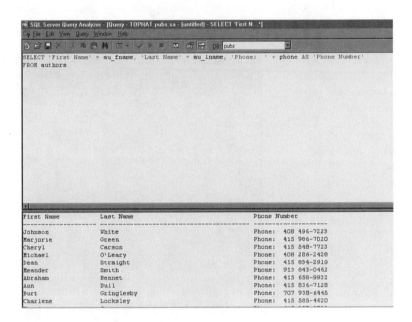

In this scenario, you are probably thinking, "So what?" Admittedly, this example is not the most useful of all scenarios. But there are a lot of other possibilities for literal expressions. So far, we have been looking at creating this phone list with the first name, followed by the last name, followed by the phone number. Most people do not actually search a phone book in this way. What most people do is search the pattern "last name, first name". In the same way we added the literal value to the resultset, we can actually add two columns together with a literal thrown in for good measure. Listing 17.5 shows the use of adding literal expressions and column information together.

LISTING 17.5 Combining Columns

```
1: SELECT au_lname + ', ' + au_fname AS 'Name', phone AS 'Phone'
2: FROM authors
```

What we have done in Listing 17.5 is to use the string concatenation function to add the columns au_lname and au_fname together to form one logical column called Name. The results from the query can be seen in Figure 17.7.

FIGURE 17.7

The resultset from Listing 17.5.

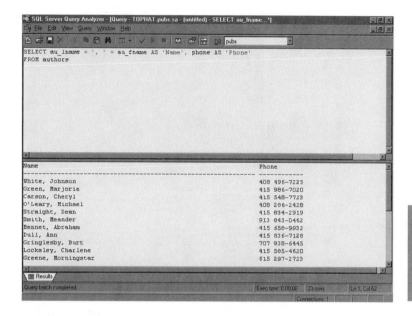

17

Changing the Order of the Rows

We now have a decent phone list. Except for one thing. The data we have returned is not in any real logical order. That is because the data in the authors table is actually sorted on a different column, called au_id. Even though we aren't SELECTing that column, the order it is sorted by is maintained. What we really want to do is reorder the names, sorting alphabetically by last name. To do this, we use a new SQL keyword called ORDER BY. To use the ORDER BY keyword, all you have to do is tell SQL Server what column, or column alias, to sort by. You can also tell SQL Server which direction you want it sorted in, either ascending or descending. In this case, we will want to sort the names ascending, or A–Z. Listing 17.6 outlines the use of the ORDER BY keyword.

LISTING 17.6 Using Order By

```
1: SELECT au_lname + ', ' + au_fname AS 'Name', phone AS 'Phone'
2: FROM authors
3: ORDER BY 'Name' ASC
```

The ORDER BY keyword, the column (or alias) to sort by, and the direction to sort in are placed after the FROM clause in the statement. This is sometimes called the ORDER BY clause. If you want to sort the same information in a descending fashion, all you would have to do is change the ASC to DESC. If you do not put either ASC or DESC in the ORDER BY clause, SQL Server will automatically sort the results in an ascending manner. The results from this statement are shown in Figure 17.8.

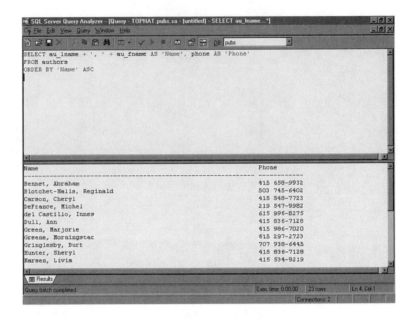

FIGURE 17.8

The resultset from Listing 17.6.

Limiting the Number of Rows

So far, we have gone over the information you need to create a SELECT statement that selects all or a subset of the columns in a table. Frequently, though, you will also want to limit the number of rows you return as well. This provides you even more control for finding specific records in the table that you are interested in. In order to do this, all we need to do is add another keyword to the SELECT statement. This is the WHERE keyword.

Comparison Operators

Normally when you are selecting a subset of rows out of a table, you are going to compare a value in a row to a known value. This is done through the use of comparison operators. A list of the comparison operators is in Table 17.1.

TABLE 17.1 SQL Server Comparison Operators

Operator	Definition
=	Equal to. This operator will return True for values that are exactly alike. For example, 1 = 1 is True.
<>	Not equal to. This operator will return True for values that are not exactly alike. For example 1 <> 3 is True.
!=	Not equal to. This operator will return True for values that are not exactly alike. This operator is the same as the <> operator. For example 1 != 3 is True.

Operator	Definition
>	Greater than. This operator will return True for values that are greater than the specified value. For example, 3 > 1 is True.
>=	Greater than or equal to. This operator will return True for values that are greater than or exactly the same as the specified value. For example, 3 >= 1 is True and 3 >= 3 is True as well.
!>	Not greater than. This operator will return True for values that are less than the specified value. For example, 1 !> 3 is True. This operator is not commonly used and is the same as the < operator.
<	Less than. This operator will return True for values that are less than the specified value. For example, 1 < 3 is True.
<=	Less than or equal to. This operator will return True for values that are less than or exactly the same as the specified value. For example, 1 <= 3 is True and 1 <= 1 is True as well.
!<	Not less than. This operator will return True for values that are greater than the specified value. For example, 3 !< 1 is True. This operator is not commonly used and is the same as using the > operator.

As you can tell, there are quite a few comparison operators that you can use. By effectively using these, you can limit the number of rows that are returned by SQL Server to the user. Let's look at a couple of these comparison operators in action. The vice president who wanted the phone list of all the authors has come back to you and decided that instead of all the authors, he just wants a list of those authors who live in the state of California. If you look back at the authors table, you will see there is a column called State. Listing 17.7 shows you how to implement the WHERE keyword in combination with the SELECT statement we used earlier to return only those authors who live in California.

LISTING 17.7   Implementing the WHERE Clause

```
1: SELECT au_lname + ', ' + au_fname AS 'Name', phone AS 'Phone'
2: FROM authors
3: WHERE state = 'CA'
4: ORDER BY 'Name' ASC
```

What we have done in this statement is to put a WHERE clause after the FROM clause of the SELECT statement. In the WHERE clause, we specify that we want only those rows where the state column in the table is exactly like CA, or the abbreviation of California. You can see that we do not have to return the column referenced in the WHERE clause to the user; it just has to be in the table. The resultset from this query is shown in Figure 17.9.

FIGURE 17.9

The resultset from Listing 17.7.

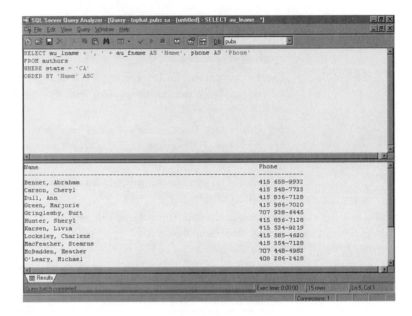

It is possible for you to specify more that one criteria in the WHERE clause through the use of Boolean operators that join the criteria together. What you are essentially telling SQL Server to do is to perform the SELECT based on multiple WHERE statements. Table 17.2 outlines the Boolean operators you can use to join together criteria in a WHERE clause.

TABLE 17.2 Boolean Operators

Operator	Description
AND	The AND Boolean operator is used to combine two criteria together and evaluates as True only if both of the specified criteria are True. For example, 1 < 6 AND 5 = 5 would be evaluated as True because both of the criteria evaluates as True.
OR	The OR Boolean operator is used to combine two criteria together and evaluates as True if either of the specified criteria is True. For example, 1 > 6 OR 5 = 5 would still evaluate as True, even though 1 > 6 is a false statement.
NOT	The NOT Boolean operator is used in conjunction with either of the other two operators listed here. What it does is negate the value of the criteria that is listed in conjunction with it. For example, 5 = 5 AND NOT 1 > 6 would be evaluated as True because 1 is not greater than 6.

These operators can be used to string together as many comparison criteria as you want. Let's say that the vice president has decided he wants all the authors who live in the state of California, have a contract status of 1, and do not live in the city of Oakland. Looking back at the authors table, you see that there are columns that track both contract status and city, so this should be relatively easy, and it is. There are a couple of ways to do it, though. The queries shown in Listing 17.8 show two different ways to perform this query. How you write it is up to you.

LISTING 17.8   Using Boolean Operators

```
 1: SELECT au_lname + ', ' + au_fname AS 'Name', phone AS 'Phone'
 2: FROM authors
 3: WHERE state = 'CA' AND
 4:       contract = 1 AND
 5:       city <> 'Oakland'
 6: ORDER BY 'Name' ASC
 7:
 8: SELECT au_lname + ', ' + au_fname AS 'Name', phone AS 'Phone'
 9: FROM authors
10: WHERE state = 'CA' AND
11:       contract <> 0 AND NOT
12:       city = 'Oakland'
13: ORDER BY 'Name' ASC
```

As you can tell, you can do quite a bit with comparison operators, especially when you know the values for which you are querying. One important thing that you should be aware of is the grouping of Boolean operators. If you remember back to your high school algebra, anything that is grouped together in parenthesis is executed first. For example, if you wanted to search for all authors who meet all of criteria outlined in Listing 17.8 or who live in Kansas, your WHERE clause would look like the following:

```
WHERE state = 'KS' OR
      (state = 'CA' AND
       contract <> 0 AND NOT
       city = 'Oakland')
```

SQL Server also provides you the ability to query data that falls between a certain range of values.

Using Ranges

Ranges provide you the ability to search for a group of unknown values that fall between two known values using the BETWEEN keyword. To perform these searches, you must know the value where you want SQL Server to start including and the top value that you want included. The minimum and maximum values are separated by the word AND. In Listing 17.7, we look at using the BETWEEN keyword to find any book names out of the titles table where the price is between $15.00 and $20.00.

LISTING 17.9   Using Ranges

```
1: SELECT title
2: FROM titles
3: WHERE price BETWEEN 15.00 AND 20.00
```

What we are telling SQL Server to do is to go out into the table and find everything where the price falls between the two prices and to return the name of those that do. We can also use the BETWEEN keyword in conjunction with the NOT keyword to return all rows that fall outside a certain range. Figure 17.10 shows the results of this query.

FIGURE 17.10

The resultset from Listing 17.9.

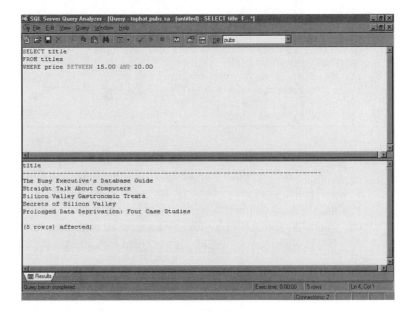

Another option that we have is to look into the tables for information that falls in a certain list.

Using Lists

SQL Server also allows you to search for values that fall within a specified list of values using the IN keyword. To perform a search like this, you need to know the values that are required. For example, back to the phone list. Let's say that the vice president now asks you to create a phone list of all authors who reside in both California and Oregon. You could do this using two comparison operators separated with the AND keyword, but using the IN keyword in this case will save you a little typing. When you start to get larger lists, it can save you a great deal of typing. Listing 17.10 shows how the IN keyword works.

LISTING 17.10 Using Lists

```
1: SELECT au_lname + ', ' + au_fname AS 'Name', phone AS 'Phone'
2: FROM authors
3: WHERE state IN ('CA', 'OR')
4: ORDER BY 'Name' ASC
```

What we have done is used the IN keyword followed by a list of the values we want to search for in parenthesis separated by commas. You can also use the NOT keyword in conjunction with the IN keyword to retrieve all rows that do not match the values in the list. The results from this query are shown in Figure 17.11.

FIGURE 17.11

The resultset from Listing 17.10.

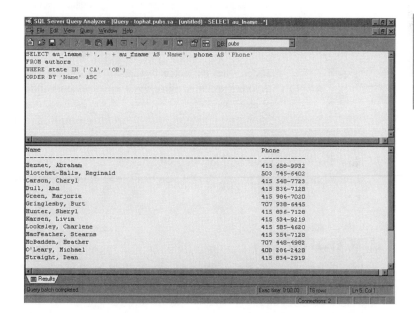

All the operations we have looked at so far for limiting the number of rows returned will work with any SQL Server datatype. One last method can be used to limit the number of rows that only works with string type data.

Using the LIKE Keyword

The LIKE keyword is used in conjunction with string data. This allows you to string columns for a certain pattern. This option allows you to use wildcard searches to find the data you are looking for. When searching with the LIKE keyword, any specific characters that you search for must match exactly, but wildcard characters can be anything. Table 17.3 lists the wildcard characters you can use in conjunction with the LIKE keyword.

TABLE 17.3 Wildcard Characters

Character	Description	Example
%	Matches any string of characters from 0 to any length.	WHERE au_lname LIKE 'M%' will retrieve rows out of the table where the author's last name starts with the character M.
_ (Underscore)	Matches any single character.	WHERE au_fname LIKE '_ean' will retrieve all rows out of the table where the author's first name begins with any letter followed by the three letters ean. For example, Dean, Sean, and Jean.
[ ]	Matches a specified range of characters or a set of characters.	WHERE phone LIKE '[0-9]19%' will retrieve all rows where the authors phone number starts with 019, 119, 219, and so on.
[^]	Matches any characters that fall outside a specified range or set of characters.	WHERE au_fname LIKE '[^ABER]%' retrieves all rows where the author's first name does not start with the characters A, B, E, or R.

Now that we have learned most of the basics of the SELECT statement, we should look at some of the different functions that you can use in conjunction with the SELECT statement.

Functions

Five different categories of functions can be used in conjunction with SQL Server SELECT statements, as well as UPDATEs and INSERTs that we will discuss later. We will discuss some of these functions in this hour.

String Functions

String functions are used to manipulate the ways that strings are returned to the user. These functions can only be used on character data. Table 17.4 outlines some of the most frequently used string functions.

TABLE 17.4 Frequently Used String Functions

Function Name	Description	Example
CHARINDEX	The CHARINDEX function is used to find the starting position of a specified character string (string1) in another string (string2). The syntax is CHARINDEX (string1, string2,start_position).	SELECT CHARINDEX ('test', 'This is a test', 1) would return 11, which is where the word test starts in the second string.
LEFT	The LEFT function is used to return the specified number of characters from the left side of a character string. The syntax is LEFT(string,number_of_ characters).	SELECT LEFT('This is a test', 4) would return the word "This" to the user.
LEN	The LEN function is used to determine the length of a character string that is passed into it. The syntax is LEN(string).	SELECT LEN('Test of LEN') would return 11, which is the total length of the string passed into it.
LOWER	The LOWER function is used to force the character string that is passed into it into all lowercase letters. The syntax of the command is LOWER(string).	SELECT LOWER ('TEST OF LOWER') would return "test of lower" to the user.
LTRIM	The LTRIM function is used to remove any blank characters from the beginning of a string that is passed into it. The syntax of the command is LTRIM(string).	SELECT LTRIM ('This is a test') would return the string "This is a test" to the user.
RIGHT	The RIGHT function is used to return the specified number of characters from the right side of the specified character string. The syntax of the command is RIGHT (string, number_of_ characters).	SELECT RIGHT ('This is a test', 4) would return the word "test" to the user.
RTRIM	The RTRIM function is used to remove any blank characters from the end of a string. The syntax of the command is RTRIM(string).	SELECT RTRIM('This is a test') would return the string 'This is a test' to the user.
UPPER	The UPPER function is used to force the character string that is passed into it into all uppercase letters. The syntax is UPPER (string).	SELECT UPPER('This is a test') would return "THIS IS A TEST" to the user.

17

Date Functions

Another class of functions that you can use are date functions. These functions are used to manipulate any datetime information that is passed into the function. Table 17.5 outlines some of the most frequently used date functions.

TABLE 17.5 Frequently Used Date Functions

Function Name	Description	Example
DATEADD	The DATEADD function is used to add an amount of time to a time that is passed in. You type in the portion of the date that you want to add. For example, if you want to add time to the year, you type the word year as the datepart. The syntax of the command is DATEADD(datepart, amount, date).	SELECT DATEADD(year, 1, GETDATE()) would add one year onto the current date.
DATEDIFF	The DATEDIFF function is used to determine the difference between two different dates using the datepart, as explained in the following. The syntax is DATEDIFF(datepart, date1, date2).	SELECT DATEDIFF(hour, '1/1/2000 12:00:00', '1/1/2000 16:00:00') would return the 4, which is the number of hours difference between the two.
DATEPART	The DATEPART function is used to return the specified portion of the date as specified by the datepart. The syntax is DATEPART(datepart, date).	SELECT DATEPART(month, '1/1/2000 00:00:00') would return 1 to the user.
DAY	The DAY function returns the number of the day of the month from a specified date. The syntax of the command is DAY(date).	SELECT DAY('5/22/1976 00:04:00') would return the number 22 to the user.
GETDATE	The GETDATE function returns the current date and time from the system. The syntax of the command is GETDATE().	SELECT GETDATE() would return the current date and time from the system.

Function Name	Description	Example
MONTH	The MONTH function returns the number of the month of the year from the specified date. The syntax of the command is MONTH(date).	SELECT MONTH('12/14/74 08:10:00') would return the number 12 to the user.
YEAR	The YEAR function returns the number of the year from the specified date. The syntax of the command is YEAR(date).	SELECT YEAR('4/12/78 10:00:00') would return the number 1978 to the user, depending on the century cutoff that is configured on the system.

Arithmetic Functions

Arithmetic functions are, of course, the same functions that you would use to add, subtract, multiply, and divide numbers. The standard arithmetic functions are outlined in Table 17.6.

TABLE 17.6 Arithmetic Functions

Function Name	Description	Example
+	The + operator is used to add numbers together.	SELECT 5 + 10 would return the number 15 to the user.
-	The - operator is used to subtract numbers from each other.	SELECT 10-5 would return the number 5 to the user.
*	The * operator is used to multiply numbers together.	SELECT 5 * 10 would return the number 50 to the user.
/	The / operator is used to divide numbers.	SELECT 10 / 5 would return the number 2 to the user.

Mathematical Functions

Mathematical functions are used to perform more complex mathematical operations such as absolute value, square, and square root. The most frequently used mathematical functions are outlined in Table 17.7.

TABLE 17.7   Mathematical Functions

Function Name	Description	Example
ABS	The ABS function returns the absolute value of a given number. The syntax of the command is ABS(number).	SELECT ABS(-10) would return the number 10 to the user.
CEILING	The CEILING function returns the largest integer value that is greater than or equal to the given numeric value. The syntax of the command is CEILING(number).	SELECT CEILING(10.50) returns the number 11 to the user.
FLOOR	The FLOOR function returns the smallest integer value that is less than or equal to the given numeric value. The syntax of the command is FLOOR(number).	SELECT FLOOR(10.50) would return the number 10 to the user.
POWER	The POWER function returns the result of a number raised to a specific value. The syntax of the command is POWER(number, power).	SELECT POWER(3, 3) returns the number 27 to the user.
ROUND	The ROUND function returns a numeric expression that has been rounded to the closest precision. The syntax of the command is ROUND(number, precision).	SELECT ROUND(10.25, 1) returns the number 10.3 to the user.
SQUARE	The SQUARE function returns the square of the number that is passed into it. The syntax of the command is SQUARE(number).	SELECT SQUARE(5) returns the number 25 to the user.
SQRT	The SQRT function returns the square root of the number that is passed into it. The syntax of the command is SQRT(number).	SELECT SQRT(25) returns the number 5 to the user.

System Functions

The last category of frequently used functions is system functions. These functions are used to get system information about objects and settings in the SQL Server. Some of the most frequently used system functions are outlined in Table 17.8.

TABLE 17.8   System Functions

Function Name	Description	Example
CONVERT	The CONVERT function is used to change an expression of one datatype into another datatype. The syntax of the command is CONVERT (datatype, expression).	SELECT CONVERT(VARCHAR(5), 12345) would return the string "12345" to the user.
CURRENT_USER	The CURRET_USER function returns the name of the current user. The syntax of the command is CURRENT_USER().	SELECT CURRENT_USER would return the name of the user that you logged in as.
DATALENGTH	The DATALENGTH function returns the number of bytes that is used to represent the expression that is passed in. The syntax of the command is DATALENGTH (expression).	SELECT DATALENGTH('Test') would return the number 4 to the user.
HOST_NAME	The HOST_NAME function returns the name of the computer that the current user is logged in from. The syntax of the command is HOST_NAME().	SELECT HOST_NAME() would return the name of the computer that you are logged in from.
SYSTEM_USER	The SYSTEM_USER function returns the name of the user that is currently logged in. The syntax of the command is SYSTEM_USER().	SELECT SYSTEM_USER would return the name of the user that you are currently logged in as.
USER_NAME	The USER_NAME function is used to return the username of the person from a given user ID number.	SELECT USER_NAME(1) would return "dbo" in any database.

17

Summary

In this section we have covered the basics of the SELECT statement. Quite a bit more can be done with it, and we will cover more of it in the next hour. After we covered the SELECT statement, we looked as some of the most frequently used functions that can be used with the SELECT statement.

Q&A

Q Is there a limit to the number of rows that you can return using a SELECT statement?

A The only limit is the amount of times that you want to wait and the number of rows in the table. If the table that you are working with contains 1 million rows, a SELECT out of that table could return all 1 million rows.

Q Are SELECT statements very resource intensive?

A In and of themselves, SELECT statements are not very resource intensive. When you start working with highly utilized systems with a large number of users, SELECT statements can take a toll on the system, especially when you are returning huge amounts of data. You should be very careful to limit the number of rows that you return in these situations.

Workshop

The quiz and the exercise are provided for your further understanding. The answers can be found in Appendix A, "Answers."

Quiz

1. What is the statement that you can use to retrieve data out of a table?
2. What is the portion of a SELECT statement that tells SQL Server where you want to retrieve data from?
3. How can you limit the number of rows that you can return from the SQL Server?
4. How can you change the order of the rows that are returned from a SELECT statement?
5. What datatype is used with the LIKE keyword?
6. What function would you use to remove extra spaces from the end of a string?
7. What function can you use to change an expression from one datatype to another?

Exercise

Write a SELECT statement that pulls the last name, first name, and hire date of all employees that started before January 1, 1990. Make sure that you use the CONVERT function to change the string date to datetime.

17

HOUR **18**

Advanced SELECT Statements

Last hour I introduced the SELECT statement, and I barely scratched the surface of what you can do with it. You can do much more with the SELECT statement, including retrieving data from multiple tables, using functions to aggregate data, and using subqueries to build query criteria.

The highlights of this hour include

- Eliminating Duplicate Rows
- Aggregate Functions
- Correlating Data
- Subqueries
- SELECT INTO
- UNION

Quick Review

Before you jump into this too far, you should go back and quickly review the SELECT statement. Three basic portions of the SELECT statement exist. The SELECT clause contains the SELECT keyword and the name of the columns that you want to retrieve. The FROM clause contains the name of the table from which you want to retrieve data. The WHERE clause is used to narrow down the number of rows that are returned to the user. I will use these terms quite a bit in this hour, so they are important to remember.

Eliminating Duplicate Rows

Frequently, you will want to return only the unique rows out of a table. For example, this time the vice president asks you to compile a list of the categories of books that your company produces. Through all the statements that I have discussed before, you should be able to figure out the first part of this. You will want to write a SELECT statement that pulls the type column out of the titles table. That much is easy. When you run that query, you will return 18 rows, of which there are only 6 truly different categories of books. To narrow this down, you could run the query, load the data into Microsoft Excel, and figure out which ones are unique.

Because I am covering this here, there must be an easier way to do this. The easiest way to do this is to use the DISTINCT keyword in the SELECT clause, which tells SQL Server that you only want distinct rows. Listing 18.1 shows the usage of the DISTINCT keyword.

LISTING 18.1   DISTINCT Usage

```
1: SELECT DISTINCT(type)
2: FROM titles
```

What I have done here is to place the column that I am looking for—only the distinct, or unique, rows from the column type—in the table titles. The results from this query are shown in Figure 18.1.

Figure 18.1

*The results from the
query in Listing 18.1.*

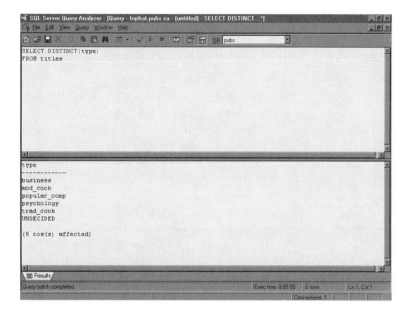

Aggregate Functions

Aggregate functions are used to perform calculations on a set of values and return a
value. For the most part, all of these functions ignore all NULL values that are passed
into them. The exception to this rule is the COUNT() function. Aggregate functions are
sometimes used with the GROUP BY clause, which I will discuss later in the GROUP BY
and HAVING section. Several rules correspond with the use of aggregate functions, and
they are as follows:

- Aggregate functions are allowed in the select list of a SELECT statement.
- Aggregate functions are allowed in the select list of a COMPUTE or COMPUTE BY
  clause.
- Aggregate functions are allowed in a HAVING clause, which I will discuss later
  in this hour.

A list of the most frequently used aggregate functions is shown in Table 18.1.

TABLE 18.1   Frequently Used Aggregate Functions

Function	Description Name
AVG	The AVG function is used to return the average of all values in a group of values. All NULL values in the group are ignored. There are two options for use with this function: ALL and DISTINCT. When you use ALL, SQL Server will aggregate all of the data into an average. ALL is the default. If you use the DISTINCT keyword, SQL Server will only average the distinct values, no matter how many times the value shows up in the table. The syntax of this command is AVG(ALL¦DISTINCT expression).
COUNT	The COUNT function is used to return the number of values in a group of values. This function is normally used to count the number of rows in a table. NULL values in groups are counted. Like AVG, two options are available to you: ALL and DISTINCT. If you use ALL, SQL Server counts all values. If you specify DISTINCT, SQL Server counts only the distinct values. The syntax of the command is COUNT(ALL¦DISTINCT expression¦*). The expression will normally be a column. If you specify *, SQL Server will count all rows in a table. The * parameter cannot be used with the ALL keyword.
MAX	The MAX function is used to find the highest value out of a list of values, which is a column. The syntax of the command is MAX(expression), where expression is the name of the column in which you want to find the maximum value.
MIN	The MIN function is used to return the lowest value out of a list of values, which is a column. The syntax of the command is MIN(expression), where expression is the name of the column in which you want to find the minimum value.
SUM	The SUM function is used to return the SUM of all values in a list of values. The SUM function can only be used with numeric values and all NULL values are ignored. There are two options that you can pass into the function: ALL and DISTINCT. If you specify the ALL option, SQL Server will apply the aggregate to all values in the table. ALL is the default value. If you specify DISTINCT, SQL Server will take only those values that are unique into consideration. The syntax of the command is SUM(ALL¦DISTINCT expression), where expression is the name of the column that you want.

Take a look at using these aggregate functions in simple SELECT statements. In Listing 18.2, I will use the AVG function to get the average cost of all books in the titles table. The results follow the query in the same listing. Note that SQL Server will warn you that it has eliminated at least one NULL value from the result.

LISTING 18.2 AVG Function in Use

```
1: SELECT AVG(price)
2: FROM titles
3:
4: --    Results Start Here --
5:
6: --  --  --  --  --  --  --  --  --  --  -
7: 14.7662
8:
9: (1 row(s) affected)
10:
11: Warning: Null value eliminated from aggregate.
```

In Listing 18.3, I will use the COUNT function to count the number of titles in the titles table. The results follow the query in the same listing.

LISTING 18.3 The COUNT Function in Use

```
1: SELECT COUNT(*)
2: FROM titles
3:
4: --    Results Start Here --
5:
6: --  --  --  --  --  -
7: 18
8:
9: (1 row(s) affected)
```

18

Listing 18.4 demonstrates the use of the MAX function to determine the cost of the most expensive book in the titles table. The results follow the query in the same listing. Note that SQL Server will warn you that it has eliminated at least one NULL value from the result.

LISTING 18.4 The MAX Function

```
1: SELECT MAX(price)
2: FROM titles
3:
4: --    Results Start Here --
5:
6: --  --  --  --  --  --  --  --  --  --  -
7: 22.9500
8:
9: (1 row(s) affected)
10:
11: Warning: Null value eliminated from aggregate.
```

In Listing 18.5, I investigate the use of the MIN function to determine the cost of the least expensive book in the titles table. The results follow the query in the same listing. Note that SQL Server will warn you that it has eliminated at least one NULL value from the result.

LISTING 18.5 The MIN Function

```
 1: SELECT MIN(price)
 2: FROM titles
 3:
 4: --   Results Start Here --
 5:
 6: --  --  --  --  --  --  --  --  --  --  -
 7: 2.9900
 8:
 9: (1 row(s) affected)
10:
11: Warning: Null value eliminated from aggregate.
```

Finally, Listing 18.6 demonstrates the use of the SUM function to determine the total cost of all the books in the titles table. The results follow the query in the same listing. Note that SQL Server will warn you that it has eliminated at least one NULL value from the result.

LISTING 18.6 The SUM Function

```
 1: SELECT SUM(price)
 2: FROM titles
 3:
 4: --   Results Start Here --
 5:
 6: --  --  --  --  --  --  --  --  --  --  -
 7: 236.2600
 8:
 9: (1 row(s) affected)
10:
11: Warning: Null value eliminated from aggregate.
```

Now that you have looked at the usage of the aggregate functions, you will look at generating more meaningful data using the GROUP BY and HAVING clauses.

GROUP BY and HAVING

The GROUP BY and HAVING clauses are used to further extend the functionality of the aggregate functions. GROUP BY is used to specify groups in which you want output rows to be placed, and when you use any aggregates, it will calculate summary data for the group. You have to pay attention to a couple of rules when you are using GROUP BY. First of all, any item in the select list must return only one value to be valid in the GROUP BY clause. You will look at this in just a minute. The GROUP BY clause must also have one of the following:

- The GROUP BY clause must contain one or more aggregate free expressions that are contained in the select list.

- The GROUP BY clause can optionally use the ALL keyword to specify that SQL Server should create all groups, even if they do not have any rows that meet the search condition.

These rules sound difficult, but in reality they are not. Normally, the second rule, dealing with the ALL keyword, is not used. You will normally perform your groupings off of specific columns in the SELECT statement. Any of the nonaggregate columns that are listed in the SELECT statement must be listed in the GROUP BY clause.

For example, imagine that you are the director of purchasing for a book store, and you want to know the average price of all the categories of books that you buy. You can accomplish this by executing the query that is shown in Listing 18.7.

LISTING 18.7   GROUP BY Clause

```
1: SELECT type AS 'Book Category', AVG(price) AS 'Average Price'
2: FROM titles
3: GROUP BY type
```

This query will return the exact information you want. The results from this query can be seen in Figure 18.2.

Now, as is the case with most book stores, you will probably buy books that come from more than one publisher. You decide you want to also add the publisher ID to this query, so you can find the average price of the different categories and publishers of books. You could do this by just adding the pub_id field to the select list, but this will generate the following error:

```
Server: Msg 8120, Level 16, State 1, Line 1
Column 'titles.pub_id' is invalid in the select list because it is
not contained in either an aggregate function or the GROUP BY clause.
```

FIGURE 18.2

The results from the query in Listing 18.7.

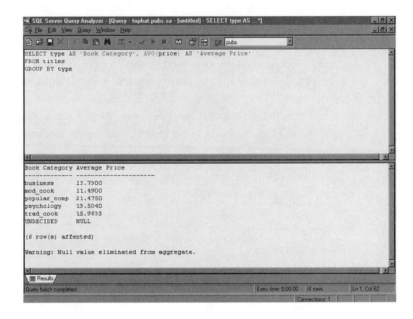

This is because of the rule that says any item in the select list must only return one value to the GROUP BY clause. SQL Server does not know whether this is the case; in this case it isn't, so it will generate an error. The way to fix this is to add the new column into the GROUP BY clause as well, as shown in Listing 18.8.

LISTING 18.8 GROUP BY Multiple Columns

```
1: SELECT type AS 'Book Category', pub_id AS 'Publisher ID', AVG(price)
2: ➥AS 'Average Price'
3: FROM titles
4: GROUP BY type, pub_id
```

What you are telling SQL Server is that you want to get the average price of the categories of books by the publisher. The results of this query can be seen in Figure 18.3.

FIGURE 18.3

The results from the query in Listing 18.8.

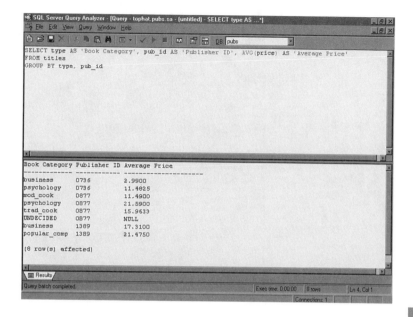

The GROUP BY clause is frequently used in conjunction with the HAVING clause. The HAVING clause specifies a search condition for a group or an aggregate. The HAVING clause can only be used with the SELECT statement, and—if a GROUP BY clause is not used—it behaves exactly like the WHERE clause. When you do have a GROUP BY clause, though, this will help you limit the number of rows that have been returned from the aggregate function. Listing 18.9 shows the use of the HAVING clause.

LISTING 18.9   GROUP BY with HAVING Clause

```
1: SELECT type AS 'Book Category', pub_id AS 'Publisher ID', AVG(price)
2: ➥AS 'Average Price'
3: FROM titles
4: GROUP BY type, pub_id
5: HAVING AVG(price) > 12.00
```

This query will only return the rows where the average price is greater than $12.00. The results of this query are shown in Figure 18.4.

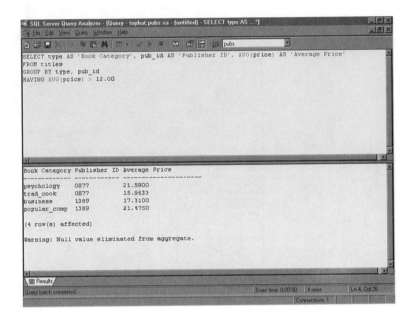

FIGURE 18.4

The results from the query in Listing 18.9.

So far, in all the statements and queries that you have looked at, I have only covered retrieving data from one table at a time. With properly normalized tables, this can be next to impossible.

Correlating Data

SQL Server can correlate and return data from multiple tables to the user through the use of a join, as long as some logical connection exists between the tables that are participating in the join. Joins can be specified either in the FROM clause of a SELECT statement or in the WHERE clause. It is good practice to try to keep your joins in the FROM clause because that is what the SQL standard specifies. Three primary join types that you can use are as follows:

- INNER JOIN—The INNER JOIN is the most common join operation that you will use. It will use a comparison operator like equal (=) or not equal (<>). An INNER JOIN operation will match rows from two tables based on common values in both tables. An example of this would be to retrieve all rows from the database in which the author ID is contained in both the authors table and the titles table.

- OUTER JOIN—The OUTER JOIN is a less common form of comparison that you will use. This type of JOIN comes in three different flavors: the RIGHT JOIN, LEFT JOIN, and FULL JOIN.

  The LEFT JOIN will retrieve all rows from the table on the left side of the join, not just the ones that match. If a row in the left table does not have a matching row in the right table, its results are returned with NULL values contained in the columns that would have been returned from the right column. This join could be used to return a list of all books in a library. If the book is checked out, the name of the person who has checked it out would be in the right column: Otherwise, the field is NULL.

  The RIGHT JOIN will retrieve all the rows from the table on the right side and only those on the left side that match. If the row on the right side does not have a match on the left side, a NULL value is returned in its place.

  The INNER JOIN will retrieve all the rows from both tables, no matter whether there is a match on either side.

- CROSS JOIN—A CROSS JOIN is a special type of join that returns all the rows from the left table, matched up with all the rows from the right table. If there are 10 rows in the right table and 10 rows in the left table, SQL Server will return 100 rows. The results of a CROSS JOIN are also known as a Cartesian product.

18

Now that you have looked at what a join is, it is time to look at some of them in action. In the first join, shown in Listing 18.10, you will use an INNER JOIN to find out which authors work for publishers in the same state they live in and which publishing company that is.

LISTING 18.10   INNER JOIN Clause

```
1: SELECT authors.au_lname + ', ' + authors.au_fname AS 'Name',
2:         publishers.pub_name, publishers.state
3: FROM      authors INNER JOIN publishers
4:           ON authors.state = publishers.state
5: ORDER BY 'Name'
```

The results of this query will show you that there are 15 authors who work in the same state as their publishing company, and they all work for the same company, Algodata Infosystems. The results of this query are shown in Figure 18.5.

FIGURE **18.5**

The results from the query shown in Listing 18.10.

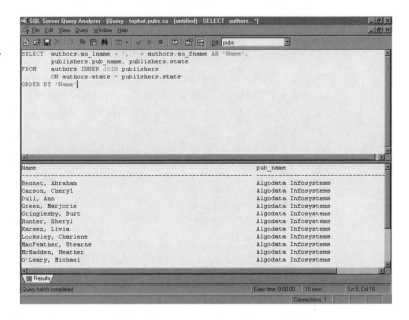

In the second JOIN, as shown in Listing 18.11, you will change the INNER JOIN that was used previously into a LEFT JOIN. This will return all the authors and only those publishing companies where the author and the publishing company are in the same state.

LISTING **18.11**   LEFT JOIN Clause

```
1: SELECT authors.au_lname + ', ' + authors.au_fname AS 'Name',
2:         publishers.pub_name, publishers.state
3: FROM      authors LEFT JOIN publishers
4:           ON authors.state = publishers.state
5: ORDER BY 'Name'
```

In this case, you have returned 23 rows. The 15 rows that are not NULL values in the publishing company side still exist. The results of this query are shown in Figure 18.6.

FIGURE 18.6

The results from the query shown in Listing 18.11.

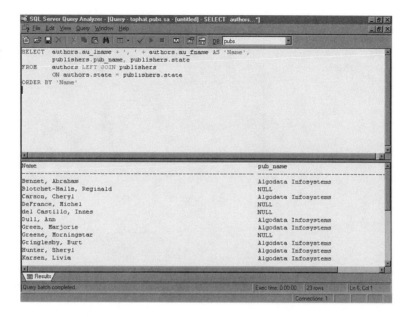

The third join that you will look at, as shown in Listing 18.12, is a RIGHT JOIN. This will return all the publishing company names and only those author names that reside in the same state as their publishing company.

LISTING 18.12 RIGHT JOIN Clause

```
1: SELECT authors.au_lname + ', ' + authors.au_fname AS 'Name',
2:         publishers.pub_name, publishers.state
3: FROM     authors RIGHT JOIN publishers
4:          ON authors.state = publishers.state
5: ORDER BY 'Name'
```

This time, you have returned 22 rows. All the publishers' names are on the right side and only those authors who work for a publishing company that resides in the same state they do are on the left. Note that these are the same authors who were returned from the query in Listing 18.10. The results from this query are shown in Figure 18.7.

FIGURE 18.7

The results from the query shown in Listing 18.12.

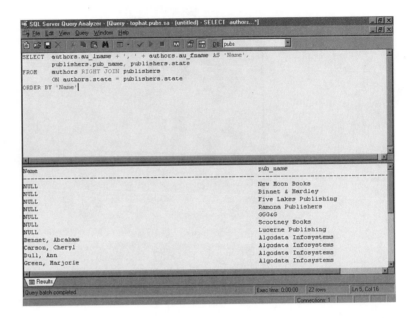

In the last join that you are going to look at, as shown in Listing 18.13, you will change the query that you have been using over to a CROSS JOIN. This will return all the rows from the authors table matched with all the rows from the publishers table. Note that you have taken out the columns you are joining on because they are not needed for this type of join.

LISTING 18.12 CROSS JOIN Clause

```
1: SELECT authors.au_lname + ', ' + authors.au_fname AS 'Name',
2:          publishers.pub_name, publishers.state
3: FROM       authors CROSS JOIN publishers
4: ORDER BY 'Name'
```

This query will return 184 rows, as seen in Figure 18.8, which is the total product of both these tables put together. You would have to perform this type of query in very few situations; although in those few situations that do require it, you will be happy that it exists.

FIGURE **18.8**

*The results from the
query shown in
Listing 18.13.*

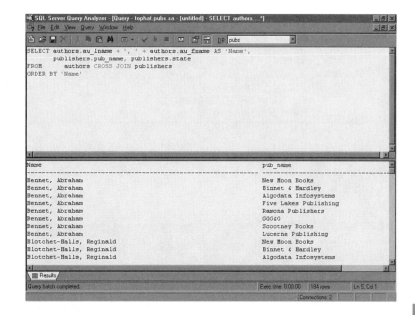

FIGURE **18.8**

*The results from the
query shown in
Listing 18.13.*

You are reaching the home stretch on the SELECT statement, and only a couple of last
things need to be discussed.

Subqueries

Subqueries are the process of returning rows out of one table based on rows that you
select from another table. Many times, the same resultset that is returned from the use
of subqueries can be returned using some type of join. Several rules must be followed
when using subqueries, but only one of them is important to you today: The results from
a subquery can only include one column name.

As I mentioned previously, most SELECT statements that involve subqueries can be written as some type of join. Usually, this will give you more functionality than a subquery.
Take for example, the problem you had before of trying to determine which authors work
for a publisher that resides in the same state that they do. The query shown in Listing
18.14 retrieves the same authors' names, but it does not tell you what publishing company they work for. I have also used the IN keyword in this scenario because the subquery is going to return a list of states that contain publishing companies.

LISTING 18.14   Sub Query

```
1: SELECT authors.au_lname + ', ' + authors.au_fname AS 'Name',
2:         authors.state
3: FROM    authors
4: WHERE   authors.state IN
5:         (SELECT DISTINCT(state)
6:          FROM publishers)
```

The results of this query can be seen in Figure 18.9. As you can see, you do get to see the authors and the states they live in, but you cannot see for which publishing company they work.

FIGURE 18.9

The results from the query shown in Listing 18.13.

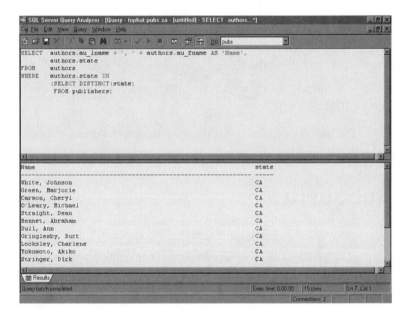

SELECT INTO

The SELECT INTO statement is a very special type of SELECT statement. This statement is used to take the resultset generated by a regular SELECT statement and place it in a new table that is created by the statement. This statement will create a brand new table in the database with the exact same column types and headings that you specify. SELECT INTO is a good way to create an exact copy of a table, except for the indexes and triggers, without having to reproduce the script for the table. All you need to do is perform a SELECT INTO with a False WHERE clause. We will look at this in a minute. The table that you name for the purposes of the SELECT INTO must not already exist in the database, or an error will be generated. Like everything else, several rules must be followed when using this statement. They are as follows:

- The person who is executing the SELECT INTO statement must have create table permissions in the database in which the SELECT INTO is being run.
- SELECT INTO is a nonlogged process, and therefore, you must take extra precautions when running this on a production system because you cannot roll it back.
- The Select Into/Bulk Copy database option needs to be turned on in the database that SELECT INTO is being run in.

An example of this would be to create a list of all the authors' first and last names and put them in their own table. You could perform this by using the SELECT INTO statement, as seen in Listing 18.15. Type this query in and run it to see the results.

Listing 18.15   SELECT INTO Clause

```
1: SELECT au_fname, au_lname
2: INTO    author_names
3: FROM    authors
4: GO
5: SELECT *
6: FROM    author_names
7: GO
```

18

As I mentioned before, to create a copy of another table with no data in it, run the SELECT INTO with a FALSE statement in the WHERE clause, as seen in Listing 18.16.

LISTING 18.16   SELECT INTO with a False WHERE Clause

```
1: SELECT *
2: INTO    empty_authors
3: FROM    authors
4: WHERE   1 = 0
```

This statement will create an empty copy of the authors table.

UNION

Last, but not least, is the UNION statement. The UNION statement is used to add the result-sets from two different queries together to form a single resultset. The biggest limitation to this rule is that the information returned from both queries has to be similar in the number of columns and have similar datatypes.

This can be especially useful when you are dealing with historical copies of a table. It is not uncommon for companies to create a new table for every year's sales data that they are collecting. If they want to retrieve the past two years worth of data, they can either run two SELECT statements and manually add them together, or they can run a single SELECT statement and join it with the UNION statement.

For example, your company tracks every sale that it makes in a table called sales_data. At the end of every year, it performs a SELECT INTO a table that is called sales_data_<year>, where <year> is the year that the company is archiving and then they delete all the data in the sales_data table. You are asked to pull a query for all sales information from the years 1996 and 1997. You could do this with the query in Listing 18.17.

LISTING 18.17   UNION Clause

```
1: SELECT * FROM sales_data_1996
2: UNION
3: SELECT * FROM sales_data_1997
```

The results would be a single set of data that you could then send back.

Summary

There you have it. A long and meandering journey through the world of the SELECT statement. As you can tell, quite a bit can be done with it. In this hour, I covered aggregate functions and generating summary data using the GROUP BY and HAVING clauses. Then I covered correlating data using joins. Finally, I wrapped up by covering some of the miscellaneous functionality of the SELECT statement. In the next hour, I will cover statements that can modify data.

Q&A

Q Can the MAX and MIN statements only be used with numeric data?

A No. If you use the MAX and MIN statements with string data, SQL Server will pick the maximum or minimum value in the table based on the sort order that is installed on the server, which is usually alphabetically.

Workshop

The quiz and the exercises are provided for your further understanding. The answers can be found in Appendix A, "Answers."

Quiz

1. What keyword can be used in a SELECT statement to eliminate duplicate rows?

2. What aggregate function can you use to add up all the values in a numeric column?

3. What aggregate function can you use to determine how many rows are contained in a table?

4. What is the GROUP BY clause used for in a SELECT statement containing an aggregate function?

5. What type of join would you use if you only want to see the rows that contain a match in both joined tables?

6. What type of join produces what is known as a Cartesian product?

7. What statement can be used to create a table based on the resultset that you queried?

8. What statement can be used to join two like resultsets?

Exercises

Write a SELECT statement that uses an INNER JOIN to determine which stores have ordered which books from the publisher. You should return the stor_id, the number ordered, and the name of the book. The two tables that will participate in the join are the sales table and the titles table.

18

HOUR 19

Modifying Data

In most business applications, your users will modify your database tables through the application itself. Nevertheless, it is important that you know how to manually modify the data that is contained in the tables. When we talk about modifying data, we are actually talking about inserting data, updating data, and deleting data. This is important so you can clean up mis-entered data, update any data that is outdated, or simply delete old data.

The highlights of this hour include

- Where Do We Start?
- Inserting Data
- Updating Data
- Locking

Where Do We Start?

When looking at all the aspects of data modification, this is a great question. The reason you have a database is to collect and gather data that will be useful to your company. This data can be order data, product performance data, or customer trend data. In the past, a lot of this same data was collected, filed away, and forgotten about. Now, with the advent of electronic databases, you can store that data away and use it to generate trends and create reports for the management. At this point, you are probably thinking "Exactly where are you headed with this?" What you should remember right now is that all the data contained in all your user databases is extremely important, and you should be very careful and take the utmost care of that data.

Many of the topics we are going to cover this hour are very useful, but you should never attempt them on productional databases as practice. The two system installed user databases, pubs and Northwind, are there for you to play with and to destroy, if necessary. It is very simple to recreate them, if you have to. It is much more difficult to rebuild or recreate data in productional systems and usually very difficult to explain, especially when you were just playing. That warning aside, it is time to get into data modification.

Inserting Data

As the name of this operation implies, we are going to cover getting data into the database in this section. Although this is not necessarily data modification, more like data creation, it is the first step in all other data modification queries. After all, the data in the tables has to come from somewhere. Getting the data into the table is done through the use of the SQL INSERT statement. This statement is relatively easy, and very few rules go along with it.

The primary rule you have to remember is when you perform an INSERT into a table, you are actually inserting an entire row into the table. If you have not specified values to go in certain fields in the table, SQL Server will either supply a default value if one was defined for that field or it will INSERT a NULL value, if one is allowed in that column. If you do not specify a value for a specific field and you have defined the field to not allow NULL, SQL Server will generate an error and halt all execution of the statement. In other words, none of the values will be put in the table.

As we mentioned previously, the INSERT statement is a relatively simple statement. It only contains two parts, as seen in Listing 19.1. The first part of the statement is the INSERT keyword itself, followed by the name of the table that is being inserted into. Optionally, you can use the keyword INTO between the INSERT keyword and the name of the table. It is not required, but if it helps you keep things straight, you can do it. If you

are not going to insert values into all fields in a table, you can list the columns you will
be entering data into in parenthesis following the name of the table. This first part is
sometimes called the INSERT clause. The second part of this statement is the keyword
VALUES followed by a list of all the values that will be put in the row. This is usually
called the values clause or values list.

LISTING 19.1   INSERT Syntax

```
1: INSERT [INTO] <table_name> [(col1, col2, col3,...)]
2: VALUES(value1, value2, value3, ...)
```

If you have not specified the names of the columns that the values are going to be
inserted into, you must have one value for every column in the table. For example, if
your table has five columns in it, you must list five values that will be inserted into that
table, or you will get an error. If you do list columns that will be inserted into, you also
need to make sure that you have listed the same number of values in the values list, or
you will get an error.

One question that you might have is how to determine the nullability behavior of specific
columns in a table. When you are working in SQL Query Analyzer, there is a very easy
way to do this. The sp_help system stored procedure can be used to determine all kinds
of useful information about the tables that you are going to be working with. Listing 19.2
shows the usage of the sp_help stored procedure using the authors table in the pubs database.

LISTING 19.2   sp_help Syntax

```
sp_help authors
```

19

When you execute this, SQL Server will return a large amount of information about the
table and its structure. You can find out all the column names, the datatype that the column is, what the nullability behavior is, what indexes are on the table, and much more.
This data is returned in a very wide format (426 characters wide), so you will have to do
a great deal of scrolling back and forth to find all the information you need, but it can be
worth it. Some of the results from Listing 19.2 can be seen in Figure 19.1.

FIGURE **19.1**

*The results from the
query in Listing 19.2.*

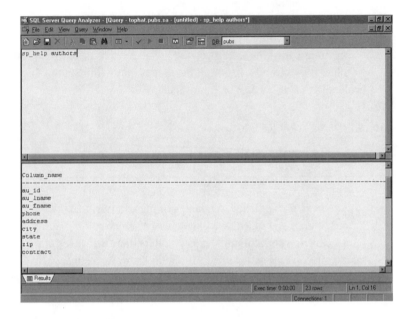

Now that you have seen what the INSERT statement looks like and where to go to find out
information about the tables, let's look at putting some data in a database. We will use
the pubs database for many of these examples. Remember, don't experiment with any of
these statements on productional systems.

In the first example, as seen in Listing 19.3, we are going to perform an INSERT into the
authors table. Let's say that this new author got all her information to the right people in
time, so when we put them in the database, we have everything that we need. In this
case, we do not have to list all the columns because we are going to perform an INSERT
into all of them.

LISTING 19.3   INSERT into a Limited Number of Columns

```
1: INSERT authors VALUES ('515-12-7654', 'Chester', 'Brooke',
2: ➡'406-555-8932', '5691 North South St.', 'Ford',
3: ➡ 'WA', '56571', 0)
```

If you type in this statement and execute it, you should get a message saying that there
was one row affected. Currently, this is not that important; but as we move forward into
the UPDATE and DELETE statements, if you are only expecting to update two rows and it
tells you that it has updated 200, you need to start investigating.

The query in Listing 19.3 is pretty straightforward. We have told SQL Server to put the values listed into the table in the order they are listed. Note that the data being inserted into columns is of string datatypes, such as CHAR or VARCHAR, and is included in single quote marks. Any data that is being inserted into numeric columns is not included in quote marks. From here, we will look at a query, where we insert data into the authors table again, but this time we didn't get all the data from the author that we should have. This time, all we have is the author's name. If you look at the table, you will see that the au_id column and the contract column are also not nullable. The author ID is a unique number that is used to identify the author. In the data that we have in the table, we have been using the author's social security number, but if we do not have that, we can make up a number, as long as it is unique. As for the contract column, you are the editor and you will know that. Now, we have to write the INSERT statement that will put that data into the columns. Listing 19.4 outlines the query.

LISTING 19.4   INSERT into Required Columns

```
1: INSERT authors (au_id, au_lname, au_fname, contract) VALUES
2: ➡('123-45-6789', 'Angel', 'Becky', 1)
```

What we have done in Listing 19.4 is listed out all the columns in which we are going to put the values that are in the VALUES list. Because the other columns in the table allow NULL values, the INSERT statement worked. Because we only inserted into those five columns, what was put into the other columns? If you run the query in Listing 19.5, you can take a look and see.

LISTING 19.5   Checking Defaults

```
1: SELECT *
2: FROM authors
3: WHERE au_id = '123-45-6789'
```

If you look at the results from this query, as seen in Figure 19.2, you will see that most of the columns in which you did not put a value contain NULL values. There is one slightly odd case, though. If you look at the phone column, you will see that the word UNKNOWN is listed as the value. This is not special to SQL Server. Instead, this is because the person who created the table defined a default value of UNKNOWN that is to be inserted into the table whenever a NULL is inserted.

19

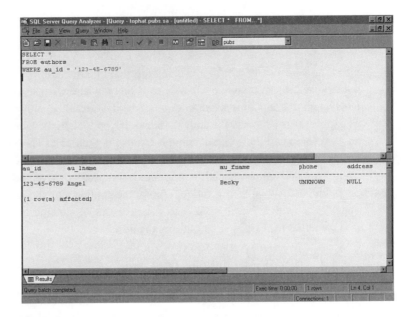

FIGURE **19.2**

The results from the query in Listing 19.5.

Default Values

It is not uncommon for database developers to determine that certain values, when all else fails, need to be inserted into their tables. These values can be anything from the UNKNOWN, which we have seen entered into the phone column in the authors table, to the username and date that a column is inserted. We have already seen how to get default values to show up when you are performing an INSERT in which you list the columns. You simply leave out the column from the column list and SQL Server will do the rest for you. But what happens if you want to perform an INSERT where you do not list all the columns that you are inserting into, as seen in Listing 19.3? In this case, you would want to use the DEFAULT keyword. For example, let's go back and look at the INSERT statement in Listing 19.3. In this case, we know all the values that we are going to insert, except for the phone number. You would probably not want to list all the column names except for that one—that would be a lot of unnecessary typing. Instead, you could do what we have done in Listing 19.6. Note that we have changed the au_id in this example. Otherwise, you would not be able to run it.

LISTING 19.6 Using the DEFAULT Keyword

```
1: INSERT authors VALUES ('511-12-7654', 'Chester', 'Brooke',
2: ➡ DEFAULT, '5691 North South St.', 'Ford',
3: ➡ 'WA', '56571', 0)
```

We have told SQL Server that we want to INSERT whatever the default value is into that column. When working with default values, remember the following things:

- If the column has been defined with a default value, the default value will be inserted into that column.

- If the column does not have a default value, but the column does allow NULLs, NULL will be INSERTed into the column.

- If the column is created with the timestamp datatype, the next valid timestamp will be INSERTed.

- If the column does not meet any of the preceding requirements, the INSERT will fail with an error.

The other option you have when INSERTing data into a table that contains default values is only open to you if all the columns in the table contain default values, which in truth is not very often. Nevertheless, if this is the case and you want to perform an INSERT that just puts the default values into the table, all you have to do is run the following:

```
INSERT <table_name> DEFAULT VALUES
```

where <table_name> is the name of the table.

INSERT Using a SELECT Statement

The last method of inserting data into a table that we will look at is performing an INSERT based on data that we SELECT from another table. This method can be used to create summary data or for filling new copies of tables. The syntax for performing an INSERT based on a SELECT is slightly different from performing a standard INSERT statement. The syntax of the statement is

```
INSERT <table_name>
    SELECT <columns> FROM <other_table_name>
```

Take, for example, the SELECT statement that we worked with in Hour 17, "Querying Data." We were writing a SELECT statement that returned the names and phone numbers of all the authors in the authors table. It could be pretty handy to have all those names and numbers stored in their own table, right? The code in Listing 19.7 will create a table called phone_list with two columns in it called author_name and phone_number. After the table is created, it will then INSERT the proper data into the table, based on the same SELECT statement that we used to gather all that same data before. Last, we then SELECT all the rows and columns out of the new table.

19

LISTING 19.7   INSERT Based on a SELECT Statement

```
 1: CREATE TABLE phone_list
 2: (
 3:      author_name     VARCHAR(32),
 4:      phone_number    VARCHAR(18)
 5: )
 6: GO
 7:
 8: INSERT phone_list
 9:      SELECT au_lname + ', ' + au_fname AS 'Author Name', phone AS 'Phone'
10:      FROM authors
11:      ORDER BY 'Author Name'
12: GO
13:
14: SELECT * FROM phone_list
15: GO
```

If you type this in and run it, and you have run all the other INSERTs, you should get a message back that says 26 rows were affected, followed by those 26 rows.

By now, you should have a pretty good handle on INSERT statements. Now we need to look at tackling the problem of modifying data that is already in the tables.

Updating Data

Businesses gather data and put it into databases. One of the golden rules of this data is that it will probably change. For the most part, most of the data contained in almost all user databases will be modified at some point. Take, for example, a database that contains supplier information. In this table, there is a record for a computer company by the name of Gateway. Up until a little over a year ago, most people would have permanently cemented that company's headquarters address in the state of North Dakota. Recently, though, Gateway moved its headquarters from North Dakota to San Diego. Now this might seem like an odd history lesson here, but if there were no way to update this address in the database, we could have some definite troubles.

In order to change existing data in the database, the UPDATE statement is used. This statement, although it has some complicated options, is actually one of the easiest statements for you to learn. This is because, for the most part, the advanced portions of this statement are rarely used. From the user's point of view, the UPDATE statement simply changes the data that is contained in the specified row. In the background, though, SQL Server actually deletes the old row from the database and then inserts a new one.

The syntax of the UPDATE statement is

```
UPDATE <table_name>
SET <column_name> = <value>
WHERE <search_condition>
```

Where the following are the options:

Option	Description
<table_name>	Is the name of the table that contains the column where you are going to change the values.
<column_name>	Is the name of the column where you are going to modify the data.
<value>	Is the new value that you want to place in the column.
<search_condition>	This is really the most important part of the UPDATE statement. Through specifying a good search condition, you are able to limit the number of rows in the table that are modified. If you did not specify a search condition, SQL Server would update every row in the table to the new value.

From here, it is time to look at actually modifying some rows in a table. Remember the author we inserted into the table when we did not know the phone number or any other information? We can't continue any sort of business relationship with that person if we do not have any way to contact her. Luckily, she calls back and gives you her phone number. We have a column in the table that contains a unique value for each row contained in the table, so we can easily write an UPDATE statement that will change only the information for her row. Listing 19.8 will first select that row from the table, update that row, and then select that same row again to show the differences.

LISTING 19.8 The UPDATE Statement in Use

```
1: SELECT *
2: FROM authors
3: WHERE au_id = '123-45-6789'
4: GO
5:
6: UPDATE authors
7: SET phone = '785-625-1212'
```

continues

LISTING 19.8 continued

```
 8: WHERE au_id = '123-45-6789'
 9: GO
10:
11: SELECT *
12: FROM authors
13: WHERE au_id = '123-45-6789'
14: GO
```

The results of this query, as shown in Figure 19.3, show that the same row you retrieved the first time has been updated to a new value.

FIGURE 19.3

The results from the query in Listing 19.8.

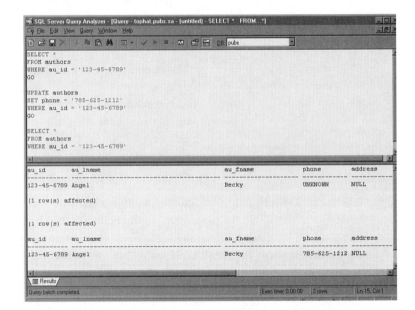

Now, let's go back and take a look at the titles table. If you needed to update every row in the table with a new value or if you needed to up the price of every book that was sold by 10 percent, would you have to write individual UPDATE statements for each row? In this case, there would not be very many UPDATE statements to write, but in larger tables this could be a problem. The answer to the question is no. All you would have to do is write an UPDATE statement that does not specify a column to update, as seen in Listing 19.9.

LISTING 19.9 UPDATE Statement Without a WHERE Clause

```
UPDATE titles
SET price = price * .10
```

After you have typed in and run this query, it should return that it has updated 18 rows. This is a useful feature, which can be turned off. You can use it to check your work and make sure that you have made the correct changes to the tables.

From here, it is time to move on to the last data modification statement, the DELETE statement.

Deleting Data

Like the INSERT statement, the DELETE statement does not actually modify data in the table. Rather, it removes rows from the table that you do not want. So, in a sense, you are modifying data by making it unavailable to other users. Take, for example, a database that contains supplier information. If a supplier that your company uses suddenly goes out of business, you no longer need those rows in the table. You would probably just delete that supplier out of your database.

Like the UPDATE command, you need to be very careful when using the DELETE statement. It is very possible for you to delete everything in the table if you do not properly form your DELETE statement. You might think that we are going over this too much, but it is very important that you realize the criticality of your data and that you do not do anything that can damage it. That warning out of the way, let's look at the syntax of the DELETE statement:

```
DELETE [FROM] <table_name>
WHERE <search_condition>
```

Where the following are the options:

Option	Description
<table_name>	Is the name of the table that contains the row or rows that you are going to delete.
[FROM]	This optional keyword is used to specify the name of the table that you are going to delete from.
<search_condition>	This is really the most important part of the DELETE statement. Through specifying a good search condition, you are able to limit the number of rows in the table that you are going to delete. If you do not specify a search condition, SQL Server will delete every row in the table.

19

So there aren't a lot of options to the DELETE statement and they are pretty self-explanatory. There are still a couple of examples that we need to look at. In the first—Listing 19.10—we will look at deleting all the rows in a table.

LISTING 19.10   Unqualified DELETE Statement

```
DELETE phone_list
```

In Listing 19.10, we will delete all the rows in this table. As you can tell, this is a pretty powerful statement. Normally, you will not want to delete all the rows in a table. Instead, you will want to delete a targeted number of rows. To do this, you would specify a search condition using any of the comparison operators that we looked at when we were discussing the SELECT statement. For example, you could delete all the books in the titles table that are less than $12.00 using the following search condition:

```
WHERE price < 12
```

The code shown in Listing 19.11 will delete a single row in the authors table.

LISTING 19.11   Deleting a Single Row

```
DELETE authors
WHERE au_id = '511-12-7654'
```

The previous listing deletes a single row in the authors table based off the au_id. In the previous example, we base this off the au_id; this is an identifying column in the table. In other words, there will be only one row in the table with an au_id of '511-12-7654'.

Locking

When any type of data modification is taking place in the database, SQL Server performs some special operations to ensure that no other user modifies or readsthe same row that is being modified. SQL Server will lock database objects and data at several levels, based on the needs of the operation that is being run. Table 19.1 outlines the different lock types that SQL Server can use.

TABLE 19.1 Lockable Resources and Descriptions

Resource Type	Description
RID	A RID, or Row Identifier, is used to lock individual rows within a table. This allows for rows to be updated, inserted, and deleted without locking entire pages.
Key	A key lock is a row lock in an index. These locks are acquired only while SQL Server is updating an index.
Page	A page lock locks an entire 8KB page in a table or an index, including all rows on that page. This is done while one user is updating more than one row on a page and it is more efficient to lock the entire page than to lock all the individual rows.
Extent	An extent lock locks a contiguous group of eight pages. As with a page lock, it locks all rows contained on all pages within the extent. These types of locks are acquired when data spans more than several pages, and it is more efficient to lock the entire extent than to lock each individual page.
Table	A table lock locks an entire table, including all the data and indexes in the table. These types of locks are required when a data modification affects a great deal of data in a table and SQL Server decides that it is much easier to lock the entire table than to lock any of the smaller objects.
DB	A DB, or database lock, locks an entire database and all tables in the database. These locks are only required during operations that affect the entire database, such as database restores.

SQL Server will lock the preceding resources using different lock modes based on the type of activity that is being performed. Table 19.2 outlines the lock modes that SQL Server can use.

TABLE 19.2 Lock Modes and Descriptions

Lock Mode	Description
Shared	Shared locks are used for operations that do not modify data, such as SELECT statements. Shared locks are released as soon as the data has been read. Multiple users can acquire shared locks on the same objects.
Update	Update locks are used when an UPDATE operation takes place. These are needed to stop a specific type of deadlock that can occur during an UPDATE. During an UPDATE operation, SQL Server will read a record, which acquires a shared lock on the affected records and then actually modify the records, which uses an exclusive lock. If two users attempt this scenario, a deadlock can occur. Only one user can acquire an update lock on an object. If the data modification actually occurs, the lock is upgraded to an exclusive lock.

continues

TABLE 19.2 continued

Lock Mode	Description
Exclusive	Exclusive locks are used during data modification operations such as INSERTs, UPDATEs, and DELETEs. This type of lock ensures that no other user can access the object that is locked.
Intent Shared	Intent Shared locks indicate that the transaction intends to place shared locks on some but not all the resources lower down the hierarchy. For example, a transaction might place an intent shared lock on a table if it appears that most of the rows in a table are going to be read.
Intent Exclusive	Intent Exclusive locks are used to indicate that a transaction to modify some but not all the resources lower down the hierarchy.
Shares with Intent Exclusive	This type of lock indicates that a transaction will read all the resources further down the hierarchy and modify some of them by placing Intent Exclusive locks on them.

Summary

In this hour, we have looked at data modification. First, we looked at inserting new data into the database. Then, we looked at updating existing data in the database. After that, we investigated the deletion of data in databases. Last, we looked at how SQL Server uses locking mechanisms to keep other users from accessing data when a user is making modifications.

Q&A

Q **Is there a way to INSERT multiple rows into a table with one statement, similar to the way an UPDATE or an INSERT can affect several rows at the same time?**

A No. The only way to INSERT multiple rows into a table is to write several INSERT statements.

Q **Is there any way around restoring an entire database if you have performed an UPDATE or DELETE that affects more rows that you expected it to?**

A With the tools that we have discussed so far, no. We will get into using explicit transactions in Hour 21, "Programming with SQL Server." You can use explicit transactions to cancel an accidental UPDATE or DELETE, but you must start the transaction before you run the statement.

Workshop

The quiz and the exercises are provided for your further understanding. The answers can be found in Appendix A, "Answers."

Quiz

1. What is the INSERT statement used for?

2. If you list six columns in the INSERT statement, how many values must you supply?

3. What occurs if you INSERT a NULL value into a column that does not contain a default value and does not allow NULLs?

4. What is the UPDATE statement used for?

5. Why is it important for you to provide a WHERE clause when using the UPDATE statement?

6. What is the DELETE statement used for?

7. Is it possible to delete more than one row at a time using the DELETE statement?

8. What are locks used for?

Exercises

Write an INSERT statement that will put the following values into the authors table in the pubs database:

Column	Value
au_id	925-12-3456
au_lname	Jones
au_fname	Melissa
phone	913-722-0909
address	94 W. 163rd St.
city	Lenexa
state	KS
zip	66213
contract	1

19

Write an UPDATE statement that will change Melissa's data to the following:

Column	Value
au_lname	Jones
phone	913-663-1234
address	9134 E. 178th St.

Finally, write a DELETE statement that will delete Melissa's data out of the authors table.

HOUR 20

Stored Procedures

Stored procedures are a very useful feature in SQL Server. A stored procedure is a group of SQL statements that are compiled together and can be executed by calling a single command. They are useful for maintaining some of the code required to run an application on the SQL Server. SQL Server also comes preinstalled with many system stored procedures that are designed to gather specific information about the server on which they are being executed.

This highlights of this hour include

- What Is a Stored Procedure?
- Uses for Stored Procedures
- Creating and Modifying Stored Procedures
- Running Stored Procedures
- Dropping Stored Procedures

What Is a Stored Procedure?

As we mentioned earlier, a stored procedure is simply a grouping of SQL statements that are compiled together and can be executed using a single command. Stored procedures can be used for returning data to the user, inserting new data into tables, modifying data, and performing system functions and administrative tasks. Overall, they are a very powerful part of SQL Server that can be used to make your life much easier. Stored procedures can be used to store the business logic and functionality of your applications on the SQL Server itself, allowing some of the decisions that need to be made about the data to be made at the server level, instead of returning the results to the client. Two major camps have sprung up in the past few years regarding using stored procedures to provide this type of functionality.

The first camp has decided it is best to place as much of the functionality in the stored procedures as possible. This group believes that stored procedures should be written to provide everything from database INSERTs and UPDATEs, to data validation. The pro to this sort of solution is if a business rule changes, all you have to do is change the stored procedure at the server level, and no changes must be made at the client level. The con to this type of solution is that putting all the application logic into the database can slow down the database itself. Many people are moving away from this type of approach and to the next one.

The second camp contends that all functionality that deals with the actual application should be left out of the stored procedures and dealt with outside the database. This group basically believes that the only thing that should be in stored procedures are the actual UPDATEs, INSERTs, and DELETEs. Any business logic such as data validation should be left within a middle tier or at the actual application level. The pros of this type of solution are that it is usually extremely fast and the database is used only for the purpose of storing data. The con of this type of approach is that if all your business logic is stored in the front-end application, any changes to the business logic will require a rewrite, recompile, and redistribution of the application. The other major issue with this type of approach is that when all the logic of the application is stored within the database itself, it makes it very difficult to migrate the database from one platform to another. This issue is usually solved through the use of a middle-tier application that contains all the business logic.

SQL Server stored procedures can return data to the user in one of several ways:

* A resultset from any SELECT statement that is contained in the stored procedure.
* Return codes, which are integer values.

- Output parameters, which can contain integer or character data that can be picked up to be the user application.
- A cursor that can be referenced outside the stored procedure.

In previous versions of SQL Server, stored procedures were a way to speed up the execution of the SQL statements that are contained in them by partially compiling the execution plan. When the stored procedure was created, the partially compiled execution plan was stored. When the stored procedure was executed, the partially compiled execution plan was retrieved and then optimized. After the stored procedure was executed and optimized, the execution plan was stored in the procedure cache. When other processes or users execute that stored procedure, that plan is simply retrieved from the procedure cache and executed.

In this version of SQL Server, stored procedures are handled in a completely different way. SQL Server 7.0 does not store any of the execution plan for the stored procedures. Instead, when the procedure is executed, SQL Server retrieves the code, compiles, optimizes, and executes it. This execution plan is then stored in the procedure cache for further execution.

Uses for Stored Procedures

The possibilities for stored procedures are nearly limitless. You can use stored procedures for anything from returning the results of a SELECT statement for user reporting to performing complex data validation. Partially, some of the decision as to what stored procedures can do for you depends on which one of the two camps previously listed you fall into. If you are a person who believes that all application functionality should be contained in stored procedures, this is possible. If you only believe that SQL Server should be used to store data, this is an option as well. Some of the uses for, and benefits of, stored procedures are as follows:

- Modular Programming—After you create a stored procedure, it is stored in the database and it can be called from your application any number of times. These procedures can encapsulate the database functionality and can be modified independently of the application code, as long as the application always knows what the data being returned will do.

- Fast Execution—When a stored procedure is compiled and stored in the procedure cache, it can be executed with extreme efficiency. This is because SQL Server will not have to continually recompile the stored procedure.

- Network Traffic—Frequently, you will have SQL statements that can be hundreds of lines long. If you can encapsulate that functionality into a stored procedure, you

20

can save a great deal of network bandwidth by sending the SQL Server one line of code, as opposed to hundreds of lines of code. When you are looking at a small number of users who are running the application, this impact is minimal; but if you scale the application to handle hundreds or thousands of users, this impact could be extreme.

- Security—Stored procedures can be used as a security mechanism. When you assign permissions for a user or group of users to execute a stored procedure, they will be able to execute even if they do not have permissions to the underlying objects that are accessed in the stored procedure. For example, if you create a stored procedure that returns all the rows in the authors table of the pubs database and assign permissions for a user named Joe to execute that stored procedure, he will be able to retrieve all the rows from the authors table even if he does not have permission to do so directly.

Now that you have an idea of what stored procedures can do for you, we will look at creating and modifying stored procedures.

Creating and Modifying Stored Procedures

Before you can actually use a stored procedure in your user application, you will need to create the stored procedure. This process for creating a stored procedure is actually a pretty easy one. The first thing you need to do is to write the query you are going to run inside the stored procedure. For example, if you are going to create a stored procedure that returns the results of a complex SELECT statement to the user, the first thing that you need to do is to write and test the SELECT statement. After you have created and tested the SELECT statement, you will actually create the stored procedure using the CREATE PROCEDURE statement.

Creating a Stored Procedure

The CREATE PROCEDURE statement is used to actually create the stored procedure from the SQL statements that you have already tested. This is actually a pretty simple process. The syntax of the CREATE PROCEDURE statement is as follows:

```
CREATE PROCEDURE <procedure_name>
{<@parameter> <datatype>} [VARYING] [= default] [OUTPUT]][,...n]
[WITH {RECOMPILE ¦ ENCRYPTION ¦ RECOMPILE, ENCRYPTION}]
AS
<sql_statements>
```

Where the following are the options:

Option	Description
<procedure_name>	This is the name that you want to call the stored procedure. We will cover naming conventions of stored procedures in a little bit.
<@parameter>	If you want to pass parameters into a stored procedure, you must define them in the declaration of the stored procedure. This declaration includes the name of the parameter, the datatype of the parameter, and a few other special options.
<datatype>	If you specify a parameter, you must specify the datatype of that parameter. This can be any valid datatype, including text and image.
[VARYING]	This option is specified when you are returning a cursor as a parameter. This option tells SQL Server that the row set for the returned cursor may vary.
[= default]	This option is used to specify a default value for a particular parameter. If the procedure is executed without specifying a value for the parameter, this value will be used instead. This can be a NULL or any other valid value for that datatype. For string data, this can include wildcards if the parameter is used in conjunction with the LIKE parameter.
[OUTPUT]	This optional keyword is used to specify that the parameter is a return parameter. The value of this parameter can then be returned to the executing procedure when execution has completed. Text or image datatypes cannot be used as OUTPUT parameters.
[,...]	This symbol indicates that you can specify multiple parameters with a stored procedure. SQL Server allows up to 1,024 parameters for use in a single stored procedure.
WITH RECOMPILE	This option forces SQL Server to recompile the stored procedure every time it is executed. You should use this when you are using temporary values and objects.

20

continues

Option	Description
WITH ENCRYPTION	This option forces SQL Server to encrypt the text of the stored procedure that is stored in the syscomments table. This allows you to create and redistribute a database without having to worry about users figuring out the source code of your stored procedures.
WITH RECOMPILE, ENCRYPTION	This option forces SQL Server to recompile and encrypt the stored procedure.
AS	This indicates that the definition of the stored procedure is about to begin.
<sql_statements>	This is a placeholder for the different statements that will make up the stored procedure.

Before we get too far into creating stored procedures, we need to look at naming conventions. All the stored procedures that come with SQL Server have the prefix of sp_. This convention should be reserved for system stored procedures. This does not mean that SQL Server will stop you from creating a user stored procedure with the prefix of sp_. It will still let you create them, but there can be issues with third-party tools. Most of these third-party tools will ignore all system objects, and because SQL Server system stored procedures have the prefix of sp_, these tools will ignore them as well. A good practice is to name user stored procedures with any other prefix. In this hour, we will use the prefix usp_ to designate user stored procedures.

Now that you have seen the command required to create a stored procedure, let's look at actually creating some. We will actually use some of the SELECT statements that we looked at and created back in Hour 17, "Querying Data." In the example shown in Listing 20.1, we will take the query that brought back all the authors and their phone numbers and make it into a stored procedure called usp_get_phone_list.

LISTING 20.1 Creating a Simple Stored Procedure

```
1: CREATE PROCEDURE usp_get_phone_list
2: AS
3: SELECT au_lname + ', ' + au_fname AS 'Name', phone AS 'Phone'
4: FROM authors
5: ORDER BY 'Name' ASC
```

This will create a stored procedure called usp_get_phone_list. To execute and test this stored procedure, open another query windowand type in the name of the stored procedure and execute it. The results from executing this stored procedure, as seen in Figure 20.1, are exactly the same as if you were to run the SELECT statement.

FIGURE 20.1

The results from the query in Listing 20.1.

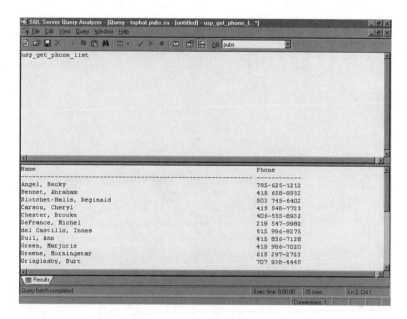

Although the preceding stored procedure can be useful, you can do quite a bit more with stored procedures. For example, what would you do if you wanted to look for a specific author's phone number by the author's last name? We can do this by passing a parameter into the stored procedure. In Listing 20.2, we will create a user stored procedure called usp_get_author_phone that will expect a parameter called @last_name to be passed into it. It will then use this parameter to find the author's phone number in the authors table.

LISTING 20.2 Passing Parameters to a Stored Procedure

```
1: CREATE PROCEDURE usp_get_author_phone
2:      @last_name       VARCHAR(32)
3: AS
4: SELECT au_lname + ', ' + au_fname AS 'Name', phone AS 'Phone'
5: FROM authors
6: WHERE au_lname = @last_name
7: ORDER BY 'Name' ASC
```

20

What we have done in this stored procedure is told SQL Server that when it is executed, we will pass in an author's last name for it to find using a WHERE clause in the SELECT statement. When you execute this stored procedure, you must pass in the last name of the author or SQL Server will return an error telling you that it expects you to pass something in. The results from executing this stored procedure are shown in Figure 20.2.

FIGURE 20.2

The results from the query in Listing 20.2.

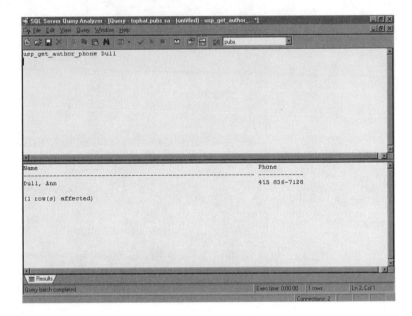

For the most part, this could be a pretty useful query. There are those times, though, when you do not know how to spell the name of the author. We can get around this by putting a LIKE clause in the SELECT query. We will have to do a little manipulation of the search string that the user passes into the stored procedure. What we will have to do is append a percent sign (%) to the end of the string so that SQL Server interprets it as a wildcard. Listing 20.3 shows how to create the stored procedure that we have previously outlined.

LISTING 20.3   Wildcard Characters in Stored Procedures

```
1: CREATE PROCEDURE usp_get_author_phone2
2:     @last_name      VARCHAR(32)
3: AS
4: SELECT @last_name = @last_name + '%'
5:
6: SELECT au_lname + ', ' + au_fname AS 'Name', phone AS 'Phone'
7: FROM authors
8: WHERE au_lname LIKE @last_name
9: ORDER BY 'Name' ASC
```

This stored procedure allows you to search for any part of the author's last name, from the first letter on. The results of the execution of this stored procedure, searching for a last name starting with "D", are shown in Figure 20.3.

FIGURE 20.3

The results from the query in Listing 20.3.

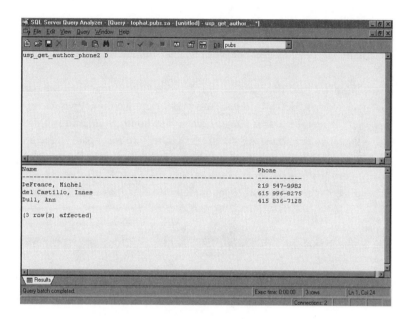

So far, we have looked at creating stored procedures that retrieve data from a table. What if we want to create a stored procedure that inserts data into a table? Let's look at creating a stored procedure that inserts data into the authors table. In this stored procedure, we will force the user to supply an identification number and the author's first and last name. If they pass in any other information, we will insert that into the table. If they do not pass any other information in, we will have to deal with that by setting up defaults in the parameters of the stored procedure. Listing 20.4 outlines the creation of a user stored procedure called usp_insert_new_author.

20

LISTING 20.4 Inserting Data Using a Stored Procedure

```
1: CREATE PROCEDURE usp_insert_new_author
2:     @au_id          VARCHAR(11),
3:     @au_lname       VARCHAR(40),
4:     @au_fname       VARCHAR(20),
5:     @phone          CHAR(12) = 'UNKNOWN',
6:     @address        VARCHAR(40) = NULL,
7:     @city           VARCHAR(20) = NULL,
8:     @state          CHAR(2) = NULL,
```

continues

LISTING 20.4 continued

```
 9:        @zip          CHAR(5) = NULL,
10:        @contract     BIT = 0
11: AS
12: INSERT INTO authors
13: VALUES(@au_id, @au_lname, @au_fname, @phone, @address, @city,
14:        @state, @zip, @contract)
```

What we have done in this stored procedure is created all the parameters we require
without any default values. Any parameters we do not require to be inserted into the table
are then created with NULL defaults. The contract column is created with a default of 0.
When you execute this stored procedure, you must pass in the author ID, the first name,
and the last name. All other columns are optional. In Figure 20.4, you can see where the
query has been executed by inserting the name Bill Jones into the table, and then by
using the usp_get_author_phone2 to see what has been inserted into the table.

FIGURE 20.4

*The results from the
query in Listing 20.4.*

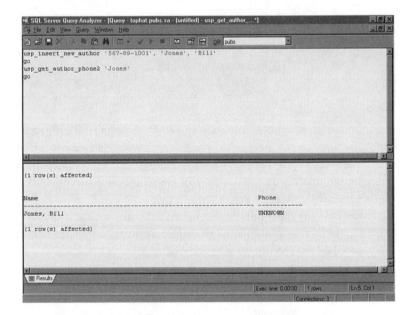

As you can tell, you can do quite a bit with stored procedures. We have barely scratched
the surface of what they can do here, but with some practice, you should be able to determine quite a bit about them.

Modifying Stored Procedures

After you have created a stored procedure, it will be inevitable that someone will want you to change it. In previous versions of SQL Server when you wanted to modify a stored procedure, you would have had to drop the procedure and then recreate it. When you drop a stored procedure, you lose all permissions that were assigned to that procedure as well as all your dependency information. Dependencies are information that SQL Server gathers about each object in the database. If a stored procedure references a table, it is said to depend on that table. For more information on dependencies, search for sp_depends in SQL Server Books Online.

In SQL Server 7.0, Microsoft has added a very useful command that will keep you from losing all this information. This is the ALTER PROCEDURE command. To use this command, you will still have to recreate all the code associated with the procedure, but you will not lose the permissions or dependencies.

A system stored procedure will assist you in recreating the code associated with a stored procedure. This system stored procedure is called sp_helptext. This procedure will return all the code associated with a stored procedure assuming that the stored procedure has not been encrypted. The syntax of the command is

```
sp_helptext <procedure_name>
```

Where <procedure_name> is the name of the procedure for which you want to retrieve the code. The output of an example of this can be seen in Figure 20.5.

FIGURE 20.5

The results from sp_helptext.

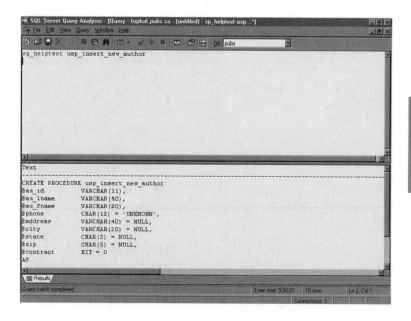

20

Now that you have the code from .the stored procedure, you can alter it rather easily. The syntax of the ALTER PROCEDURE command is as follows:

```
ALTER PROCEDURE <procedure_name>
{<@parameter> <datatype>} [VARYING] [= default] [OUTPUT]][,...n]
[WITH {RECOMPILE ¦ ENCRYPTION ¦ RECOMPILE, ENCRYPTION}]
AS
<sql_statements>
```

Where the following are the options:

Option	Description
<procedure_name>	This is the name of the stored procedure that you are going to alter.
<@parameter>	If you want to pass parameters into a stored procedure, you must define them in the declaration of the stored procedure. This declaration includes the name of the parameter, the datatype of the parameter, and a few other special options depending on their use.
<datatype>	If you specify a parameter, you must specify the datatype of that parameter. This can be any valid datatype, including text and image.
[VARYING]	This option is specified when you are returning a cursor as a parameter.
[= default]	This option is used to specify a default value for a particular parameter. If the procedure is executed without specifying a value for the parameter, this value will be used instead. This can be a NULL or any other valid value for that datatype. For string data, this can include wildcards if the parameter is used in conjunction with the LIKE parameter.
[OUTPUT]	This optional keyword is used to specify that the parameter is a return parameter. The value of this parameter can then be returned to the executing procedure when execution has completed. Text or image datatypes cannot be used as OUTPUT parameters.
[,...]	This symbol indicates that you can specify multiple parameters with a stored procedure. SQL Server allows up to 1,024 parameters for use in a single stored procedure.

Option	Description
WITH RECOMPILE	This option forces SQL Server to recompile the stored procedure every time that it is executed. You should use this when you are using temporary values and objects.
WITH ENCRYPTION	This option forces SQL Server to encrypt the text of the stored procedure that is stored in the syscomments table. This allows you to create and redistribute a database without having to worry about users figuring out the source code of your stored procedures.
WITH RECOMPILE, ENCRYPTION	This option forces SQL Server to recompile and encrypt the stored procedure.
AS	This indicates that the definition of the stored procedure is about to begin.
<sql_statements>	This is a placeholder for the different statements that will make up the stored procedure.

For example, to alter the procedure we created earlier called usp_insert_new_author—which inserts, as a default state, CA into the state column—you would run the query in Listing 20.5.

LISTING 20.5 ALTER PROCEDURE in Use

```
 1: ALTER PROCEDURE usp_insert_new_author
 2: @au_id          VARCHAR(11),
 3: @au_lname       VARCHAR(40),
 4: @au_fname       VARCHAR(20),
 5: @phone          CHAR(12) = 'UNKNOWN',
 6: @address        VARCHAR(40) = NULL,
 7: @city           VARCHAR(20) = NULL,
 8: @state          CHAR(2) = 'CA',
 9: @zip            CHAR(5) = NULL,
10: @contract       BIT = 0
11: AS
12: INSERT INTO authors
13: VALUES(@au_id, @au_lname, @au_fname, @phone, @address, @city,
14:        @state, @zip, @contract)
```

20

This will alter the procedure without changing any of the dependencies or permissions. Now that we have created a few procedures, we need to look at running them.

Running Stored Procedures

As we have already seen, running stored procedures is actually pretty simple. You have two options. First, you can execute a stored procedure by typing the name of theprocedure into the query window of SQL Server Query Analyzer and executing it. This option will work if the stored procedure is the only thing that is being run. If other portions of the batch contain the stored procedure, this will cause a problem. You will have to use the EXECUTE statement. The syntax of the EXECUTE statement is as follows:

```
EXECUTE <procedure_name>
```

where <procedure_name> is the name of the procedure that you want to execute.

Dropping Stored Procedures

As with all things, a time will come when most stored procedures will need to be dropped from the system. This might be because your business has outgrown the procedure or because the functionality is just no longer needed. If you are sure that you no longer need the functionality performed by the stored procedure, you can drop it from the system. Note that it is very important that you make sure that the functionality provided by the stored procedure is no longer needed because you will have to recreate the stored procedure if you actually do need it. To drop a stored procedure, you will use the DROP PROCEDURE command. The syntax of the command is as follows:

```
DROP PROCEDURE <procedure_name>
```

where <procedure_name> is the name of the procedure that you will be removing from the system. Remember that this removal is permanent, and you must recreate it if you later find out you need it.

Summary

Stored procedures can be a very powerful feature of SQL Server if you plan it correctly. Stored procedures can be used for anything from simple queries to application logic, depending on your implementation. In this hour, we looked at creating stored procedures using the CREATE PROCEDURE command and modifying them using the ALTER PROCEDURE command. Next, we looked at executing stored procedures. Finally, we looked at dropping old stored procedures using the DROP PROCEDURE command.

Q&A

Q **How much storage space in the database does it take to store each stored procedure?**

A Stored procedures are not allocated space directly in the server. You can estimate how much space is going to be required for the stored procedure by determining the size of the script required to create the stored procedure.

Q **Is it a bad thing to put application logic in stored procedures?**

A It is not necessarily a bad thing, but in most cases, you should investigate keeping the logic in either a middle tier or in the application itself (as you can tell, I am using SQL Server for storing data only).

Workshop

The quiz and the exercise are provided for your further understanding. The answers can be found in Appendix A, "Answers."

Quiz

1. What is a stored procedure?
2. What command is used to create a stored procedure?
3. What can you use to pass data into a stored procedure?
4. What command can you use to modify a stored procedure?
5. What do you gain from modifying a stored procedure, as opposed to dropping and recreating it?
6. What is a dependency?
7. What command do you use to drop a stored procedure from the system?

Exercise

Create a stored procedure that returns all the address information about an author if the person who executes it passes in any part of the author's last name.

20

HOUR 21

Programming SQL Server

In the past few hours, you have covered pretty much everything that you must know to write SQL Server scripts. These scripts can also incorporate some basic logic that can turn them into rather powerful applications. SQL Server provides several different logic statements that can be added to your scripts. These include if-then logic and while constructs for looping. SQL Server also provides functionality for you to create error messages that you can return to the user.

The highlights of this hour include

- Programming in General
- Batches
- Transactions
- Control-of-Flow
- Comments
- Variables

Programming in General

SQL Server can be used to create extremely powerful applications. Most of this is done through the use of scripts, stored procedures, triggers, and views. You must be very careful when you are designing these applications for the first time. These type of applications, those that rely on SQL Server for all their functionality, tend to scale very well for small installations. The problem is when you scale these to larger installations. In these cases, performance sometimes suffers.

In this hour, we are going to cover many of the programmatical terms and structures that can be implemented using SQL Server. If you have never programmed before, some of these structures could seem rather daunting. You should not worry about this, though, because the only databases you should be working with at this point are nonproductional systems that contain no real business data.

Batches

In SQL Server programming, the term batch will be thrown around quite a bit. Two possible scenarios can be used to define this term. The first refers to batch processing. Batch processing is somewhat of a holdover term from the mainframe days. Because of limited processor cycles during business hours, only the bare minimum of changes were made to the live system. Batches were then run during off hours to pick up the rest of the changes and populate them into their respective areas and systems. Although this type of processing in SQL Server is still called batch processing, this is not what we will normally be referring to when we speak of batches.

The other way that batches will be described in SQL Server is when the term is used to define a unit of work. A batch is a group of SQL statements that are sent at the same time from an application for SQL Server to process. SQL Server takes all the statements in the batch and compiles them into an executable unit. This executable unit is called an execution plan. SQL Server then executes all statements in the execution plan at one time.

SQL Server handles errors that occur within batches in several ways:

- If a syntax error occurs within any statement in a batch, SQL Server will not create the execution plan, and therefore none of the statements in the batch are run. An example of a syntax error is misspelling the word SELECT.
- Most runtime errors, such as arithmetic overflow errors, stop the currently executing statement and halt all execution after that statement.

- Most CREATE statements cannot be combined in the same batch as they are used. In other words, you cannot run a CREATE TABLE statement and any other statement within the same batch.

- You cannot run an ALTER TABLE command and then reference any new columns that are added to the table in the same batch. This is because SQL Server compiles the batch ahead of time and looks for the columns in the table. Because the columns do not exist yet, the compilation fails.

- If you are running multiple stored procedures within the same batch, SQL Server requires that they be run with the EXECUTE statement.

In order to delimit a batch in an SQL script, SQL Server uses the GO keyword. To use this keyword, all you have to do is place it after a series of statements that are going to be run as a single batch. For example, in Listing 21.1, we first USE a database in one batch; CREATE a table in another batch; perform an INSERT, an UPDATE, and a DELETE in another batch; and then finally DROP the table we just created. These all can be run at one shot: SQL Server just interprets them as different portions.

LISTING 21.1 Example of Batch Statements

```
 1: USE pubs
 2: GO
 3:
 4: CREATE TABLE TestTable
 5: (
 6:     column1    INT,
 7:     column2    VARCHAR(32)
 8: )
 9: GO
10:
11: INSERT INTO TestTable VALUES(1, 'Test Value 1')
12: UPDATE TestTable SET column2 = 'Updated Test Value 1'
13: DELETE TestTable WHERE column1 = 1
14: GO
15:
16: DROP TABLE TestTable
17: GO
```

Another good thing about batches is that they can break up your code into smaller sections that will continue to run even if one of the previous sections fails, which leads us perfectly into transactions.

21

Transactions

Transactions are the basic fundamental of how SQL Server protects your data from getting into what is called an inconsistent state. We have gone over how transactions actually work. In this section, we will look at how to make transactions work for you in your SQL Server development. Transactions in SQL Server come in two basic flavors. These are implicit transactions and explicit transactions.

Implicit Transactions

An implicit transaction, as the name implies, is one that SQL Server just does for you. These transactions are also known as autocommit transactions. If you simply run an INSERT statement, SQL Server wraps it up into a transaction, so if the INSERT statement fails, SQL Server rolls back, or cancels, the transaction. Every SQL Statement that is executed is treated as its own transaction. For example, in Listing 21.2, there are four INSERT statements. The first, second, and fourth INSERT statements are valid. The third statement, though, is invalid. It violates a constraint on the table that says that the author ID must be unique. When this is run, the first, second, and fourth statements succeed and are inserted into the table. The third statement fails and is rolled back.

LISTING 21.2 Implicit Transactions

```
 1: INSERT authors VALUES('111-11-1111', 'Davis', 'Mark',
 2:      '816-459-1111', '321 N. South St.', 'Kansas City', 'MO',
 3:      '68901', 1)
 4: INSERT authors VALUES('222-22-2222', 'Johnston', 'Doug',
 5:      '816-459-2222', '678 0 Boy St.', 'Gods Country', 'MO',
 6:      '69699', 1)
 7: INSERT authors VALUES('341-22-1782', 'Smith', 'Meander',
 8:      '913 843-0462', '10 Mississippi Dr.', 'Lawrence', 'KS',
 9:      '66044', 0)
10: INSERT authors VALUES('333-33-3333', 'Peterson', 'Joel',
11:      '816-459-3333', '345 E. West St.', 'Far Away', 'MO',
12:      '67234', 1)
```

In normal day-to-day scripted operation, you will probably rely on implicit transactions. In third-party applications, the developers of those applications will probably use explicit transactions.

Explicit Transactions

An explicit transaction is a transaction that you specify. These transactions allow you to determine which amounts of work must complete successfully, or all portions of it will fail. To delimit your own transactions, you can use the BEGIN TRANSACTION and the ROLLBACK TRANSACTION or COMMIT TRANSACTION keywords.

- BEGIN TRANSACTION—This key phrase is used to tell SQL Server that a transaction is about to being. Every SQL statement that occurs after the BEGIN TRANSACTION will be considered a part of the same transaction.

- ROLLBACK TRANSACTION—This key phrase is used to tell SQL Server that all the work that has been done since the BEGIN TRANSACTION was issued should be cancelled. Any changes that have been made to the data in the database is changed back and any objects that have been created or dropped are deleted or brought back.

- COMMIT TRANSACTION—This key phrase is used to tell SQL Server that all the work that has been done since the BEGIN TRANSACTION is to be completed and made a permanent part of the database. You cannot issue both a COMMIT TRANSACTION and a ROLLBACK TRANSACTION in reference to the same transaction.

It is very important you realize that, even if there are errors in your script, and you tell SQL Server to commit the transaction, it will do so. You must build error checking into your scripts if you are going to rely on explicit transactions to ensure data integrity. The code shown in Listing 21.3 shows the use of explicit transactions to roll back a change made to the employees table.

LISTING 21.3 Explicit Transactions

```
 1: BEGIN TRANSACTION
 2: GO
 3: DELETE employee
 4: GO
 5: SELECT 'Before ROLLBACK'
 6: SELECT * FROM employee
 7: GO
 8: ROLLBACK TRANSACTION
 9: GO
10: SELECT 'After ROLLBACK'
11: SELECT * FROM employee
12: GO
```

The results of this query can be seen in Figure 21.1.

21

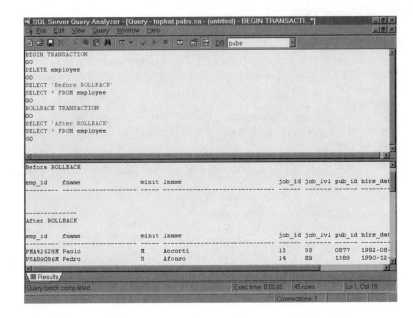

FIGURE **21.1**

The results from the
query in Listing 21.3.

As you can see in the results, we did not get any rows back from the SELECT statement
after the delete has been made. This shows they are really gone. If we would have issued
a COMMIT TRANSACTION instead of a ROLLBACK, SQL Server would have made those
changes permanent. This type of statement is useful when you are making UPDATEs and
DELETEs to a table. If you begin a transaction and then issue the UPDATE or DELETE, you
can then roll back the transaction if you accidentally deleted or updated more rows than
you expected. It is also important to note that during the time between the BEGIN
TRANSACTION and the COMMIT or ROLLBACK, any data that is affected by the transaction
is not visible to any other session on the server.

Control-of-Flow

SQL Server provides several control-of-flow keywords that can be used to control how
SQL Server executes the statements in a batch or procedure. If you do not use any of the
flow control statements, SQL Server will execute each statement in the script in a
sequential manner. With control-of-flow language, you can group statements together and
control their execution based on other criteria that have been met within batch or procedure. It is important to note that, although the control-of-flow language is very powerful,
it cannot span multiple batches or procedures.

BEGIN...END

The BEGIN...END keyword pair is used to group a block of SQL statements together so that they can be executed together. This is an important set of keywords because they will be used with many of the other control-of-flow keywords. For now, just remember the syntax of the statement:

```
BEGIN
    <sql_statement>
END
```

where <sql_statement> is any valid SQL statement or group of SQL statements. The one important thing to remember with this is that this must be contained in a single batch.

IF...ELSE

The IF...ELSE construct will be recognized by most people who have been exposed to even a little bit of programming. This statement is usually known as an IF...THEN...ELSE statement, but in SQL Server we leave out the THEN. This construct is used to evaluate a condition and then, based on the results of that evaluation, will either execute the code following the IF statement or the code after the optional ELSE statement. If you do not include an ELSE statement, SQL Server will simply skip the code after the ELSE statement and continue on. The syntax of the command is as follows:

```
IF <Boolean_expression>
    <sql_statements>
ELSE
    <sql_statements>
```

Where the options are

Option	Description
<Boolean_expression>	This is an expression that is going to evaluate to either True or False. It is possible to use a SELECT statement as the Boolean expression. If you do this, you must enclose the SELECT statement within parenthesis.
<sql_statements>	This is either a single SQL statement or a group of SQL statements. If there is more than one SQL statement that follows the IF or THEN statement, you must enclose the statements in a BEGIN...END block.

21

This construct can be used to form some very powerful application code. The code in Listing 21.4 shows a simple use of the IF...ELSE statements to determine how many or whether any authors live in California.

LISTING 21.4   IF...ELSE Statement

```
1: IF (SELECT COUNT(*) FROM authors WHERE state = 'CA') > 0
2: BEGIN
3:      SELECT 'There are ' + CONVERT(VARCHAR(8), COUNT(*)) +
4:              ' authors in the state of CA'
5:      FROM authors
6:      WHERE state = 'CA'
7: END
8: ELSE
9:      SELECT 'There are no authors that live in CA'
```

As you can tell, this can be a very powerful way to determine how you are going to perform WHICH statements.

WHILE

The WHILE statement is used to create a loop in which SQL Server will continue performing a function until the condition of the loop is False. This type of execution is useful when you are looking for specific values to show up in a table when you are updating, or for setting up a process that loops continually. This last part can be done by setting up a condition that will always be True, such as 1=1. The syntax of the command is as follows:

```
WHILE <Boolean_expression>
    <sql_statements>
    BREAK
    <sql_statements>
    CONTINUE
```

Where the options are

Option	Description
<Boolean_expression>	This is an expression that is going to evaluate to either True or False. It is possible to use a SELECT statement as the Boolean expression. If you do this, you must enclose the SELECT statement within parenthesis.

Option	Description
`<sql_statements>`	This is either a single SQL statement or a group of SQL statements. If more than one SQL statement follows the WHILE statement, you must enclose the statements in a BEGIN...END block.
BREAK	This keyword causes the loop to halt processing. Any statements after the END statement, which marks the end of the loop, are then executed.
CONTINUE	This keyword causes the loop to restart, ignoring all statements after the CONTINUE statement.

An example of the WHILE loop is outlined in Listing 21.5. Note that all the changes are contained in a transaction, so they can be, and are, cancelled at the end of the processing.

LISTING 21.5   WHILE Loop

```
 1: SELECT MIN(price) AS 'Minimum Price', MAX(price) AS 'Max Price'
 2: FROM    titles
 3: GO
 4:
 5: BEGIN TRANSACTION
 6: GO
 7:
 8: WHILE (SELECT AVG(price) FROM titles) < $30
 9: BEGIN
10:     UPDATE titles
11:         SET price = price * 2
12:     IF (SELECT MAX(price) FROM titles) > $50
13:         BREAK
14:     ELSE
15:         CONTINUE
16: END
17:
18: SELECT MIN(price) AS 'Minimum Price', MAX(price) AS 'Max Price'
19: FROM    titles
20: GO
21:
22: SELECT 'Prices are getting out of hand'
23: GO
24:
25: ROLLBACK TRANSACTION
26: GO
```

21

GOTO and RETURN

The last control-of-flow statement is the GOTO statement. You should be very careful when using this statement because overuse can make for difficult-to-read and slow-to-execute code. This statement will commonly be used in conjunction with the RETURN statement. The GOTO statement is used to tell SQL Server to jump to a specific label in your SQL code that has been designated in the following manner:

```
label_name:
```

It is important to note that the label does nothing in the code other than give SQL Server a place to jump to. The label is not executed nor are any of the statements between the GOTO and the label. The reason that you use the RETURN statement in conjunction with the GOTO statement is that if the GOTO is not executed, when the script gets to the label, all the code in the label will be executed as well. The RETURN statement is used to unconditionally terminate a batch or stored procedure. None of the statements after the RETURN are executed. The syntax of the GOTO and RETURN statements are as follows:

```
GOTO label_name
<sql_statements>
RETURN <return_code>
label_name:
<sql_statements>
```

Where the options are

Option	Description
label_name	This is an expression that simply tells SQL Server where it is to jump to.
<sql_statements>	This is either a single SQL statement or a group of SQL statements.
<return_code>	This is an integer code that can be used in conjunction with the RETURN statement. In a stored procedure, this code can be used to return information about the execution of the procedure.

Again, you should use this statement very carefully because it can make for poor code. Another thing you should do to ensure that your code is easily readable and understandable to others is to comment your code.

Comments

Commenting your code is one of the most important things you can do to ensure that you and any others who ever read your code can know what it does. You should place comments in the code that outline what it does, what parameters it takes in, and what output it produces. You should also make comments about when the code has been changed and why.

You can also use the comment characters to temporarily disable portions of the code you do not want to run. This is especially useful when you are testing. SQL Server supports two different script characters:

- /* ... */—This comment character is used to comment an entire block of script, containing several lines. The /* is used to open the comment, and the */ is used to close the comment. It is very important to note that you cannot use the word GO in a comment. If you do, the comment pair will be broken, and SQL Server will try to execute your words, causing an error.

- - -—This comment character is used to comment out a single line. This can be used at the beginning of the line or at the end of the line. When you have multiple lines of comments, you must place the - - character before each line.

The importance of comments cannot be stressed enough. The most important part of the comments is to document the purpose of your code and how it works. If you are not around at a later date, when the code needs to be changed, the comments become even more important.

Variables

Variables are an extremely important part of programming. A variable is an entity you create that can be assigned a value. Local variables are created and assigned values by the user and can only be seen by the user who created them. Global variables are created and assigned values by a user, but they can be seen by everyone on the system. When you define a variable, you must tell SQL Server what type of data that it is going to hold by assigning a datatype to it.

Creating Variables

To create a variable in SQL Server, you have to give it a name and assign it a datatype. After the variable is created, SQL Server will assign it a value of NULL and then wait for you to assign it a value. Variables are created using the DECLARE statement. When declaring a new variable, the name must have a single at sign (@) as the first character of the name. The syntax of the statement is

```
DECLARE @variable_name datatype
```

21

Where the options are

Option	Description
@variable_name	This is the name that you will want to refer to the variable during the life of the script.
datatype	This is the datatype, as outlined in Hour 7, "Creating Tables." You will be required to assign data of this type to the variable during the life of the script.

For example, to declare a variable called author_name that will hold character data of no more than 64 characters, you would use the following:

```
DECLARE @author_name VARCHAR(64)
```

Assigning a Value

Now that you have created the variable, you can assign a value to it. As we mentioned previously, SQL Server assigns it a value of NULL. There are two ways to assign a value to a variable. The preferred method to do this is to use the SET command. The other way is to use the SELECT statement to assign the value. The syntax of the SET command is as follows:

```
SET @variable_name = <value>
```

Where the options are

Option	Description
@variable_name	This is the name of the variable to which you want to assign a value.
<value>	This is the value that you want to assign to the variable.

To assign a value to the variable that we created earlier using the SET command, you would run the following:

```
SET @author_name = 'Shepker, Matthew'
```

You can also use the SELECT keyword to assign a value to the variable, the same way you would in the SET statement. All you have to do is substitute the word SELECT for SET, as follows:

```
SELECT @author_name = 'Shepker, Matthew'
```

You can then use the variable as you would in the place of constants.

Summary

In this section, we have gone over most of the syntax that you will need to know to program using SQL Server. What we did not go into was how to program. We have gone over batches and transactions and how they interact. Then we looked at SQL Server control-of-flow language and how it works. Next we looked at one of the most important portions of writing SQL Server scripts—comments. You should comment every piece of code and script that you write. Last, we went over variables and their use.

Q&A

Q Is it possible to have a transaction that spans several batches?

A Yes, it is possible to have a transaction that spans several batches.

Q Are comments really as important as they are made out to be here?

A To put this into perspective, look back over the history of computer programming. Right now, the world is clamoring over getting the Y2K bug fixed. For those of you who have missed out on the past few years, the Y2K bug is a problem with computers and software that recognizes only the last two digits of the year. When the year 2000 rolls around, these computer programs will think that the date is 1900, potentially causing a great deal of problems. One of the problems with going back and fixing these issues is that a great deal of this software is not commented and people used strange variable names for the dates. Stories are circulating about people finding variables called anything from date to the name of the original programmer's wife or dog. If the code had been properly documented through comments, this would have been an easier problem to fix.

Workshop

The quiz and the exercise are provided for your further understanding. The answers can be found in Appendix A, "Answers."

Quiz

1. What is a batch?
2. What keyword do you use to designate a batch?
3. What is a transaction?
4. If you want to cancel a transaction, what keyword do you issue?
5. What is control-of-flow language?

21

6. What control-of-flow statement would you use to create a looping structure?

7. What characters do you use to designate a one-line comment?

8. What is a variable?

9. How do you designate a variable?

Exercise

Write a SQL Script that creates a table called TestTable with a column called column1 with a datatype of integer. Create an infinite looping structure that inserts values into the table until there are 100 numbers in the table. Use the variable to hold the number that you are going to store in the table. When the value of the variable has reached 100, use the BREAK statement to exit the loop.

Hour 22

Indexes and Data Integrity

Now that you have seen how to create most of the objects you can have in a database, and the language you can use to access those objects, you should be aware of how indexes work and how they are implemented in the server. Indexes are a way to speed up data access to your tables. Not only do indexes speed up SELECT statements, but they can also speed up UPDATE and DELETE statements when they are created correctly. This is because, like SELECT statements, UPDATE and DELETE statements have to find the affected rows in the table before they can be modified. It should be noted, though, that the more indexes you have, the more overhead it will take to keep those indexes current when data is changed and it is possible to degrade your data modification performance when you add indexes.

The highlights of this hour include

- How Are Indexes Used?
- Types of Indexes
- Creating Indexes

* Data Integrity
* Triggers

How Are Indexes Used?

Indexes are used to help SQL Server find the data in the tables for which it is looking. The simplest way to look at it is to imagine that the data in your tables is stored in a set of books, like an encyclopedia. In order to find the entry on gooney birds, you would first go the G volume. When you have that volume, you would look in alphabetical order to find gooney birds. If the data in these books were stored in random order, you would have to look through every book to find the entry that you are interested in. Indexes are the same way. If you did not have the data in any kind of order, SQL Server would have a difficult time finding the data in the tables.

Types of Indexes

SQL Server supports two basic types of indexes. On top of these two types of indexes, you can add the functionality of having a unique index, which enforces that all values inserted into the index must remain unique. The two main types of indexes are clustered and nonclustered indexes.

Clustered Indexes

A *clustered* index is a special type of index that actually stores the data in the table in the same order it is sorted in the index. A clustered index is actually similar to a dictionary. That is, all the items in the dictionary are sorted in alphabetical order. Clustered indexes actually reorganize the data in the table, so you can only have clustered indexes on the table at once.

Clustered indexes are especially useful on tables where the data is searched by ranges of values. This is because all SQL Server has to do is find the first row in the range and then all rows following until the final value in the range is found and all other values are guaranteed to fall within that range. A good example of this would be an application that searches for a list of names that fall between the letters G and P, SQL Server will find the first name that begins with a G and then pull back all the records until it finds names that start with a P and then stops. This makes the query process very efficient.

You must take into account several considerations when you are considering creating a clustered index on a table:

- You should always define a clustered index on as few columns as possible. Any other indexes that are created on the table will be larger than normal because they will not only have the other indexed values, but also the clustered index key.

- Columns that contain a relatively few number of distinct values, such as the names of the countries in the world, and then a clustered index would be a good idea.

- If there are very few values that are going to be indexed, such as a column containing all 0s and 1s, a clustered index would not be a good idea.

- If a table is accessed and returns a range of values using the BETWEEN, <, >, >=, or <= operators, a clustered index should be used.

- If the values in a table are accessed in sequential order, a clustered index should be considered.

- If the table is frequently accessed to return a large amount of data, a clustered index should probably be used.

- Tables frequently sorted by a specific column; then that column would be a good candidate for a clustered index. This is because the data in the table has already been sorted for you.

- Applications that require extremely fast, single row lookup are excellent candidates for a clustered index.

- Tables that undergo a large amount of data modifications are not good candidates for clustered indexes. This is because SQL Server will have to maintain the order of the rows in the table.

Nonclustered Indexes

A *nonclustered* index in an index in which the order of the data in the index is not stored in the same order as the data in the table. This type of index is similar to an index in a textbook. The data in the table is stored in whatever order it occurs, and the index simply has a sorted key value and a pointer to the data, in this case a page number. SQL Server uses these types of indexes in the same way that you use the index of a book. When it is looking for a specific value, it simply finds the key value and then goes to the table and retrieves the data from the location that the index specifies. If the table contains a clustered index, the index actually points to the clustered index key. If there is no clustered index on the table, the index points to the Row Identifier, or RID.

One advantage to a nonclustered index is that you can create several of them on the same table. This way, if there are several different ways that a table is accessed, you can create different indexes on the table based on those access methods.

You should take into account a couple of considerations when you create nonclustered indexes:

- Columns containing a large amount of unique values, such as names or addresses; then a clustered index can be created on that table.

- As with clustered indexes, if the table contains very few unique values, such as 0s and 1s, no index should be created.

- Queries that do not return a large amount of data are good candidates for nonclustered indexes.

- Columns that are frequently referenced in the WHERE clause of a select statement and return exact matches are good candidates for nonclustered indexes.

- Applications that require a large number of joins to create their resultsets should be considered for highly indexed tables.

It is possible to create indexes on more than one column in a table. These types of indexes are called *composite indexes*. These indexes are useful when your users include multiple columns in the WHERE clause of a SELECT statement. For example, if your users commonly search for authors who live in a specific city and in a specific state, you might want to create an index on both of those columns.

Unique Indexes

You cannot create a unique index by itself. A unique index is created as a part of a clustered or nonclustered index. Unique indexes are used to ensure that the data contained in the indexed columns is unique. If you create an index that contains several columns, a unique index will ensure that the combination of all the values contained in the index are unique. An example of a good use of unique indexes is on a column that contains social security numbers. Because, theoretically, no two people can have the same social security number, this column would be a great candidate for a unique index. On the other hand, a combination of first name and last name would not be a good candidate for a unique index because you would never be able to have two people with the same name in the table. When you create a UNIQUE or PRIMARY KEY constraint on a table, SQL Server will automatically create a unique index on the table.

Creating Indexes

Now that you have a good idea of the types of indexes you can create on a table, it is time to look at how to actually create indexes. As with most other objects that can be created in the database, there are two different ways to create indexes. The first is to use SQL Server Enterprise Manager. The following will walk you through creating indexes using SQL Enterprise Manager:

1. Open SQL Server Enterprise Manager and connect to the server containing the database that has the tables on which you want to create indexes. For the purposes of this tutorial, we will use the pubs database on the server that you have been using all along.

2. Click on the plus sign next to the name of the server. Then click in the plus sign next to the database folder. This opens a list of all the databases on the server.

3. Click on the plus sign next to the tables folder. This opens a list of all the tables contained in the database that you chose, as seen in Figure 22.1. Click on the name of the table on which you want to create an index.

FIGURE 22.1

A list of all the tables contained in the database.

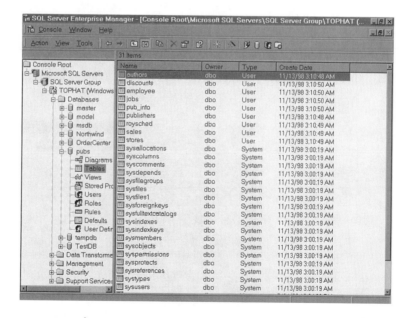

4. Choose the table that you want to create an index on and then select Wizards from the Tools menu. This opens the Select Wizard dialog, as seen in Figure 22.2.

FIGURE 22.2

The Select Wizard dialog.

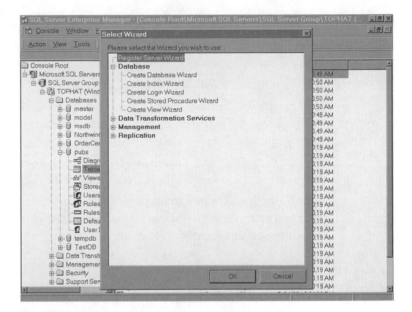

5. Click on the plus sign next to the Database option and then click on the Create Index Wizard. This opens an introductory screen, as seen in Figure 22.3.

FIGURE 22.3

The Create Index Wizard introductory screen.

6. The next screen, as shown in Figure 22.4, allows you to select the name of the database and the name of the table on which you want to create the index. If you did not select the database and table as outlined in step 3, you can select it now.

FIGURE 22.4

The Select Database and Table dialog.

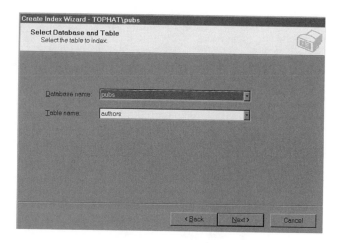

7. The next screen is the Current Index Information dialog, as seen in Figure 22.5. If there are any indexes already created on the table, you will see these in this dialog.

FIGURE 22.5

The Current Index Information dialog.

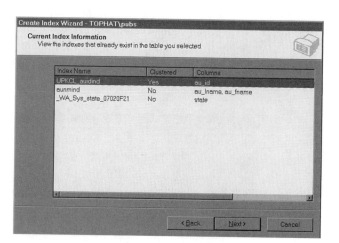

8. The next screen is the Select Columns dialog, as seen in Figure 22.6. From this screen, you will be able to select any of the columns in the table that can be indexed. For the purposes of this tutorial, select the zip column.

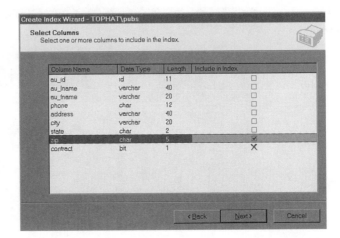

9. The next screen, the Specify Index Options, as seen in Figure 22.7, allows you to indicate any specific options for this index. You can specify that this index is a clustered index if one does not exist on the table already and you can also make this a unique index if you want. The section below these options allows you to specify a Fill Factor for the index. The Fill Factor is the percentage that SQL Server will fill the index pages to. The best option you have is to allow SQL Server to fill the index page to the optimal level.

10. The next screen, the Completing the Create Index Wizard dialog, as seen in Figure 22.8, outlines the columns you are adding to the index and allows you to specify a name for the index.

FIGURE 22.8

The Completing the Create Index Wizard dialog.

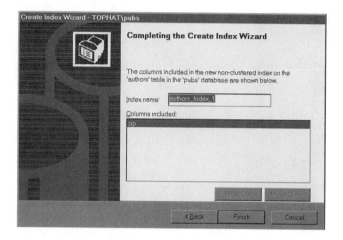

11. When you have finished filling out this information, click on the Finish button and SQL Server will create the index for you, and when it has completed, SQL Server will pop up a message box telling you that the index has been created.

The other option you have in creating a new index on a table is to use SQL Query Analyzer with the CREATE INDEX command. The syntax of this command is as follows:

```
CREATE [UNIQUE] [CLUSTERED ¦ NONCLUSTERED]
INDEX <index_name> ON <table> (<column> [,...n])
[WITH
    [PAD_INDEX]
    [[,] FILLFACTOR = <fillfactor>]
    [[,] IGNORE_DUP_KEY]
    [[,] DROP_EXISTING]
    [[,] STATISTICS_NORECOMPUTE]]
[ON <filegroup>]
```

Option	Description
UNIQUE	This keyword is used to specify that the index you are creating is to be a UNIQUE index. The keyword must be used in conjunction with one of the other index creation keywords.

continues

Option	Description
CLUSTERED	This keyword is used to specify that the index you are creating is to be a clustered index. This keyword cannot be used in conjunction with the nonclustered keyword. You can only create one clustered index on any table.
NONCLUSTERED	This keyword is used to specify that the index that you are creating is to be a nonclustered index. This keyword cannot be used in conjunction with the clustered keyword. You can have as many as 249 nonclustered indexes per table.
<index_name>	This is the name that you want to call the index. The index name must comply to the naming standards outlined in earlier hours.
<table>	This is the name of the table on which you are going to create the index.
<column>	This is the name of the column that is going to be included in the index. The sum of the total lengths of the columns in a composite index can be no longer than 900 bytes.
,...n	This indicates that you can add multiple columns in an index key.
PAD_INDEX	This option is used to tell SQL Server that you want to leave space on each page of the index. This feature is only useful when you specify a fill factor. By default, SQL Server will allow enough room on each page for there to be one row to be inserted.
FILLFACTOR	This option tells SQL Server what percentage to leave the leaf pages in the index free during the initial creation of the index. This option is useful when you are creating an index on a table that is frequently inserted into. This can be useful because when the pages are full, SQL Server must split the index page to make space for the new index row. You must specify a value from 1 to 100 for this percentage. You should not specify a percentage of 100 unless there are no INSERTs or UPDATEs made against the table.

Option	Description
IGNORE_DUP_KEY	This option is used to control what happens when an insert is being made into UNIQUE index. If this option is specified and a duplicate row is inserted into the table, SQL Server will issue a warning and then ignore the duplicate row. If this option was not specified, SQL Server will issue a warning and then ROLLBACK the insert statement.
DROP_EXISTING	This option allows you to force SQL Server to drop and rebuild the index you have named in the statement. Note that any NONCLUSTERED indexes created on a table, which has a CLUSTERED index on it that is being rebuilt, will also cause the NONCLUSTERED indexes to be rebuilt as well.
STATISTICS_NORECOMPUTE	This option tells SQL Server that it should not automatically recompute the usage statistics on the index. If you specify this option, you must run the UPDATE STATISTICS command on the table in order to maintain up-to-date statistics on the index.
<filegoup>	This option tells SQL Server to build the index on a specific filegroup.

A lot of options are available to you in creating an index via a script; you will use only a couple of these in normal usage. The code in Listing 22.1 will create a nonclustered index on the state column of the authors table.

LISTING 22.1   Creating an Index

```
CREATE INDEX nci_state ON authors(state)
```

Data Integrity

Data integrity refers to the accuracy and reliability of the data contained in the database. Data integrity is extremely important in all user environments, but becomes extremely important in multiuser environments where data is shared. In every relational database management system, data integrity is the most important concern.

Data integrity is the process of ensuring that the data in the database is of the highest quality. Several different types of data integrity exist. For example, if you have a book in the titles table with a title_id of 56734, you should not be able to enter another title into that table with an id of 56734. Another example of data integrity is the ability to force SQL Server to only allow a specific value into a column while disallowing others. Another type of data integrity is the ability to tell SQL Server that, if a value does not exist in a column in one table, that same value cannot exist in another table.

These three examples of data integrity fall into one of four different definitions of data integrity:

- Entity Integrity—Entity integrity is the process of forcing SQL Server to maintain unique values in specific columns of a table. You can enforce entity integrity through the use of PRIMARY KEY constraints and UNIQUE constraints.

- Domain Integrity—Domain integrity is the process of enforcing the validity of the values in a column. You can do this by restricting the type of data that can be entered into a table using datatypes, the actual format of the data in the table through the use of CHECK constraints, and by allowing only a certain number of values in a column through the use of FOREIGN KEY constraints, DEFAULT values, CHECK constraints, and NOT NULL constraints.

- Referential Integrity—Referential integrity is the process of maintaining relationships between tables. Referential integrity is maintained through the use of FOREIGN KEY constraints that reference PRIMARY KEY constraints. This relationship keeps SQL Server from adding records to a related table that do not have records in the primary tables, changing values in either table that would result in orphaned records, or from deleting records from either table that will leave orphaned records in the table.

- User Defined Integrity—User defined integrity is enforced through the use of triggers and stored procedures. These allow you to create business rules to validate values that do not fall in any of these other ranges.

Triggers

Last but not least, you need to learn about triggers. Triggers are similar to stored procedures in the fact that they are a grouping of SQL statements. The major difference is how triggers are executed. Triggers are executed when a row is inserted, updated, or deleted from a table, depending on how the trigger was created. Triggers are a powerful way to enforce business rules when data is modified. A single table can have up to three different triggers on it. You can have a trigger that fires when an UPDATE occurs, one that fires

22

when an INSERT occurs, and one that fires when a DELETE occurs. Triggers can be a way that the SQL Server automates business processes. For example, when an author has sold enough books to cover the advance that the publishing company paid, a trigger could be used to automatically begin calculating the royalty payments. Triggers fire after the record has been successfully modified in the table. If the modification fails because of a syntax error or constraint violation, the trigger is not fired.

You need to be aware of one point of caution when dealing with triggers. Although triggers can be very powerful, they can also be very damaging to the performance of your server. Be very careful that you do not try to put too much functionality into your triggers because it will slow down response and can really frustrate your users.

Summary

In this hour, we have looked at indexes and have discussed what they can do for you. It is important to remember to add indexes to your tables when you create databases. When you do create indexes, you must check to see how your users are going to interact with the tables.

Q&A

Q Can I have too many indexes?

A Although indexes are very important to have, it is very possible for you to have too many indexes. This is because SQL Server has to maintain all the indexes that you have, and this does cause some overhead on the server. The more indexes that you have, the more overhead you will incur on the server. The best option that you have is to determine the way that your tables are accessed and then index those columns.

Q Is it better to enforce data integrity through the use of triggers or other constraints?

A If at all possible, you should attempt to enforce data integrity on your tables through the use of constraints. This is because there is very little server overhead incurred when using constraints as opposed to triggers.

Workshop

The quiz and the exercise are provided for your further understanding. The answers can be found in Appendix A, "Answers."

Quiz

1. What are indexes?

2. What is a clustered index?

3. What is a nonclustered index?

4. How many clustered indexes can you have on one table?

5. What type of data integrity are you using if you are ensuring that any data entered into one table has a matching record in another table?

6. What is entity integrity?

7. What are triggers used for?

Exercise

Create a composite nonclustered index on the city and state columns in the authors table.

Hour **23**

Optimization and Tuning

No matter how well designed your databases and applications are, there will always be room to improve on the performance. There are several ways to do this, anywhere from increasing the physical performance of the server, to changing server level options, to changing the physical database. SQL Server provides several ways for you to do this. In SQL Server 7.0, many of the server level options are automatically managed for you. This makes the life of the DBA much easier.

The highlights of this hour include

- Advances in SQL Server Tuning
- Why Should You Tune Your Server?
- Establishing a Baseline
- SQL Server Performance Monitor
- Using the SQL Server Profiler
- Using the Index Tuning Wizard

Advances in SQL Server Tuning

As I mentioned earlier, Microsoft has made many advances in tuning. If you have ever worked with previous versions of SQL Server, or any other RDBMS, performance tuning and optimization, also known as PTO or PT&O, can be a very complicated process with literally hundreds of different variables to investigate. For example, in previous versions of SQL Server, you had to tell it exactly how much memory it was going to use. It was not smart enough to figure out that if the server had 4GB of memory, it could use more than 32MB. In SQL Server 7.0, it will automatically allocate and deallocate memory as needed. For example, if you start Microsoft Word on the same computer that SQL Server is running on, it will deallocate enough memory for Word to use.

So what do these advances mean for you? Overall it is going to mean less work. SQL Server is going to automatically configure nearly all the server configuration options. Even though you can modify all these options, you should really leave them at the default values that allow SQL Server to automatically tune based on runtime server conditions. The following lists several options that you might want to set, depending on your needs:

- SQL Server Memory—Sometimes, it is necessary for you to configure maximum and minimum memory for use by SQL Server.
- I/O Subsystem—Frequently when you set up a SQL Server, you will install it on a very powerful and sophisticated server. These types of servers usually configure the hard drives in a special configuration called RAID. This configuration enables the server to look at all the hard drives in the computer as one single hard drive and also provides redundancy in the fact that one hard drive can be lost without losing all the data. This speeds up reads to the I/O subsystems. When your server is configured in this way, you might want to change some SQL Server options to enable it to make more reads that the computer can issue against a file.
- Windows NT Options—When SQL Server is the only application running on a Windows NT Server, several options can be changed that will allow SQL Server to run faster and better on the server. These options include setting up the server to maximize network throughput and to run server tasks more quickly.

Why Should You Tune Your Server?

Whether you are a manager, a database administrator, or a database user, there is a universal reason for you to want to tune your SQL Server and that is performance. When you have properly tuned the resources on the server, you will notice performance increases. Performance increases will become apparent in faster return on queries, data modifications, and overall, happier users. Users will be the first people to let you know if a server isn't performing up to their expectations.

One of the biggest things that you can do is to start considering performance issues while the application is being developed, not when the system is being implemented. You will find out that many developers and implementers do not consider performance issues until problems arise. These problems can appear anywhere from slow user response times to potential corruption in the database, and they are extremely difficult to troubleshoot and fix. The good thing about it from a user standpoint is that, usually, performance can only go up, and any increase that you get will seem significant.

23

Establishing a Baseline

As with anything else, you have to start someplace. When dealing with performance tuning and optimization, this is especially important. Before you start tuning, you have to determine which areas are working well and which ones you will need to focus on. This is done by determining a baseline. You will use the baseline to determine whether your SQL Server is performing optimally. When generating a baseline, you will monitor statistics on your server and its performance over time and then compare them. After you have determined what your server performance baseline is, you will then compare the current performance with that baseline. If you begin to see major differences, those areas should be investigated. To establish a baseline, you should routinely monitor the following:

- Server performance
- User activity
- SQL Server error log and Windows NT Event log

To have an effective baseline, you should monitor your server over a period of time and while performing a variety of tasks. While creating a baseline, the server performance should meet your users' needs, and most importantly, their expectations. You should make sure to note peak and off-peak hours of operation, query response times, and database dumps and loads. After you have determined a baseline, you will then want to compare it to information that you gather further down the road. If you begin to see large variances in either direction, you should investigate them.

Creating a baseline involves using Performance Monitor to log server performance, as outlined later in this hour. The type of information that you should monitor includes:

- Processor
- Memory
- Physical Disk

Monitoring Server Performance

As a DBA, you should create a schedule in which you monitor your SQL Server frequently to determine whether it is performing the way that you and your users expect. SQL Server provides several graphical utilities and some text-based ways to monitor your server. Table 23.1 lists the various utilities and ways to monitor your server.

TABLE 23.1 Ways to Monitor Your Server

Utility	Description
SQL Server Performance Monitor	This utility enables you to monitor server performance using predefined objects and counters. It enables you to monitor both SQL Server and Windows NT at the same time. You can also set thresholds that will generate alerts to notify operators and fire off applications when the threshold is reached. It will log information to a data file for later analysis or in a graphical fashion on the screen.
Current Activity window	This utility provides a graphical representation of the users who are logged in, blocking processes and commands that are running. You also have the ability to send messages to users and to stop processes.
SQL Server Profiler Server	This is a new and powerful tool added to SQL 7.0. This utility provides a way to profile both server resources and database activity. This information can be fed into a table in a SQL Server database or into a log file for analysis by external applications.
sp_monitor	This system stored procedure displays statistics about how busy SQL Server has been since the last time it was started. This provides the same sort of information that is available to you when you run SQL Server Performance Monitor.
sp_spaceused	This system stored procedure will provide an estimate of how much physical space a table or database is taking up on disk. It is important to realize that this number is not always accurate.
sp_who	The sp_who system stored procedure is used to check the current user and status information. This provides the same information that is available to you when viewing the Current Activity window in SQL Enterprise Manager.
sp_lock	The sp_lock system stored procedure is used to view the current lock and block information. This provides the same information that is available to you when viewing lock activity in the Current Activity window in SQL Enterprise Manager.
DBCC commands	The Database Consistency Checker, or DBCC, is a set of commands that provides the ability to check performance statistics, check table and database consistency, and complete a wide number of general housecleaning functions.

One of the main tools that you will use to monitor your server is SQL Server Performance Monitor.

SQL Server Performance Monitor

SQL Server Performance Monitor is an extension of the Windows NT Performance Monitor that can be used to track up-to-the-minute information and statistics about SQL Server. You can use this data to provide feedback on the performance of your server and view it as a graph or store it for future use.

23

Monitoring Counters

Performance Monitor gathers information from SQL Server using counters. Counters are individual items that are monitored. For ease of use, counters are grouped together in objects. Objects are simply groups of similar counters.

When SQL Server Performance Monitor starts, it monitors five default counters, which are outlined in the following. You can configure SQL Server Performance Monitor to track other counters aside from the default.

- Cache Hit Ratio—The percentage of data that was found in data cache instead of having to be read from disk. When you see low values for this counter, in the range of 90 percent, it usually means that you need to add more memory to the server. If you start to monitor this value right after SQL Server starts, it will be very low because data is just being read from the disk.

- I/O - Transaction/sec—The number of transactions that are completed each second. This gives you a ballpark figure on how much data your users are sending to the server.

- I/O - Page Reads/sec—The number of physical disk reads per second. This tells you how frequently SQL Server has to go the disk to read information. If you see a large amount of disk reads in conjunction with a low cache hit ratio, it is usually a sign that you need to add more memory to the server.

- I/O - Single Page Writes/sec—The number of single page writes performed per second. This is the number of times that SQL Server takes a page of data out of memory and writes it to the hard disk.

- User Connections—The number of users who are currently connected to the SQL Server at any point in time. This value can be useful when you are trying to determine the capacity of the server. If the server is overworked while you are at half your expected user count, you know your server will not work properly when you have all your users logged in.

Sixteen different objects, outlined in Table 23.2, can be used to track SQL Server statistics. Each object can contain at least one counter.

TABLE 23.2 SQL Server Counters

Object Name	Description
SQL Server: Access Methods	Provides information about searches and allocations of database objects.
SQL Server: Backup Device	Provides information about the status of backup devices.
SQL Server: Buffer Manager	Provides information about the usage of memory buffers by SQL Server, including the amount of free memory.
SQL Server: Cache Manager	Provides information about the procedure cache.
SQL Server: Databases	Provides information about user databases, including the size of the transaction log.
SQL Server: General Statistics	Provides server-wide statistics, such as the number of users logged into the server.
SQL Server: Latches	Provides information about latches on internal resources that are being used by SQL Server.
SQL Server: Locks	Provides information about locks that are being requested by SQL Server, including timeouts and deadlocks.
SQL Server: Memory Manager	Provides information about SQL Server memory usage.
SQL Server: Replication Agents	Provides information about any currently running replication agents.
SQL Server: Replication Dist.	Provides information on the number of transactions that are read from the distribution database and sent to the subscriber databases.
SQL Server: Replication Logreader	Provides information on the number of transactions that are read from the published databases and sent to the distribution database.
SQL Server: Replication Merge	Provides information about SQL Server Merge Replication.
SQL Server: Replication Snapshot	Provides information about SQL Server Snapshot Replication.
SQL Server: SQL Server Statistics	Provides information about SQL Queries that have been sent to the server.
SQL Server: User Settable	Provides the capability to perform custom monitoring. Each counter can be a query or stored procedure that returns a value to Performance Monitor.

Running SQL Server Performance Monitor

If you have installed SQL Server 7.0 on a Windows NT computer, you will have access to SQL Server Performance Monitor. The following will walk you through running SQL Server Performance Monitor:

1. Click the Start button, go to Programs, Microsoft SQL Server 7.0, and click on SQL Server Performance Monitor. This will open the SQL Server Performance Monitor, as seen in Figure 23.1.

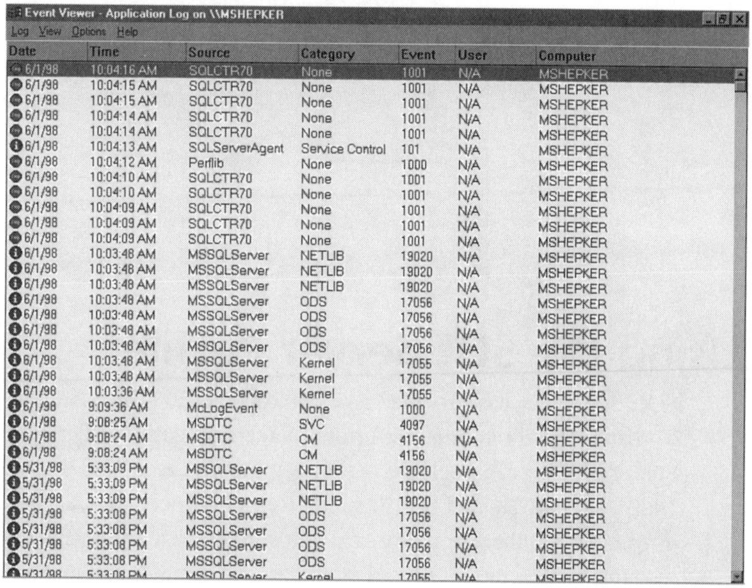

23

FIGURE 23.1

The SQL Server Performance Monitor.

2. As I mentioned before, this automatically begins monitoring several default counters. If you want to add additional counters, click the plus sign (+) on the toolbar. This will open the Add Counters dialog, as seen in Figure 23.2.

3. From the Object drop-down box, select the base object that you want to monitor. For these purposes, select SQL Server: Locks. You will use information contained in this counter when you are troubleshooting poorly written queries.

4. From the Counters box, select Users Blocked. This counter lets you know whenever one user is blocking another. After you have selected the counter, click OK to close the window and begin monitoring that counter.

5. When you are monitoring a large number of counters, it can be difficult to determine which line belongs to which counter. To assist you in determining this, you can highlight the counter that you want to see and press CTRL+H. This turns the line associated with that counter white, allowing you to choose it.

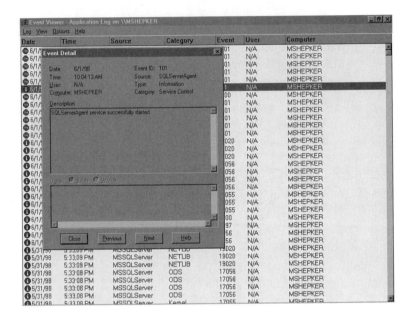

FIGURE 23.2

The Add Counter dialog.

Using the SQL Server Profiler

SQL Server 7.0 has provided a new and powerful utility that enables a DBA to collect data and monitor system performance and user activity. The types of events that SQL Server Profiler can track are login attempts; connects and disconnects; Transact-SQL INSERTs, UPDATEs, and DELETEs; and Remote Procedure Call batch status. After collecting information in the form of traces, you can then use the traces to analyze and fix server resource issues, monitor login attempts, and correct locking and blocking issues. A trace is simply a file in which you capture server activity and events for later use.

What to Trace

SQL Server Profiler can collect specific data about server activity. Although you are new to SQL Server, you will probably be using SQL Server Profiler in conjunction with the Index Tuning Wizard, which is discussed in the section called "Using the Index Tuning Wizard." For the Index Tuning Wizard to work, you must have a workload created. A workload is a file that contains either a script or an SQL Server Profiler Trace that contains a group of SQL statements or Remote Procedure Calls. Ideally, this workload would mimic the actions that your users are making against the database. The following walks you through creating a workload using SQL Server Profiler:

1. Start SQL Enterprise Manager and connect to the server on which you will be running a trace. From the Tools menu, choose SQL Server Profiler. The SQL Server Profiler application, shown in Figure 23.3, will open.

FIGURE 23.3

The SQL Server Profiler application enables a DBA to collect data and monitor system performance and user activity.

23

2. If you want to start a predefined trace, select File, Open, and select Trace Definition.

3. To create a new trace, click the New Trace button on the toolbar, or click the File menu and then choose New, Trace. The Trace Properties dialog box, shown in Figure 23.4, opens.

FIGURE 23.4

In the General dialog box, you define what the trace will capture.

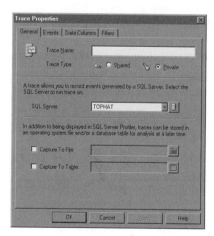

4. In the Name box, type the name that you will use to identify the trace.

5. In the Type area, choose either a Private trace or a Shared trace. If the trace is going to be used by people other than the user who created it, choose Shared. The default is a Private trace.

6. The General tab also enables you to choose where you want the captured data to go. If you want to record the data for later analysis, choose to capture the file either to a table or to a file. The default option is to simply record events to the screen.

7. On the Events tab, shown in Figure 23.5, you can specify which SQL Server events you want to trace. In this dialog, you can choose specific options that you want to record. For the sake of this exercise, choose SQL Operators and click the Add button. This will track all SQL Statements such as INSERTs, UPDATEs, SELECTs, and DELETEs that are made against your database.

FIGURE 23.5

On the Events tab, you can choose events to monitor.

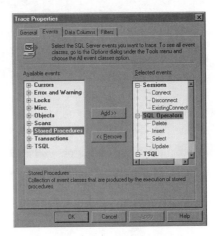

8. On the Data Columns tab, shown in Figure 23.6, you can select the data you want to capture for each traced event. This includes information about the user and any server objects that are accessed. In most cases, you will not need to change anything in this tab.

FIGURE 23.6

On the Data Columns tab, you can select which data you can collect.

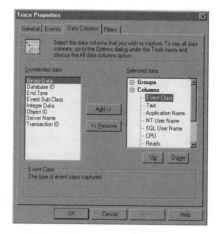

23

9. On the Filters tab, shown in Figure 23.7, you can choose specific criteria to include or exclude. For example, by default, any events that are generated by SQL Server Profiler are ignored. For these purposes, you will leave this with its default settings.

FIGURE 23.7

On the Filters tab, you can choose criteria for determining which events to capture.

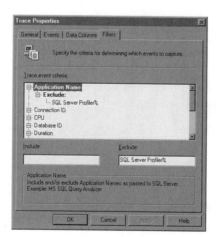

10. After you have set the options, click the OK button and the trace will automatically start. If you are tracing to the screen, you will begin to see information.

Using the Index Tuning Wizard

The Index Tuning Wizard is a tool new to SQL Server 7.0 that enables administrators to create and modify indexes without knowledge of the structure of the database, hardware platforms and components, or how end-user applications interact with the database. The wizard analyzes data that is collected with the SQL Server Profiler and then makes recommendations about the effectiveness of the indexes that are on the system and any new ones that might need to be created. These recommendations are in the form of a script that can be run to drop and re-create indexes on the system, as shown in the following steps:

1. From SQL Enterprise Manager, click the Tools drop-down box and select Wizards. This opens the Select Wizard dialog box, as seen in Figure 23.8. Click the plus sign next to Management and select Index Tuning Wizard; then click the OK button.

FIGURE 23.8

The Select Wizard dialog.

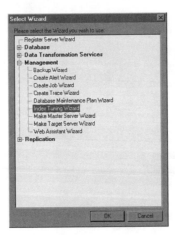

2. The first screen is a summary of what is going to be done. Click the Next button.

3. In the Select Server and Database dialog, as seen in Figure 23.9, choose the name of the SQL Server and the name of the database that you will be analyzing and click the Next button.

FIGURE 23.9

The Select Server and
Database dialog.

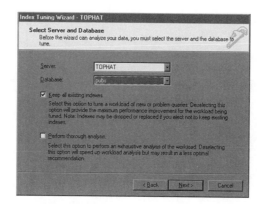

23

4. From the Identify Workload dialog, as seen in Figure 23.10, choose I Have a Saved Workload File if you have already created one using SQL Profiler. If you have not, choose the I Will Create a Workload File On My Own option. This opens SQL Profiler for you to create a workload file. For these purposes, I will assume that you already have a workload file.

FIGURE 23.10

The Identify Workload
dialog.

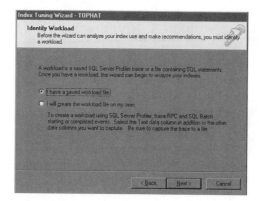

5. From the Specify Workload screen, as seen in Figure 23.11, select either the file or the SQL Server table that contains the trace information and click the Next button.

FIGURE 23.11

The Specify Workload dialog.

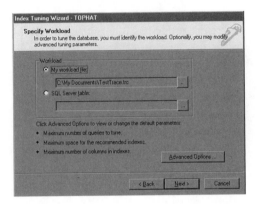

6. In the Select Tables to Tune dialog, as seen in Figure 23.12, SQL Server will automatically choose all the tables in the database for tuning. If you want to exclude any tables, you do so here.

FIGURE 23.12

The Select Tables to Tune dialog.

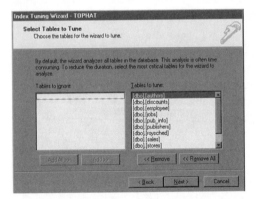

7. When you click the Next button, the Index Tuning Wizard begins to analyze the data you collected and specifies indexes based on that. When it has completed analyzing, it will open the Index Recommendations dialog box, as seen in Figure 23.13, specifying which indexes need changed or added. Examine this information and click Next.

23

FIGURE 23.13

The Index Tuning Wizard analyzing data.

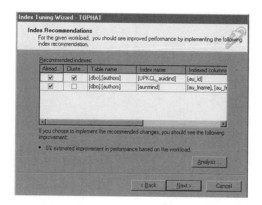

8. The next dialog enables you to choose either to save the changes as a script file that enables you to apply the changes when you want, or allow SQL Server to make the changes for you.

Summary

In this hour, I have covered a few of the things that you would do to monitor and optimize your server. Performance Tuning and Optimization is a very complex subject. In this hour, you have barely scratched the surface. If you would like to read more information on Performance Tuning and Optimization, you should look at *Using SQL Server 7.0* or *SQL Server 7.0 Unleashed.*

Q&A

Q Should I attempt to configure the memory, locks, and user count on the server, or should I let SQL Server handle it?

A Under most circumstances, you should let SQL Server dynamically configure most of the resources on SQL Server. At certain times you will need to configure the resource allocations, but these are few and far between.

Q My SQL Server has been running well for several months now, and in the past couple of days, my users have started to complain about response times. What should I look at first?

A The first thing that you should investigate is the overall performance of the computer itself. The best tool for this is SQL Server Performance Monitor. Using this, you will be able to determine some issues, such as user count, processor usage, and memory usage.

Workshop

The quiz and the exercise are provided for your further understanding. The answers can be found in Appendix A, "Answers."

Quiz

1. Why should you monitor and tune your SQL Server?

2. What is a baseline used for?

3. What is SQL Server Performance Monitor used for?

4. What is a counter?

5. What is SQL Server Profiler used for?

6. What is a workload?

7. What is this Index Tuning Wizard used for?

Exercise

Create a workload file using SQL Server Profiler monitoring the pubs database while you run select statements against different tables. When you have a trace created, use the Index Tuning Wizard to determine which, if any, new indexes might be needed on the tables.

HOUR 24

Troubleshooting

Sometime during your life as an SQL Server DBA, one of your worst nightmares is going to happen—one of your user databases is going to crash. It is not a question of if, it is a question of when. This can be a very trying time for you. Your users are going to be asking when is it going to be up, the management is going to be asking what happened and who can they blame, and you are going to be asking yourself what you should do now. In this hour, I will go over some of the basic troubleshooting steps and tools that you have at your disposal. Troubleshooting can be a very complicated task, and, unfortunately, the only thing that can make you an expert is to actually do it.

The highlights of this hour include

- "It's All Down!"
- The Troubleshooting Process
- SQL Server Information Sources
- SQL Server Error Messages
- Dealing with Corrupt Databases

- The Database Consistency Checker
- Using Trace Flags
- Other Sources of Information

"It's All Down!"

For many SQL Server DBAs, the first report of a problem comes from the user. It is usually a knock on your door followed with "The server is down", or "Nothing works." This is usually followed by a momentary panic on your part wondering what went wrong and how many hours of sleep you are going to lose trying to get it fixed. Like I mentioned earlier, this can be an extremely trying time. You really do not have any idea, at this point, what is going on. That is why the troubleshooting process is so important. Although fixing an SQL Server can be very difficult, the steps to gathering information and finding what went wrong is really not that difficult.

The Troubleshooting Process

Very few steps to the troubleshooting process exist, and these steps can be used on any server, not just SQL Server. These are very methodical steps that involve gathering information about the problem, using that data to figure out what went wrong, attempting a fix, and then monitoring to ensure that what you tried actually fixed the problem.

Documentation

Believe it or not, the first step in troubleshooting is one that you should be performing long before you have a problem. This is documentation. You should keep track of everything that you ever do to the server. One of the ways that you can accomplish this is to keep a notebook next to every server that you have. When you make a change, no matter how inconsequential it might seem, write it down in your book. This can be anything from creating new user logins, to changing permissions, to applying the latest service pack. You can use the information contained in this notebook when an error occurs to track down what changes have been made before problems started occurring.

You should also be very careful in documenting everything that you do during the troubleshooting process for two major reasons. The first is the ability to return to a specific point. For example, when troubleshooting a specific problem, you attempt a fix, and it does not help. Although this seems minor, it is possible that your attempted fix could leave the server in an unknown state. You can use the information about what you tried to get back to where you started. The second reason is the ability to reproduce a specific fix. If you manage to get a certain problem fixed, and you have documented the steps you took to get the problem fixed, it is very simple to just look up the solution if the problem ever occurs again.

Find the Facts

Like almost every other type of server problem, the majority of time the first report of a problem has occurred comes from the user. This is both a good and bad thing. The best part of this is that you will find out about almost every error as soon as it occurs. The bad part of this is, for the most part, errors tend to be reported inaccurately and be overexaggerated. It does not mean that you should disregard everything a user tells you; rather, you should take what he says with a grain of salt.

For example, take Bob in accounting. Bob is the type of person who should stick to doing all his accounting using a ledger book and slide rule. We all know users like Bob. One afternoon, Bob comes into your office and tells you that the accounting server is down and no one can do anything. An error message said something about violating something, but he thought it was best to clear the error and come get you.

After you have calmed your heart and gotten past the surge of adrenaline, it is time to start examining what you know. From what Bob told you, you know that something went wrong for him, and he is logged into the accounting server. Now what? It is time to put on your investigator's hat and go to work. The first thing you should do is go to the accounting department and see, firsthand, what is going on. In this case, when you get to the accounting department, you discover that everyone else is working just fine. When you go over to Bob's workstation, you notice that he is entering new vendors into the system, and you ask him to redo exactly what he was going before he came to get you. He picks up a vendor slip and types in all the relevant information. When he clicks the OK button, an error pops onto his screen. The error reads `Violation of PRIMARY KEY Constraints 'PK_Vendor': Attempt to insert duplicate key into object 'Vendors'`. Aha! You have managed to find the error for yourself. This error is a rather simple one to fix, but at least you know what it is.

Now, what happens if the user cannot reproduce the error while you are standing there? You should council your users that, in the event of an error, they should write down the entire text of the message, including all numbers associated with the error, and then report it to you.

Identify the Problem

Now that you know what error messages the users are getting, it is time to find out what the underlying issue is. In Bob's case, he is simply trying to enter the same vendor into the system multiple times. Other times, this can be a very difficult problem. The reason behind this is that developers do not always return the exact error message that was generated by the server to the users. Instead, they return their own error messages and numbers. By doing this, they might not be telling the user everything that SQL Server is.

Two basic ways exist to determine the exact error that the user is getting. The first is to start the application the user is using and attempt to recreate the problem. Although this might not tell you exactly what the problem is, it can help you find out where it is. Instead of using the application the user is using, you can use SQL Query Analyzer to perform the same operations against the database. This option will help you determine the exact error message. The second option you have in determining the problem is to investigate the SQL Server error log and Windows NT Event Viewer. Most error messages that require DBA intervention will be written to the error log.

Attempt a Fix

After you have determined the exact error that your users are getting, it is time to try to get it fixed. In most cases, the solution to simple problems can be found in the SQL Server Books Online or in Microsoft TechNet. In the event you cannot find the solution in either of these locations, the best thing you can do is to call your primary support provider or Microsoft's technical support. Especially when dealing with Microsoft, they will usually have solutions for almost any problem you can come up against.

SQL Server Information Sources

Several resources can be used when looking for information about SQL Server and any errors that have occurred. When troubleshooting any SQL Server error, you should consult all of these to see what information you can get.

SQL Server Error Log

The error log is where SQL Server writes startup information, error messages, and informational messages that occur during everyday operation. This file is a text file that can be viewed with a text editor or from within SQL Enterprise Manager. The location of the file is determined in the registry, and the default path for the error log is C:\MSSQL7\LOGS\ERRORLOG. SQL Server creates a new error log every time it is restarted. The previous six error logs are saved with extensions numbering .1 through .6.

When you are troubleshooting SQL Server, you will need to view the error log. The easiest way to do this is within SQL Enterprise Manager. The following will walk you through viewing the SQL Server error log from within SQL Enterprise Manager:

1. Start SQL Enterprise Manager and connect to the server on which you will be viewing the error log.

2. Click the plus sign next to the name of the server to expand the view.

3. Click on the plus sign next to the Error Logs entry. This will expand the entry to list the current error log entry, as well as the previous six entries.

4. You can choose which error log to view by clicking on its name in the list. When you choose one, the contents of the log are displayed in the panel on the right side, as seen in Figure 24.1.

FIGURE 24.1

After choosing an error log, the contents of the log are displayed in the panel on the right side.

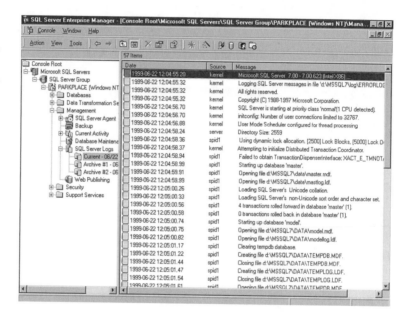

5. If the text of the error message is too long to be displayed in the window, you can double-click the message to pop up a box containing the full text of the message, as seen in Figure 24.2.

FIGURE 24.2

You can pop up a box displaying the full text of the error message by double-clicking on it.

Windows NT Event Log

Another valuable source of information about SQL Server is the Windows NT Application log. Not only will there be information about SQL Server, but it will also contain information about Windows NT Server and any other application that is running on the server. This can be especially useful if there is an outside event or series of events that is affecting SQL Server. The following will walk you through viewing the Windows NT Application log:

1. Click the Start menu, go to Programs; then go to Administrative Tools (Common), and choose Event Viewer. This opens the Windows NT Event viewer, as seen in Figure 24.3.

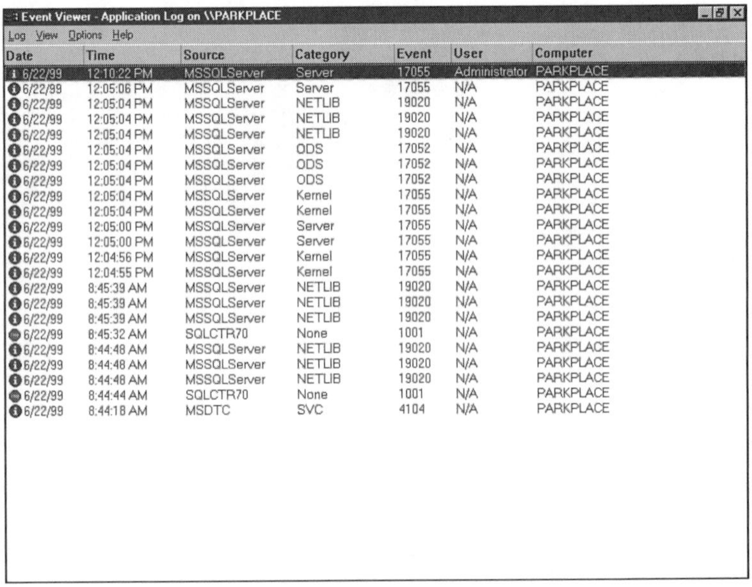

Date	Time	Source	Category	Event	User	Computer
6/22/99	12:10:22 PM	MSSQLServer	Server	17055	Administrator	PARKPLACE
6/22/99	12:05:06 PM	MSSQLServer	Server	17055	N/A	PARKPLACE
6/22/99	12:05:04 PM	MSSQLServer	NETLIB	19020	N/A	PARKPLACE
6/22/99	12:05:04 PM	MSSQLServer	NETLIB	19020	N/A	PARKPLACE
6/22/99	12:05:04 PM	MSSQLServer	NETLIB	19020	N/A	PARKPLACE
6/22/99	12:05:04 PM	MSSQLServer	ODS	17052	N/A	PARKPLACE
6/22/99	12:05:04 PM	MSSQLServer	ODS	17052	N/A	PARKPLACE
6/22/99	12:05:04 PM	MSSQLServer	ODS	17052	N/A	PARKPLACE
6/22/99	12:05:04 PM	MSSQLServer	Kernel	17055	N/A	PARKPLACE
6/22/99	12:05:04 PM	MSSQLServer	Kernel	17055	N/A	PARKPLACE
6/22/99	12:05:00 PM	MSSQLServer	Server	17055	N/A	PARKPLACE
6/22/99	12:05:00 PM	MSSQLServer	Server	17055	N/A	PARKPLACE
6/22/99	12:04:56 PM	MSSQLServer	Kernel	17055	N/A	PARKPLACE
6/22/99	12:04:55 PM	MSSQLServer	Kernel	17055	N/A	PARKPLACE
6/22/99	8:45:39 AM	MSSQLServer	NETLIB	19020	N/A	PARKPLACE
6/22/99	8:45:39 AM	MSSQLServer	NETLIB	19020	N/A	PARKPLACE
6/22/99	8:45:39 AM	MSSQLServer	NETLIB	19020	N/A	PARKPLACE
6/22/99	8:45:32 AM	SQLCTR70	None	1001	N/A	PARKPLACE
6/22/99	8:44:48 AM	MSSQLServer	NETLIB	19020	N/A	PARKPLACE
6/22/99	8:44:48 AM	MSSQLServer	NETLIB	19020	N/A	PARKPLACE
6/22/99	8:44:48 AM	MSSQLServer	NETLIB	19020	N/A	PARKPLACE
6/22/99	8:44:44 AM	SQLCTR70	None	1001	N/A	PARKPLACE
6/22/99	8:44:18 AM	MSDTC	SVC	4104	N/A	PARKPLACE

FIGURE 24.3
The Windows NT Event Viewer contains information from all applications running on the server, as well as information about the server itself.

2. From the Log menu, click Application. This changes the contents of the screen to show only the information about the applications that are running on the server and not from Windows NT itself.
3. To view more information about an event, double-click the event and it will open up the Event Detail window, as seen in Figure 24.4, which contains the event description.

FIGURE 24.4

The Event Detail window provides you with more information, including an event description.

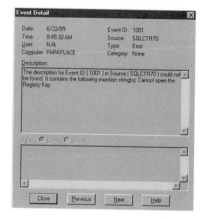

When viewing the Windows NT event log, you will find that because so much information is written there, it is difficult to discern what information comes from SQL Server and what does not. You can alleviate this by filtering the source of the event information to show only the SQL Server events. The following will walk you through filtering the Windows NT Application log to show only the SQL Server events:

1. Open the Windows NT Event Viewer and view the Application log as outlined in the previous tutorial.

2. From the View menu, choose the Filter Events option. The Filter dialog box, as seen in Figure 24.5, appears..

FIGURE 24.5

The Filter dialog box allows you to choose the Source of events that you view.

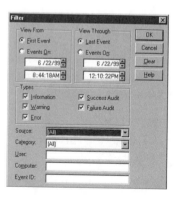

3. In the Source drop-down box, choose MSSQLServer. This filters out all events except for the ones that are coming from the MSSQLServer service.

4. In the Category dialog box, you can narrow down the filter into categories such as Backup, Network Libraries, and Server events.

5. After you have chosen the Source and Category, if you choose to filter by category, click the OK button. The Application Log will be filtered, as seen in Figure 24.6, to show only the events that you have selected.

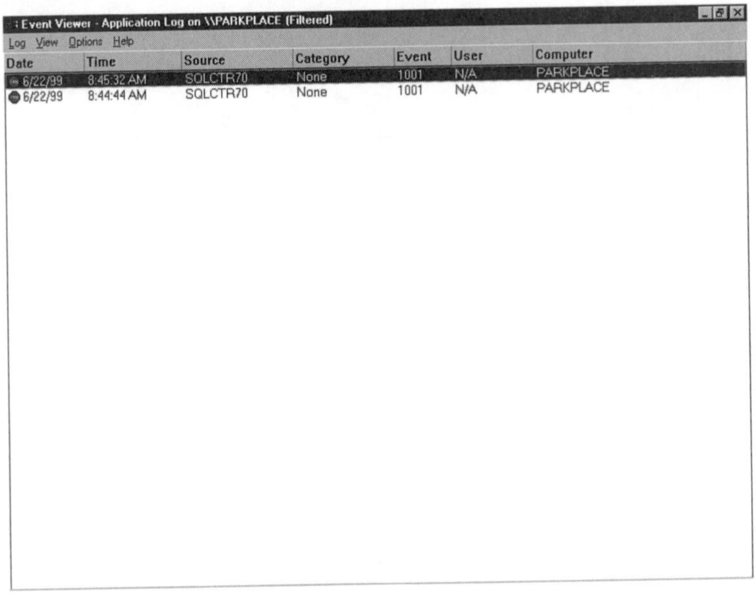

FIGURE 24.6

After filtering the Application Log, it becomes much easier to discern which events come from SQL Server.

SQL Server Error Messages

When SQL Server encounters an error, it will either write a message to the error log, send a message back to the user, or both, depending on the severity level. Every SQL Server error message contains the following information:

- A unique number that identifies the message.
- A number that identifies the severity level of the error.
- A number that identifies the source of the error.
- An informational message that tells you about the error and, depending on the error, some steps you can take to fix the error.

All error messages are stored in the sysmessages table in the master database. To view a complete list of all messages, run the query from Listing 24.1.

LISTING 24.1 You Can Get a Complete Listing of all Error Messages by Running the Following Query

```
1: use master
2: go
3: select * from sysmessages
4: go
```

Severity Levels

Every SQL Server error message contains a severity level that indicates the type of problem that SQL Server has encountered and how bad the problem can be. Error messages can be divided into two categories: nonfatal errors and fatal errors.

Nonfatal Errors

Nonfatal errors are errors that have severity levels of 0 and 10 through 18. Often, nonfatal errors are user correctable errors. These errors do not cause the connection to SQL Server to be dropped. Table 24.1 shows some examples of nonfatal errors.

TABLE 24.1 SQL Server Nonfatal Errors

Severity Level	Definition	Example
0 or 10	These messages are not errors. These are informational messages that do not require any user correction.	Msg 2528, Level 10 State 1. DBCC execution completed. If DBCC printed error messages, see your System Administrator.
11–16	These errors are user correctable errors. Most often, these are because of syntax or logic errors in SQL statements.	Msg 109, Level 15, State 1. More columns are in the INSERT statement than the values specified in theVALUES clause. The number of values in the VALUES clause must match the number of columns.
17	Indicates that SQL Server has run out of some resource. This can be physical resources, such as disk space, or configurable resources, such as locks.	Msg 1105, Level 17, State 1. Can't allocate space for object SYSLOGS in database PUBS because the syslogs segment is full. If you ran out of space in Syslogs, dump the transaction log. Otherwise, use ALTER DATABASE or sp_extendsegment to increase the size of the segment.

continues

TABLE 24.1   continued

Severity Level	Definition	Example
18	Indicates that an internal error has kept SQL Server from completing the statement, but the connection to the server is not terminated.	Msg 1521, Level 18, State 1. Sort failed because a table in tempdb used for the processing of the query had a bad data page count. Tempdb should not have been damaged.

Fatal Errors

Fatal errors are errors with severity levels of 19 or greater. When a fatal error occurs, the user's connection to SQL Server is terminated. Correcting these errors often requires the database to be taken offline and the SQL Administrator to perform corrective actions. Table 24.2 shows some examples of fatal errors.

TABLE 24.2   SQL Server Fatal Errors

Severity	Definition	Example
19	These errors indicate a nonconfigurable internal limit has been reached. These errors rarely happen.	Msg 422, Level 19, State 1. Too many nested expressions or logical operators to compile. Try splitting query or limiting ANDs and ORs.
20	These errors indicate that the error was in the current process. These affect only the current process, and the database was probably not damaged.	Msg 405, Level 20, State 1. Cannot route query results—query internal representation corrupted.
21	These errors indicate that a problem has occurred that affects all processes in the current database. There was likely no corruption in the database though.	Msg 611, Level 21, State 1. Attempt made to end a transaction that is idle or in the middle of an update.
22	These indicate that the integrity of a table is suspect. Level 22 errors are rare.	Msg 904, Level 22, State 1. Unable to find master database row in Sysdatabases. Cannot open master database.

Severity	Definition	Example
23	These messages indicate that the integrity of an entire database is suspect. These errors are rare.	Msg 277, Level 23, State 1. A transaction that began in this stored procedure which did updates in tempdb is still active. This causes corruption in tempdb that will exist until the server is rebooted. All BEGIN TRANs and END TRANs must have matching COMMITs and ROLLBACKs.
24	These messages indicate some sort of media failure. It might be necessary to replace hardware and reload the database.	Msg 902, Level 24, State 1. Hardware error detected reading logical page 24145, virtual page 340782 in database PUBS.
25	These messages indicate some sort of system error internal to SQL Server.	Msg 3508, Level 25, State 1. Attempt to set PUBS database to single user mode failed because the usage count is 2. Make sure that no users are currently using this database and rerun CHECK POINT.

It is important to investigate all fatal errors that happen. This often involves taking the database offline and running diagnostics. Some fatal errors will occur and then, during diagnostics, will not reappear. It is better to investigate the errors when you first find them and not allow them to get any worse.

Dealing with Corrupt Databases

Sometimes, after you have begun troubleshooting, you will find that your problems do not lie with configuration issues or user training issues: You find actual corruption in the database. After you have found corruption, the next step you must take is decide what to do about it. When making this decision, you must take into account the amount of time the database has been offline, the amount of time it will take for you to find the problem, and the amount of time it will take to correct. Sometimes, restoring from the last known good backup is the best option. Note that even if SQL Server has marked a database as inaccessible, Microsoft has ways of getting to the data. If this is the case, you might want to contact Microsoft for assistance. The information that I cover in the next couple of sections is pretty high level. Being new to SQL Server, the first couple of times, you should consider calling Microsoft Technical Support or a local consulting company for assistance with getting your database working again.

Fixing Corrupt User Tables

When dealing with corrupt user tables, it is important to remember that, although they contain all the information that your users have collected, they are the easier of the two types of tables to repair.

The first step in repairing a corrupt user table is to make a full backup of the database in the current state. This backup should be clearly marked and put in a safe place. This backup will provide a two-fold purpose. First, it will be a record of what was wrong in the database. This can be useful at a later time when you have more time to investigate exactly what was wrong with the database. Secondly, it can be used to restore the database after you have attempted a fix that did not work.

The second step is to figure out exactly where in the table the corruption lies. If the corruption lies within an index on the table, oftentimes dropping and recreating the index will fix the problem. If the corruption lies in the table itself, you will need to drop and recreate the table.

Dropping and recreating a table is not as easy as it sounds. Before dropping the table, you must figure out what to do with the data contained in the table. Depending on the age of the last backup and the activity level in the database, you might be able to restore the information from backup. Unfortunately, this is not always an option. If the activity level in the database is not that great, you might be able to have the users recreate the data by re-entering it. Otherwise, you will need to use the Bulk Copy Program, or BCP, to get the data out.

After you have gotten the data out of the corrupt table, the last step is to drop and recreate the table. After that is complete and you have loaded the data back into the table, you should run DBCCs on the database to ensure that there are no more errors.

Fixing Corrupt System Tables

Corrupt system tables, although they contain no user data, are the most difficult failures to recover from. The system tables contain all the data that make the rest of the tables in your database work. When a system table fails, the results can be catastrophic.

The first step is to make a backup of the database in its nonfunctional state. As with corrupted user tables, you will need this as a record of the state that the database was in when you started troubleshooting.

The next step you should take is to call your primary support provider or Microsoft's technical support. A number of undocumented DBCC commands and trace flags might be able to help you to repair your database.

Next, restore a previous backup and run a Database Consistency Checker (DBCC) against it. System table corruption does not always make itself evident as soon as it occurs. If you are running DBCCs on a daily basis, you might have caught the corruption on the day that it occurred. If not, do not be overly surprised if your previous backups were corrupt too.

As a last resort, you might need to BCP all the data out of your user tables. After all the data is out, you should drop the database, the devices that it resided on, and completely recreate the database. When the database has been recreated, you can BCP the data back in.

The Database Consistency Checker

The DBCC was originally intended to simply check the consistency of the database. Over time, Microsoft has added many useful features to DBCC that can be used when troubleshooting SQL Server problems.

DBCC is the most useful and powerful tool when trying to isolate and repair problems that you are having within your databases. Aside from the supported DBCC commands, many others are undocumented and unsupported by Microsoft. If you come across any of these, it is best to use them with caution and only after contacting your primary support provider. When repairing an error, some of the commands could cause more problems to your database because of other underlying problems. For more information on the syntax of using DBCC, consult SQL Server Books Online.

Using Trace Flags

When coding SQL Server for public release, Microsoft determines a default amount of functionality and error recording that meets the needs of most of the people most of the time. At times, though, SQL Administrators will need more than the default. Microsoft has provided a way to add extra functionality through the use of trace flags. There are many trace flags, and like the DBCCs, there are many that are undocumented. For more information on trace flags, consult SQL Server Books Online.

Other Sources of Information

When you are troubleshooting an SQL Server problem, you can get information from several places. Normally, the first place you will look is within SQL Server Books Online. Unfortunately, Books Online is created and released when SQL Server is. That means the information contained therein can be several months or even years old when you are in need of information. Several other sources of information can be used to assist you in troubleshooting.

Microsoft Support Online

Microsoft Support Online is one of the best free resources available to you when you are troubleshooting SQL Server. This resource is frequently updated and well maintained. On this Web site, you can access all the latest bug notices, fixes, and tips. You can access this Web site by pointing your Web browser at `http://www.microsoft.com/support`.

Microsoft Newsgroups

Another great source of information is the Microsoft public access newsgroups. These are available by pointing your newsreader at `msnews.microsoft.com`. Hundreds of groups are available that you can post to and ask questions. One thing to remember is that some people who respond to your posts might not always know the correct answer to your questions. In other words, take their advice with a grain of salt.

MSDN and TechNet

MSDN and TechNet are both valuable subscription resources that you can get. They both contain articles, white papers, and knowledge base articles on all of Microsoft's products. MSDN is updated on a quarterly basis and is primarily targeted for developers. TechNet, on the other hand, is targeted for administrators and is updated on a monthly basis. To get more information on MSDN or TechNet, you can visit `http://www.microsoft.com/msdn` or `http://www.microsoft.com/technet`.

Microsoft Technical Support

When you have tried everything you know and have run out of resources, there is one last option. This option, as much as we all hate to admit it, is to call technical support. Admittedly, when we have to call someone to help us, we feel like we have failed. Remember one important thing about calling Microsoft Technical Support; although they might not always have all the answers, they do have something that no one else has—access to the developers. They will be able to help you implement many undocumented fixes and features in SQL Server that would normally be unavailable to you.

Summary

Troubleshooting can be one of the most difficult things you have to do. The good thing about troubleshooting, though, is that you will learn more then than you ever will during the normal process. Make sure that during the troubleshooting process, you keep your eye on the objective and remember not to panic.

Q&A

Q What is the best option that I have when a user database fails?

A Usually, the best option that you have is to restore the database from the most current backup.

Q I have an SQL Server that has crashed, and the managers in my company want to know when it is going to be back up. What should I tell them?

A As always, the first thing you should do is to keep your head. You should tell the managers that you will give them an answer as soon as you have investigated the error and determined how to fix it. The other option is to pretend you are Mister Scott from *Star Trek*—tell them that it is going to be 10 hours, fix it in 10 minutes, and be a hero.

24

Workshop

The quiz and the exercise are provided for your further understanding. The answers can be found in Appendix A, "Answers."

Quiz

1. A user has called you and has an error on his screen. What should you tell him to do?

2. A user has called you and reported that she has received an error with a severity level of 24. What does this error mean?

3. Where are the two important places that you can look for information about SQL Server?

4. What is one thing that you should always do, even before you have a server problem?

5. When consulting the Microsoft Public Newsgroups, what should you bear in mind before attempting anything that someone tells you?

6. What is the best free resource that you have available to you?

7. When all else has failed and you have run out of resources, what should you do?

Exercise

Start a documentation trail of all your servers and look through the Windows NT Event log and the SQL Server Application log. Become familiar with them and how to use them before a problem occurs.

APPENDIX A

Answers for Hour 1

Quiz

1. What is an RDBMS?

   An RDBMS, or Relational Database Management System, is an engine that is used to store and manage databases.

2. What platforms does SQL Server 7.0 run on?

   SQL Server 7.0 will run on Windows NT or Windows 95/98.

3. What is a DBA?

   A DBA, or Database Administrator, is a person who manages and maintains a database server.

4. What management tool is used to manage SQL Server?

   SQL Server is managed through the SQL Enterprise Manager, which is a plug-in to the Microsoft Management Console.

5. How did SQL Server get started?

   SQL Server got started as a joint venture between Microsoft and Sybase in 1988.

6. What does it mean to have an N-Tier application?

An N-Tier application is an application that has been divided up into at least three different layers: consisting of the presentation layer, the business layer, and the data layer.

Exercises

No answer to exercise.

Answers for Hour 2

Quiz

1. What are the minimum processor requirements for SQL Server 7.0?

SQL Server 7.0 requires an Alpha-based processor or an Intel Pentium-based (Pentium, Pentium Pro, Pentium II, or Pentium III) or other compatible running at 166 MHz or faster.

2. How much disk space does a typical installation of SQL Server 7.0 take?

A typical installation of SQL Server 7.0 takes about 165MB of hard drive space.

3. What operating system does SQL Server 7.0 Enterprise Edition run on?

SQL Server 7.0 Enterprise Edition requires Windows NT 4.0 Enterprise Edition.

4. What is the major limitation that you must take into account when you are using SQL Server 7.0 Desktop Edition?

One of the major limitations to running SQL Server 7.0 Desktop Edition is that databases are limited to 4GB.

5. When installing SQL Server, you get an error message; what should you do?

Copy down the error message with any associated numbers and investigate using *Books Online, TechNet* or *Microsoft Support Online*.

6. What is the biggest limitation that you have when you install SQL Server using the local system account?

The biggest limitation to using the local system account when installing SQL Server 7.0 is that it has no access to network resources.

7. What type of privileges must you be logged in with in order to install SQL Server 7.0?

You must be logged into Windows NT with an account that has administrative rights.

Exercises

No answers.

Answers for Hour 3

Quiz

1. Physically, how is a database implemented?

   A database is physically implemented in at least two files on the hard disk of the server.

2. What is a table?

   A table is a collection of columns and rows that are used to track information that is important to the organization that owns the database.

3. What can a view do for you?

   A view can be used to simplify access to data in a table.

4. What type of constraint could you use to make sure that all the rows in the table are different from each other?

   You would use a UNIQUE constraint to ensure that all the rows in a table are different from each other.

5. What type of constraint could you use to ensure that all the rows in one table have a matching row in another table?

   You would use a FOREIGN KEY constraint to ensure that all the rows in one table have a matching row in another table.

6. What is a stored procedure?

   A stored procedure is a collection of SQL statements that can be executed by running one statement.

7. What functionality does a trigger perform for you?

   A trigger is a collection of SQL statements that are executed when a specified data modification takes place in the table for which the trigger was defined.

Exercise

No answer.

A

Answers for Hour 4

Quiz

1. What is the smallest amount that SQL Server allocates space to an object in the database in, and how large is it?

   SQL Server allocates space in the database in units of a page, which is an 8KB unit of space.

2. When SQL Server first allocates space to a new database object, how does it do it?

   SQL Server allocates space out of a mixed extent, which is an extent that has information from other database objects in it. When the database object has grown to be larger than eight pages, SQL Server will move that object out of the mixed extent and into a uniform extent.

3. What is an extent, and how large is it?

   An extent is a grouping of eight contiguous 8KB pages, making it 64KB.

4. What is the purpose of the master database?

   The master database contains all the information that SQL Server needs to operate. It contains all login information, information about user databases, and information about how space is allocated on the physical hard drives.

5. What is the purpose of the msdb database?

   The msdb database is used by the SQL Server Agent to track information about jobs, alerts, and operators.

6. What is tempdb used for?

   tempdb is used as a space for sorting and for the creation of worktables that SQL Server uses during many processes.

7. What are primary database files used for?

   A primary database file is the first file that is added when you create a database. This file contains information that is gathered by the user and information about all other files that are attached to the server.

8. How many primary database files can you add to a database?

   When you create a database, a primary database file is created for that server. This file is the only primary database file that can be added to a database.

9. What is the transaction log used for?

   The transaction log is used to maintain the database in a consistent state. It is used to ensure that all changes to the database are complete, or they are cancelled.

10. What is a transaction?

A transaction is a single logical unit of work that must be 100 percent complete or be cancelled.

Exercises

No answers.

Answers for Hour 5

Quiz

1. What is the Client Configuration Utility used for?

The SQL Client Configuration Utility is used to configure the way that client computers will connect to the server machines.

2. What is SQL Enterprise Manager?

SQL Enterprise Manager is a graphical user interface for managing SQL Servers.

3. What is MMC?

MMC is the Microsoft Management Console and its function is to provide a framework for managing BackOffice products.

4. What can you do with the SQL Server Profiler?

SQL Server Profiler is used to monitor and optimize SQL Server.

5. What functionality is provided to you through SQL Query Analyzer?

SQL Query Analyzer is used to connect to SQL Servers and execute SQL Command and stored procedures.

6. Is it possible to run SQL Server 6.5 and SQL Server 7.0 on the same machine at the same time?

It is not possible to run SQL Server 6.5 and SQL Server 7.0 on the same machine at the same time. Rather, you have to run them separately and use the SQL Server—Switch application to move between them.

7. What tools do you have to troubleshoot Named Pipe issues?

You can use the makepipe and readpipe utilities to troubleshoot Named Pipe issues.

Exercises

No answers.

Answers for Hour 6

Quiz

1. What is a database file?

   A database file is a physical file that corresponds to the database.

2. What is the difference between a database file and a log file?

   The major difference between a database file and a log file is that a database file contains only data from the database and a log file can only contain transaction log information.

3. What is a filegroup?

   A filegroup is a logical grouping of database files used to improve management.

4. If you do not specify the logical name for the log file when creating a database using the CREATE DATABASE statement, what is the maximum length of the name of the database?

   If you do not specify the logical name for the log file when you are creating a database using the CREATE DATABASE statement, the maximum length of the database name is 123 characters.

5. What is the Auto Create Statistics database option used for?

   The Auto Create Statistics database option is used to force SQL Server to create statistics on the database tables.

6. What database option would you use if the database you are working on is a non-productional development database?

   One of the database options that you should make sure is turned on in this environment is the Truncate Log on Checkpoint option.

7. When shrinking a database, how would you tell SQL Server to leave 50 percent of the existing free space in the database available.

   You would use the DBCC SHRINKDATABASE command specifying a target percentage.

Exercises

No answers.

Answers for Hour 7

Quiz

1. What is a table?

   A table is where all data is stored in an SQL Server database. This data is stored in a row and column array.

2. What is a column?

   A column is a singe category of data that is collected in an SQL Server table.

3. Is the column name &Column 1 a valid column name? Why or why not?

   No. The column name starts with an illegal character and it contains a space.

4. What are datatypes used for?

   Datatypes are used by SQL Server to determine what type of data is going to be stored in a column.

5. What does the CREATE TABLE statement do?

   The CREATE TABLE statement is used to create a table.

6. If you do not specify NULL or NOT NULL when creating a table, what will SQL Server use as the default?

   SQL Server will use NULL as the default nullability behavior when one is not specified.

7. What is the command for altering a table called Table1 and adding a column called Column3 with a datatype of int?

   The command is ALTER TABLE Table1 ADD Column1 INT.

8. If you mistakenly drop a table from a database, what must you do to get it back?

   If you mistakenly drop a table, the only way to get that table back is to restore from backup.

Exercises

2.

```
CREATE TABLE Sales
(
    OrderID INT NOT NULL ,
    CustomerID INT NOT NULL ,
    OrderTotal MONEY NOT NULL ,
    ShipMethod VARCHAR(32) NOT NULL ,
    Shipped BIT NOT NULL
)
```

A

```
CREATE TABLE SalesDetail
(
    OrderID INT NOT NULL ,
    Quantity INT NOT NULL,
    ProductID INT NOT NULL ,
    ExtendedPrice MONEY NOT NULL
)
```

Answers for Hour 8

Quiz

1. Why is security important?

   Security is important because you want to keep unwanted users from accessing data that they are not supposed to and from keeping your regular users from accessing data that is not for their use.

2. What is a login ID?

   A login ID is used to provide access to the SQL Server.

3. What is a user ID?

   A user ID is used to provide an authenticated user access to a database.

4. What are roles used for?

   Roles are used to group users with similar work responsibilities into manageable groups.

5. What are application roles used for?

   Application roles are used to ensure that users only access the database with specific applications.

6. What is the difference between SQL Server Authentication and Windows NT Authentication?

   SQL Server Authentication is all handled internally to SQL Server, and with Windows NT Authentication, SQL Server relies on Window NT to authenticate users.

7. What is the public role used for?

   The public role is used to assign permissions to all users in the database.

Exercise

No answer.

Answers for Hour 9

Quiz

1. What are permissions used for?

   Permissions are used to allow the administrator of a system to lock specific portions of a system down to allow only certain users the ability to perform those functions.

2. What are statement permissions?

   Statement permissions are permissions that allow or disallow users to perform functions such as creating tables, views, stored procedures, and defaults.

3. What are object permissions?

   Object permissions are permissions that allow or disallow users the ability to access objects in the database.

4. What are implied permissions?

   Implied permissions are special types of permissions that are given to users who are members of certain roles.

5. What command would you use to allow a user SELECT permissions on a table?

   You would use the GRANT SELECT statement to allow users to SELECT data from a table.

6. What is an ownership chain?

   An ownership chain occurs when views or stored procedures are created. These types of objects rely on other objects in the database, thus creating an ownership chain.

7. What is a broken ownership chain?

   A broken ownership chain is created when users create objects in the database that are owned by different users.

Exercise

GRANT CREATE TABLE TO TestUser.

Answers for Hour 10

Quiz

1. Why should you back up your databases?

   You should back up your databases to protect yourself and your organization from losing data from hardware failure, natural disaster, and malicious data deletion.

2. What is acceptable loss?

   Acceptable loss is the amount of data that you can use on a database without adversely affecting your business. This will vary from database to database and is measured in an amount of time. For example, in some businesses it might be acceptable to lose 5 minutes worth of data and in others it might be acceptable to lose 5 days worth.

3. What are two situations in which running only a full database backup might be a good idea?

   Two situations in which running only full database backups might be that the data in the database does not change that frequently, or the site is a remote site with very little DBA support.

4. What is a transaction log backup?

   A transaction log backup is the process of backing up only the transaction log of a database. This allows you to perform quick and small backups, but these take longer to recover.

5. What is point-in-time recovery?

   Point-in-time recovery is the ability to recover a database up until a specific point in time, such as 15 minutes before a failure took place. This type of recovery is only available when using transaction log backups.

6. What is a differential backup?

   A differential backup is a backup in which you back up all changes that have been made in the database since the last full database backup.

7. Why is it a good idea to verify your backups?

   Verifying backups is a good idea because you can make all the backups you want, but if your hardware is not working for some reason, they will not do you any good.

8. What is a backup device?

   A backup device is a location where SQL Server can store copies of your databases when you perform a backup.

9. Why should you back up the master database?

You should perform backups of your master database because it is the most important database on the server. It contains information about all other databases on the server, and if it crashes, it is very difficult to recover all the other databases.

10. Besides the master database, which other system databases should you back up?

You should also routinely make backups of the msdb database and the publication database if the server participates in replication. If you have made changes to the model database, it is also a good idea to back it up as well.

Exercises

No answers.

Answers for Hour 11

Quiz

1. What does it mean to restore a database?

Restoring a database is the process of recreating everything in the database from a previous copy of it.

2. Is it possible for users to actively use the database when you restore it?

No, the database cannot be in use when you restore it.

3. When you are restoring transaction logs, what is the major limitation that you have?

The major limitation that you have when restoring transaction logs is that you must restore them in the same order in which they were taken.

4. Do you have to recreate the database in the same way that it was created previously before you actually restore it?

No, this limitation was removed from SQL Server 7.0.

5. What is automatic recovery?

Automatic recovery is the process of going through the SQL Server transaction log to ensure that all transactions are either 100 percent complete or they are cancelled.

6. What happens to transactions that are incomplete in the database after the database is restored?

Any transactions that are not complete in the database after it is restored are rolled back and cancelled.

A

7. What must you do to get SQL Server to start before you restore the master database?

   You must rebuild the master database to get SQL Server to start before you can actually restore the master database.

Exercise

No answer to exercise.

Answers for Hour 12

Quiz

1. Why is interoperability between systems important?

   It is important for systems to interoperate because there is frequently similar data stored in multiple systems and it is often very difficult to maintain that data on all systems.

2. What is DTS?

   DTS is the Data Transformation Services that is used to import, export, and transform data from multiple systems.

3. What is a DTS application called?

   A DTS application is called a package.

4. What are the three main functions that can be performed with DTS?

   The three main functions available in DTS are importing and exporting data, transforming data, and transferring database objects.

5. What is the bulk copy program used for?

   The bulk copy program is used to import and export data from an SQL Server.

6. What database objects can you use the BCP command with?

   You can run the BCP command in conjunction with tables and views.

7. What is the BULK INSERT command used for?

   The BULK INSERT command is used to read and load a data file directly from within an SQL script.

Exercise

No answer to exercise.

Answers for Hour 13

Quiz

1. What is SQL Server replication?

   SQL Server replication is the process of copying data from one server to another. This is used to make sure that the data needed is always available at the correct site.

2. When might you use SQL Server replication?

   You might implement SQL Server replication to off-load reporting processes from the main database server: to ensure that clients have up-to-date copies of data such as phone and prices lists, and to keep copies of the data on different servers for availability reasons.

3. What are the four main methods for distributing data?

   The four main methods for distributing data are snapshot replication, transactional replication, merge replication, and distributed transactions. Each type of data distribution requires differing amounts of server resources and setup.

4. What is the purpose of the publishing server?

   The publishing server contains the master copy of all publications. Data can be modified on any server, if it is set up correctly, and can be sent back to the publication for redistribution to all servers.

5. What is the purpose of the distribution server?

   The distribution server is used to act as a store and forward server. This server receives all changes made on the publishing server and sends them out to the subscribers. The distribution server can be a separate computer from the publishing server, but it does not have to be.

6. What is a publication?

   A publication is one or more articles that are made available for subscription. A publication is the smallest unit in which a subscriber can subscribe.

7. What is contained in an article?

   An article is a single table that is created, placed into a publication, and made available for subscription.

Exercises

No answers.

A

Answers for Hour 14

Quiz

1. What is the default replication scenario?

   The default replication scenario is the central publisher scenario.

2. When setting up replication over a slow WAN link, what is the best replication scenario to use?

   The best replication scenario for replication over a slow WAN link is the publishing subscriber scenario.

3. What type of replication scenario is best for roll-up reporting?

   The central subscriber replication scenario is best for roll-up reporting.

4. When setting up replication over the Internet, what protocol must you use?

   In order to set up replication over the Internet, you must use the TCP/IP protocol.

5. Which replication scenario involves several servers that act as both publishers and subscribers to certain data?

   The multiple publishers or multiple subscribers replication scenario involve several servers that act as both publishers and subscribers.

6. What replication security method involves a list of login IDs and passwords that are allowed to access specific publications?

   The publication access list, or PAL, contains involves a list of login IDs and passwords that are allowed to access specific publications.

7. How are Internet publications transferred?

   Internet publications are transferred using the use of the FTP protocol.

Exercises

No answers.

Answers for Hour 15

Quiz

1. When setting up replication, what is the first thing that you must have defined?

   You must define a distribution server before you can set up any of the other replication components.

2. What role must you be a member of in order to install and configure replication?

    In order to install replication, you must be a member of the sysadmins server role.

3. When you install replication on a Windows NT computer, what ways are available to you to monitor the progress of replication?

    When you install replication on a Windows NT computer, you can use SQL statements, SQL Enterprise Manager, and Windows NT Performance monitor to monitor replication.

4. When you install replication on a Windows 95/98 computer, what monitoring method is not available to you?

    When you install replication on a Windows 95/98 computer, Windows NT Performance Monitor is not available to you to monitor the status of replication.

5. What type of subscription is created from the client computer?

    Pull subscriptions are created from the client computer.

6. What type of subscription is created from the server computer?

    Push subscriptions are created from the server computer.

7. When configuring a subscription, what schedule should you set up for the replication agent to provide the lowest latency?

    When you are configuring the replication agent, the setting that provides the lowest latency is the run continuously option.

Exercise

No answer.

Answers for Hour 16

Quiz

1. What is the SQL Server Agent?

    SQL Server Agent is a process that runs in conjunction with SQL Server that is responsible for running jobs, firing alerts, and notifying operators.

2. What is a job?

    A job is a task—which can contain multiple steps—that is run on SQL Server.

3. What is an alert?

    An alert is an event that is fired in response to an SQL Server event or error.

A

4. What two things can you configure an alert to fire from?

   You can configure SQL Server to fire an alert based on an error that occurs or based off performance statistics.

5. What is an operator?

   An operator is a person who receives notifications from SQL Server.

6. How does SQL Server provide paging support?

   SQL Server provides paging support through an email paging gateway set up by your paging company.

7. What type of mail system is required for SQL Mail to work?

   SQL Mail requires that there be a MAPI mail system in order to work.

Exercise

No answer to exercise.

Answers for Hour 17

Quiz

1. What is the statement that you can use to retrieve data out of a table?

   You use the SELECT statement to retrieve data out of tables.

2. What is the portion of a SELECT statement that tells SQL Server where you want to retrieve data from?

   The portion of a SELECT statement that tells SQL Server where you want to retrieve data from is called the from clause.

3. How can you limit the number of rows that you can return from the SQL Server?

   You can limit the number of rows that you can return from a table using a WHERE clause.

4. How can you change the order of the rows that are returned from a SELECT statement?

   You can change the order of the rows that are returned from a SELECT statement using an ORDER BY clause.

5. What datatype is used with the LIKE keyword?

   The LIKE keyword is used with string datatype.

6. What function would you use to remove extra spaces from the end of a string?

   You can use the RTRIM function to remove extra spaces from the end of a string.

7. What function can you use to change an expression from one datatype to another?

The CONVERT function can be used to change an expression from one datatype to another.

Exercise

```
SELECT lname + ', ' + fname AS 'Name', hire_date AS 'Hire Date'
FROM employee
WHERE hire_date < CONVERT(DATETIME, '1/1/1990')
ORDER BY 'Name'
```

Answers for Hour 18

Quiz

1. What keyword can be used in a SELECT statement to eliminate duplicate rows?

   The DISTINCT keyword can be used to eliminate duplicate rows in a resultset.

2. What aggregate function can you use to add up all the values in a numeric column?

   The SUM keyword can be used to add up all the values in a numeric column.

3. What aggregate function can you use to determine how many rows are contained in a table?

   The COUNT function can be used to determine how many rows are in a table.

4. What is the GROUP BY clause used for in a SELECT statement containing an aggregate function?

   The GROUP BY function is used to generate summary data.

5. What type of join would you use if you only want to see the rows that contain a match in both joined tables?

   You would use an INNER JOIN to retrieve the data that matched only in both tables.

6. What type of join produces what is known as a Cartesian product?

   A CROSS JOIN will produce a Cartesian product.

7. What statement can be used to create a table based on the resultset that you queried?

   The SELECT INTO statement can be used to create a table based off a resultset.

8. What statement can be used to join two like resultsets?

   The UNION statement can be used to join two like resultsets.

A

Exercise

The following code is your answer to Exercise 1:

```
SELECT sales.stor_id, sales.qty, titles.title
FROM   sales INNER JOIN titles ON
       sales.title_id = titles.title_id
```

Answers for Hour 19

Quiz

1. What is the INSERT statement used for?

   The INSERT statement is used to put new data into a table in a database.

2. If you list six columns in the INSERT statement, how many values must you supply?

   If you list six columns in the INSERT statement, you must supply six values.

3. What occurs if you INSERT a NULL value into a column that does not contain a default value and does not allow NULLs?

   If you INSERT a NULL value into a column that does not contain a default value and does not allow NULLs, SQL Server will return an error.

4. What is the UPDATE statement used for?

   The UPDATE statement is used to modify existing data in a table.

5. Why is it important for you to provide a WHERE clause when using the UPDATE statement?

   It is important to provide a WHERE clause when using the UPDATE statement to prevent SQL Server form updating all the data in the table.

6. What is the DELETE statement used for?

   The DELETE statement is used to remove existing data from a table in the database.

7. Is it possible to delete more than one row at a time using the DELETE statement?

   You can delete more than one at a time from a row without using a WHERE clause.

8. What are locks used for?

   Locks are used to keep other users from reading or modifying data that is being modified by another user.

Exercises

```
INSERT authors VALUES('925-12-3456', 'Jones', 'Melissa',
➥ '913-722-0909', '94 W. 163rd St.', 'Lenexa',
➥ 'KS', '66213', 1)

UPDATE authors
SET    au_lname = 'Jones',
       phone = '913-663-1234',
       address = '9123 E. 178th St.'
WHERE  au_id = '925-12-3456'

DELETE authors WHERE au_id = '925-12-3456'
```

Answers for Hour 20

Quiz

1. What is a stored procedure?

   A stored procedure is a way of encapsulating complex SQL statements into a single command that can be executed from the server.

2. What command is used to create a stored procedure?

   You can use the CREATE PROCEDURE command to create a new stored procedure.

3. What can you use to pass data into a stored procedure?

   You can use parameters to pass data into a stored procedure.

4. What command can you use to modify a stored procedure?

   You can use the ALTER PROCEDURE to modify stored procedures.

5. What do you gain from modifying a stored procedure, as opposed to dropping and recreating it?

   You cannot lose permissions and dependencies when you ALTER a stored procedure.

6. What is a dependency?

   A dependency is a reference from one database object to another in the database.

7. What command do you use to drop a stored procedure from the system?

   You use the DROP PROCEDURE command to drop a stored procedure from the system.

A

Exercise

1.

```
CREATE PROCEDURE usp_get_author_address
      @last_name       VARCHAR(32)
AS
SELECT @last_name = @last_name + '%'

SELECT au_lname + ', ' + au_fname AS 'Name', address + ' ' + city +
      ', ' + state + ' ' + zip AS 'Address'
FROM authors
WHERE au_lname LIKE @last_name
ORDER BY 'Name' ASC
```

Answers for Hour 21

Quiz

1. What is a batch?

   A batch is a group of statements that are put together and executed at the same time by the SQL Server.

2. What keyword do you use to designate a batch?

   To designate a batch in SQL Server, you use the GO keyword.

3. What is a transaction?

   A transaction is a single unit of work that must all be completed or it will be canceled.

4. If you want to cancel a transaction, what keyword do you issue?

   To cancel the work that has been performed in a transaction, you use the ROLLBACK TRANSACTION statement.

5. What is control-of-flow language?

   Control-of-flow language is used to control the direction of execution that a script will take, based on values that are designated in the script.

6. What control-of-flow statement would you use to create a looping structure?

   The WHILE keyword is used to create a looping structure.

7. What characters do you use to designate a one-line comment?

   To create a one-line comment, you use two dashes (--) before the line that is going to be commented out.

8. What is a variable?

A variable is an entity that can be used to store a value for use during the processing of a script.

9. How do you designate a variable?

You designate a variable by using the DECLARE statement, giving the variable a name and assigning it a datatype.

Exercise

1.

```
CREATE TABLE TestTable
(
    column1    INTEGER
)
GO


DECLARE @InsertValue INTEGER

SET @InsertValue = 1
WHILE 1 = 1
BEGIN
    INSERT INTO TestTable VALUES(@InsertValue)
    IF @InsertValue = 100
        BREAK
    SELECT @InsertValue = @InsertValue + 1
END
GO


SELECT * FROM TestTable
GO
```

A

Answers for Hour 22

Quiz

1. What are indexes?

Indexes are structures in a database used to speed up queries against existing data in your tables.

2. What is a clustered index?

A clustered index is a structure in the database that speeds up access to the table. With a clustered index, the data in the table is in the same order as it is in the index.

3. What is a nonclustered index?

   A nonclustered index is a structure in the database used to speed up access to the table. In the case of a nonclustered index, it contains the indexed value and a pointer to that value in the table.

4. How many clustered indexes can you have on one table?

   You can only have one clustered index on any one table.

5. What type of data integrity are you using if you are ensuring that any data entered into one table has a matching record in another table?

   This type of data integrity is known as referential integrity.

6. What is entity integrity?

   Entity integrity is the process of ensuring that only one row in the table contains a specific value. This type of integrity is maintained using UNIQUE constraints.

7. What are triggers used for?

   Triggers are used to enforce business rules in your database.

Exercise

CREATE NONCLUSTERED INDEX ncl_city_state ON authors(city, state).

Answers for Hour 23

Quiz

1. Why should you monitor and tune your SQL Server?

   The main reason for monitoring and tuning your SQL Server is for performance reasons.

2. What is a baseline used for?

   A baseline is used to perform optimal performance and current performance to determine if something is not working properly.

3. What is SQL Server Performance Monitor used for?

   SQL Server Performance Monitor is used to monitor different statistics about SQL Server.

4. What is a counter?

   A counter is a single performance statistic that you can gather in SQL Server Performance Monitor.

5. What is SQL Server Profiler used for?

SQL Server Performance Monitor is used to capture SQL Server statements and execution times.

6. What is a workload?

A workload is a file that contains information gathered from SQL Server about how tables are accessed.

7. What is this Index Tuning Wizard used for?

The Index Tuning Wizard is used to create indexes on an SQL Server database without knowing any of the underlying database structure or how the data in the database is accessed.

Exercises

No answers.

Answers for Hour 24

Quiz

1. A user has called you and has an error on his screen. What should you tell him to do?

You should ask the user to read the error message and any numbers associated with it to you. You should copy that error down and use that to investigate the problem.

2. A user has called you and reported that she has received an error with a severity level of 24. What does this error mean?

An error with a severity level of 24 is a fatal error, and it means that you should investigate it immediately.

3. Where are the two important places that you can look for information about SQL Server?

Two places that you can look for information about the health of SQL Server is in the Windows NT Event Viewer and the SQL Server Error Log.

4. What is one thing that you should always do, even before you have a server problem?

You should maintain a log of everything that you do to a server, from adding user logins, to assigning permissions, to applying service packs.

5. When consulting the Microsoft Public Newsgroups, what should you bear in mind before attempting anything that someone tells you?

   You should remember that it is possible these people might not know the correct answer. They are not Microsoft Technical Support; they are just your average person.

6. What is the best free resource that you have available to you?

   Microsoft Support Online, `http://www.microsoft.com/support`, is one of the best resources available to you.

7. When all else has failed and you have run out of resources, what should you do?

   When you have run out of all options, you should call Microsoft Technical Support.

Exercise

No answer.

INDEX

Other Related Titles

Sams Teach Yourself Microsoft SQL Server 7.0 in 21 Days
0-672-31290-5
Rick Sawtell and
Richard Waymire
$39.99 USA/$57.95 CAN

Microsoft SQL Server 7 Programming Unleashed
0-672-31293-X
John Papa, et al.
$49.99 US/$71.95 CAN

Sams Teach Yourself Transact-SQL in 21 Days
0-672-31045-7
David Solomon
$35.00 USA/$49.95 CAN

Building Enterprise Solutions with Visual Studio 6
0-672-31489-4
G.A.Sullivan
$49.99 US/$71.95 CAN

Sams Teach Yourself OLE DB and ADO in 21 Days
0-672-31083-X
John Fronckowiak
$39.99 USA/$57.95 CAN

Sams Teach Yourself MFC in 24 Hours
0-672-31553-X
Michael Morrison
$24.99 USA/$37.95 CAN

Sams Teach Yourself Active Server Pages in 24 Hours
0-672-31612-9
Christop Wille and
Christian Koller
$19.99 USA/$29.95 CAN

Microsoft SQL Server 7.0 Unleashed
0-672-31227-1
Greg Mable, et. al.
$49.99 US/$71.95 CAN

Microsoft SQL Server 7.0 DBA Survival Guide
0-6722-31226-3
Mark Spenik
$49.99 US/$71.95 CAN

SAMS

www.samspublishing.com

All prices are subject to change.

Get FREE books and more...when you register this book online for our Personal Bookshelf Program

http://register.quecorp.com/

 Register online and you can sign up for our *FREE Personal Bookshelf Program...*unlimited access to the electronic version of more than 200 complete computer books—immediately! That means you'll have 100,000 pages of valuable information onscreen, at your fingertips!

 Plus, you can access product support, including complimentary downloads, technical support files, book-focused links, companion Web sites, author sites, and more!

 And you'll be automatically registered to receive a *FREE subscription to a weekly email newsletter* to help you stay current with news, announcements, sample book chapters, and special events, including sweepstakes, contests, and various product giveaways!

 We value your comments! Best of all, the entire registration process takes only a few minutes to complete, so go online and get the greatest value going—absolutely FREE!

Don't Miss Out On This Great Opportunity!

QUE® is a brand of Macmillan Computer Publishing USA.

For more information, please visit *www.mcp.com*